Gone to Hell This Morning

By

Marvel Lang

1663 LIBERTY DRIVE, SUITE 200
BLOOMINGTON, INDIANA 47403
(800) 839-8640
WWW.AUTHORHOUSE.COM

© 2005 Marvel Lang. All Rights Reserved.

No part of this book may be reproduced, stored in a retrieval system, or transmitted by any means without the written permission of the author.

First published by AuthorHouse 11/15/05

ISBN: 1-4208-2879-7 (sc)

Library of Congress Control Number: 2005900820

Printed in the United States of America
Bloomington, Indiana

This book is printed on acid-free paper.

FOREWORD

History would have many believe that the Black man in the Jim Crow segregationist South was scared, docile, subservient and in constant fear of whites and the Ku Klux Klan. Being born and reared in the South during the early 1950's until the early 1970's I saw and lived a very different experience, which may not have been the circumstances of most Black men but was certainly true for a number of them. Not all Black men in the South during the turbulent times of Jim Crow and the Civil Rights Movement yielded themselves to the humiliation, abuse and scorn of racist whites. Some took very assertive and even aggressive stances to defend themselves and to command the respect they deserved in their own ways.

My daddy, Otha Lang, Sr., was such a man. I witnessed him on many occasions defend himself and stand for what was right even in the face of what might have been certain danger or even death or incarceration. He was determined that nobody was going to disrespect, humiliate, abuse or misuse him without penalty. I saw him on numerous occasions defend himself in ways that should have cost him his life. In fact, many Black men in the South were murdered for lesser acts than what I witnessed my daddy do to defend himself. What intrigued me was that the Ku Klux Klan never came after him. As I grew older I realized why. The Ku Klux Klan and other cowardly racists only attacked in mobs and attacked those whom they perceived were not prone to fight back and defend themselves; those who were afraid to die.

When I became a man I questioned daddy about why he did the things he did to defend himself given the dangers that he might have faced. His answer was that he would rather die defending his dignity and pride than to live in fear and under the constant humiliation of being perceived as weak and helpless. Early on in life he and his family had lost everything they had during the Great Depression except their pride and dignity as men; they had lost home and land which were their means of survival. Once you have suffered such a loss, just living in honor and dignity means much more than mere survival or material possessions. Besides, he explained, nobody wants to die; not even a racist who would put a Black man to death. Once he knows that his chances of dying are just as good as yours if he attacks you, then he realizes that attacking you is not worth the risk of losing his own life.

Daddy's life is a story of extreme contrasts and contradictions. Yet, it shows how the will of God can transform a person and use his life to build character and become a living example for others to follow; even those of low and unheralded status. Daddy could be a gentle giant or a roaring lion; it all depended on how you approached him; he could be humble as a lamb or as stubborn as a mule. Still he helped two generations of men in a rural community to become self-sufficient and independent craftsmen who were able to acquire skills and pass those skills on to their sons so that they too could make a living for themselves without being at the mercy of others entirely. Those men's sons are still passing those skills on to their sons in Jasper County, Mississippi.

Daddy built buildings and he also pastored churches and helped to mold people's lives. In all that he did, he had to first teach himself what he needed to know, and that he did by availing himself of the knowledge he needed to be successful at what he did. He learned what he needed to know by investing his own time and energy in resources he provided for himself, which he did time and time again. As children we admired and feared daddy, but as adults we revered and respected him. He commanded both our reverence and respect, and our admiration and fear. Until this day we all recognize that daddy is daddy, and he will always be our daddy. This book is his story the way it was lived. Here is to you daddy.

A GIANT OF A MAN

A Tribute to my Daddy
A giant of a man
That's what my daddy was
Standing tall, strong and firm just like a tree
A giant of a man
That's what my daddy was
At least that's what he was to me.

A giant of a man
Yes, that's who he was
No, he didn't have any fear
He'd tell them all the same thing
And he didn't care what color they were.

Tall and brave and without fear
Sure, that's who he was
A lover of peace but not afraid
A man of God and a pioneer.

Desiring to go to Heaven
And not afraid to die
That was his signal call
When it came time to lay it all on the line
He'd give it his all and all.

A giant of a man
Believe me, that's who he was
But he didn't pick a fight
All he wanted from every man
Was for all to do what was right.

A lover of God and a lover of family
Earning his way and not bowing or begging
Seeking the peace and avoiding strife
Those were his joys in life
A builder of buildings and a builder of men
Yeah, a giant of a man
That's what my daddy was.

Marvel Lang, Ph.D.

I've got my mind made up and I'm ready to go to Hell this morning. Don't mess with me unless you've got your mind made up to go to hell with me, 'cause I don't plan on going by myself. I intend to take somebody with me and it might as well be you".
-Otha Lang, Sr.

I. WHEN THE KLAN COMES

I never shall forget that Saturday afternoon in May 1954. It is etched in my memory like a branding iron burns the brand on a steer to identify the ranch to which it belongs. I was only five years old at the time but I remember it well; and that afternoon is as vivid in my memory today as it has been over all those years since then.

Sitting on a low stool on the porch of our five-room green wood-framed galvanized tin-topped house on our farm in the Rock Hill Community in southwest Jasper County, Mississippi, I was being instructed in the ways of righteousness by Cousin Mary Lou Beavers. She was the old lady who lived up the road just west of our house about one-tenth of a mile with her husband, Cousin John Beavers. In our community just about every older person was called cousin even if they were no kin. You could see their house clearly from our's, it was west of us just across the field and up the hill. Cousin Mary Lou had come to our house that day to bring some peas she had picked from her garden and had more than she was going to cook; she had taken the time to visit for a while. She was sitting in a chair on the porch, I was sitting next to her on the stool, and my daddy, Otha Lang, Sr., was lying on the floor on the west end of the porch in the shade with his feet propped and slightly elevated against one of the wood posts that formed the supports across the front of the open porch.

Daddy was lying there nodding as Cousin Mary Lou was talking to me. Mama and the girls, Walterene, Brenda and Bobbie, and my brother just older than me, Otha Jr., were inside the house cleaning up after the noon meal. The three older brothers had gone back to the barn to unhitch the mules to turn them out of the barnyard into the pasture. They were done plowing and planting for the day and were going to town later in the afternoon.

Cousin Mary Lou was also my Sunday School teacher and was my surrogate grandmother. She and my mother were my first two teachers, and mama had already taught me to read fluently by the time I was five years old in 1954. As it was hot in the house, Cousin Mary Lou was sitting there listening to me read to her from the Sunday School book waiting for mama to come out of the house to sit and talk with her. Daddy was nodding because it was just after the noontime dinner meal and he was full. Daddy always found a way to take a nap after a good meal no matter where he was or whose company he was in.

On this particular Saturday, however, daddy was nodding for another reason. You see, daddy had already been drinking moonshine whiskey all day that Saturday morning. The fact was, daddy had been drinking moonshine ever since he had come home from work on the Friday before. Although daddy was not yet drunk that Saturday around 1:30 p.m. he was well on his way to tying on a good one. If it had not been for Cousin Mary Lou coming to the house just as we were finishing up the meal, daddy would have been back in the woods or out behind the smokehouse, or wherever he had hidden his whiskey jug that day and would have already started back to drinking.

But out of respect for Cousin Mary Lou he had pretended to be more sober than what he was; plus, the good meal he had just eaten was easing the effects of the whiskey from drunk to sleep, and he had been able to carry on a conversation with her before I started reading and he fell asleep. The nod had overtaken him as the heat was bearing down from the sunshine; it was a clear sunny day and the temperature was at least 95 degrees. Daddy never drank whiskey in the presence of us children, but you could tell when he had been drinking; you could smell the moonshine whiskey from seemingly 50 yards away, and you could tell by his demeanor and the look in his eyes.

It was early May but the heat was already oppressive in southeastern Mississippi. School was out for the summer which meant that my three oldest brothers, Charles, Claude and George, were now working with daddy building houses when they were not plowing, chopping or planting on the farm. The oldest brother had just graduated from high school and was working full-time with daddy every day trying to earn enough money to be able to attend Jackson College (now Jackson State University) in the fall. George and Claude, along with my three sisters, were making sure all the plowing and chopping were getting done.

In those days when there was nothing pressing to be done on the farm, the three oldest brothers would work with daddy in the building business. In the Spring of 1954 daddy had begun building a house for the young lawyer son of one of the prominent lawyers in Bay Springs. The Old man was having the house built for his son who had finished law school at Ole Miss a year or so earlier and had come home to join his father in the law practice. The son had gotten married to a local girl from one of the other prominent white families in Bay Springs and his father was furnishing the money to have a house built for them. The old man had made an agreement with daddy to build the house on a labor provision basis meaning that he would pay daddy and his helpers for their labor by the hour and he would provide all the building materials.

Back then it was almost unheard of for a black man to get a contract of any kind to build a new house for a prominent white family. Mr. Roy James, a white contractor, was the most prominent builder in the area and he built most of the houses being built by whites in the whole county. But daddy was getting a reputation as a good builder, and some of the prominent white families were contacting him to do their work; since being black his labor prices naturally were cheaper but his work was just as good or better. Daddy had recently done some work for another prominent white lawyer in town, Mr. Bob McFarland, and his young son, Attorney Joe Alex McFarland no blacks were building new houses during those times, especially not stylish houses like the one daddy was building for the young lawyer, and black carpenters were mostly relegated to doing remodeling work and building barns, smokehouses and farm buildings.

I can remember daddy talking to mama and the older boys at the dinner table after it had been cleared in the evenings about the difficulties involved in building houses for white folks during those times; especially the difficulties the white men faced trying to please the white women. It seemed that every day they would change their minds about what they wanted in the house. They could never be satisfied about what colors to paint the walls, what kind or color of paneling to put on what walls, what arrangements they wanted in the kitchen, etc. Black women of the day took no thoughts about such things and had no choices over them even if they were to build a house.

Since daddy was only concerned about providing the labor, it really didn't matter to him. There were many times I remember when daddy would come home with his truck loaded with scrap materials because the young madam had come by the job the day before and broken down in tears crying because she didn't like this or didn't like that about something she had decided on just two or three days before. Therefore, whatever it was that she didn't like had to be torn out and redone with something else that she thought she might like better. I can remember daddy mocking her and saying that she would say, "It didn't look like that in the store, I don't like that. Honey that's got to be changed."

As I recall, one stall in our barn had been set aside to collect all of the scrap lumber and materials that were being hauled home at least once a week due to the young madam's rejection. Daddy would save some of the materials, especially the framing lumber, to use somewhere else on another job or for some odd job he had to do around our house and the farmstead. The truly scrap would be used for firewood and kindling in the winter and for stove wood in the summer and winter. In 1954 we still had a wood stove on which the meals were cooked in the kitchen.

On the Friday before this particular Saturday, daddy had left the job for good. He didn't leave the job because the house was completed, he had left because of another reason. Customarily, when the older brothers were working with daddy in the summers, and since Charles was old enough to drive the truck and had his driver's license, daddy would send him back to the lumberyard in town to pick up a bill of materials. This would save daddy from having to wait to get the materials and get to the job late. During those times and even until this day there is only one major supplier of building materials in Bay Springs; that is the Alexander's Hardware and Lumber Company which is owned by the family that everybody has long considered to be the richest family in the town and county - the Alexanders.

As was the custom and the racial ethics of the times, the black carpenters and customers had to wait until all the white customers were served and waited on before they were served. It didn't matter who got there first or last, all the whites who came while the blacks were there were served first and the blacks were ignored until all the whites were finished and gone. With this being the case, daddy knew that if he had to pick up a load of materials in the morning he was going to be late getting to the job. That is why when he had his boys working with him he would go to the job first, drop-off the men who were riding on the truck with him, unload whatever tools needed to be unloaded, and then he would either go himself or send a driver to pick up a bill of materials. When Charles was available that was his job.

On that Friday in May 1954, daddy not only had his three oldest sons on the job, he also had four or five other men. One of those men was R.J. Agee who was the son of Mr. Rice Agee who lived in the Rock Hill Community. They had arrived on the job around 8:00 a.m. and daddy had sent Charles back to town to the lumberyard to pick up the materials. The old man had an open account at the Alexander's Lumber Company and had granted permission for daddy to buy whatever he needed and to charge it to that account. However, on that Friday morning it had taken Charles an unusually long time to go and pick up the materials. Usually he was back on the job by 9:45 or 10:00 o'clock. On that day it was almost 11:00 o'clock when he returned, and when he did return the truck was empty.

Of course the first thing daddy wanted to know was what took him so long and where was the load of materials he had been sent to bring. By the time Charles returned the men had used all the materials on the job, had cleaned up all the scraps and piled them, and were just waiting for him to arrive with more materials. Naturally, daddy's attitude had gotten kind of sour. Charles' explanation was that Mr. Alexander had told him that the old man had come by the store the day before and closed the account and said to not let Otha have any more materials on that job.

For a moment daddy went into a rage: "Not to let me have any more materials for the job!! I ain't building no goddamn house for me!!!" All of the men standing around became dead silent; they knew Otha was mad and nobody said a word. They stood in dead silence for a few minutes waiting for daddy to say the next words, or to see what he would do next. After the pause, daddy turned around and picked up a big stick and hit it as hard as he could to the ground. He told the men to gather up all the tools and to load them and all the scaffolding on the truck; he was going home and he had some corn he wanted to get planted before the ground got too dry. That day would be a good day to plant it.

By the time the men got all of the tools and the scaffolding loaded it was a little after noon. Daddy told them that he would bring their pay to them as soon as he had talked with the old man, and if he didn't pay him, then he would have to make some arrangements to get them their money. Usually the men were paid on Friday afternoon unless they were going to work on Saturday morning which many times they would. With all of his belongings packed up and loaded, daddy and the men departed the job that Friday never to return again.

Daddy and his boys came home and got there just as mama was putting the food for the noontime dinner meal on the table.

Daddy made it a habit of showing up on most occasions just as mama was setting the table for a meal. No matter where he had been and no matter how long he had stayed he would always show up just as the food was being put on the table for the next meal. Often times if he had been gone from home a long time and mama wanted him to come home she would fix the food and put it on the table. It always seemed that within five minutes daddy would come driving up in the yard, get out of the vehicle he was driving and come walking through the door whistling or humming his "do-do-do-do-do" tune which he still hums till this day. Still nobody knows what that tune means or from what song it was taken, but it has a specific melody that every one of my brothers and sisters knows by memory. Daddy still hums that tune when he comes to the table for a meal. And, if you really want him to show up and be upset, sit in his chair at the head of the table. That would get you a scolding for sure.

When daddy and the boys got home he was as mad as a wet setting hen. I mean he was fuming! He and the boys came into the house and prepared to eat their meal. He told them that as soon as they had finished eating he wanted them to go the pasture and round up the mules and to get started planting the corn in the field that had already been plowed and prepared for planting. Daddy had delayed planting that particular field because he and the boys had been so busy working on the house; the family was in a rush to get the house finished. The old man had been getting mighty upset with the son and his wife lately and he wanted the house to be finished and done with; but the young wife kept changing her mind. Obviously, the old man had taken all he could and had cut off the money, that's why he had closed the account at the lumberyard. But what had upset daddy was the fact that no one had the decency to let him know.

After daddy and the boys finished their meal and had gotten the mules caught and harnessed, all of us children and daddy went to the field and got started planting corn. At the time we had four mules; Frank, Henry, Dave and Nell. In those days mules and horses used for plowing were always given a name and they were just like members of the family so to speak. Each of the older brothers had a mule that he plowed and daddy had his favorite. At that time Charles plowed Frank; Claude plowed Henry; George plowed Nell; and daddy plowed Dave. When we got to the field we had the wagon loaded with fertilizer and equipment; the boys did the harrowing and ran the planter and the girls and us two younger boys put down the fertilizer in front of them.

When daddy got the planters and harrows set the way he wanted them and got us started and lined out doing what he wanted at the pace he wanted he left the field and got in the car and took off. At that time, in addition to having the green long-bed Chevrolet pick-up truck that was used for the building business, daddy also had a

1952 blue and white Pontiac four-door sedan which was the family car driven mostly on the weekends to go to town for shopping and on Sundays for taking the family to church. I am still amazed when I think about how mama and daddy and eight children could all ride in one car, but we did.

Daddy stayed gone for about two hours and when he returned he had two gallon jugs of the clearest moonshine whiskey I have ever seen. When he drove up to the house we could see him from the field where we were busy planting corn. He got out of the car and took the two jugs, one in each hand and headed to the barn to stash the whiskey in one of his favorite hiding places; probably in a corner of the crib under the corn. We never could find his whiskey he had stashed, but we didn't get caught looking for it either.

Daddy went into the barnyard carrying those two jugs of whiskey and after a few minutes he came out with only one of them in his hand and headed for the woods down in front of the house. In front of the house was a wagon road that led to the fields and to the pastures. Daddy walked down that road which lead to the field where we were planting. He walked down the road a piece until he came to a big oak tree that sat beside the road just across from the first field next to the house, but before he got to the field where we were working. He sat under that tree where there was a patch of woods between him and us. He could see us from where he was but we could not see him clearly. Daddy never did let us see him outright drinking whiskey; he considered that to be disrespectful of his family. But from where he was under the tree that afternoon he could keep an eye on us and our progress and he could see back to the house. He sat down and he began drinking out of that jug while we worked.

Daddy sat there and drank moonshine out of that jug all afternoon until it was about time for us to quit working for the day which was about 5:30 or 6:00 p.m. We worked longer than usual because we had gotten a late start and the older boys knew that daddy desperately wanted to get that corn planted as it was already late. Usually the farmers in the community wanted to get all of their corn in the ground by April; although we had gotten one field planted there was still a lot left to be planted. When we were heading home daddy saw us coming and got up, he must have fallen asleep under that tree.

Anyway, he headed back to the house in front of us and you could tell by the way he walked that he was almost staggering drunk. He staggered into that patch of woods and hid his jug somewhere where we could not see it when we passed by, then he headed on up to the house.

Daddy must have picked that spot so he could see if anybody drove up in the driveway at the house, and so that he could keep an eye on what was going on in the field. Usually he would have been in the field with all the rest of us helping to get the planting done and supervising the work. But we all knew that daddy was raging mad and was just waiting for the opportunity to go off on somebody.

When we got back to the house, daddy had already washed up but he did not go to the table to eat right away. Mama had the supper on the table for she knew we would be ready to eat once we got home; she could see us leaving the field from the kitchen window which looked out from the east side of the house toward the fields and pastures. First the mules had to be unharnessed, watered and fed and put in their stables for the night. By this time of the year only the milk cows were fed and stabled at night; their calves were left in the barnyard all day while they grazed in the pasture, that way they were sure to come back to the barn in the evening. While one or two of the boys would take care of the mules the others would take care of the cows and feed the chickens. The girls would go inside and prepare to help mother serve the meal and get ready to wash the pots and pans and dishes she had used to prepare the meal.

When we got to the dinner table everybody was cautious and as quiet as possible; we knew not to disturb daddy or to provoke him when he was mad like this. Even at five years old I already knew when to be quiet and when to talk around daddy; if he was not saying anything the best thing to do was to keep quiet. Daddy didn't say much while he ate. You could tell as he ate that the whiskey was taking its toll, but he managed to eat anyway. Once he finished he got up from the table and walked out on the front porch and sat in a chair as if he was waiting for somebody to show up. But nobody ever came that evening.

On that Saturday morning the family got up and had breakfast and prepared to go back to the field to finish the planting. Daddy told the boys that when they came home at noon they could take the rest of the day off and they could go to town if they wanted to. Saturday afternoons were always the time that was set aside to go to town and to do whatever shopping had to be done. Either daddy and mama would go together with the older boys and the girls, or some would stay home with the younger of us children, or mama and one or two of the older boys and one or two of the sisters would go.

We went back to the field that morning and worked until noon. Daddy had gone and found his second jug of whiskey that morning and started sipping on it until the noon meal when we came home from the field. By noon daddy was feeling pretty good from his whiskey again.

As he and I and Cousin Mary Lou were there on the porch around 1:30 o'clock that afternoon all of a sudden a black shiny 1954 Pontiac sedan turned off the main road and came into the road to our house and into the driveway as if all hell had broken loose. As the dust settled, this young white man, the young lawyer, got out of the car and began screaming and cursing to the top of his voice: "Goddammit nigger why did you walk off my job yesterday, don't you know I got to get my house built?" The young Lawyer couldn't have been much more than 26 or 27 years old at the time, he looked about the same age to me as one of my older brothers.

Before he could say much else, daddy had gotten up off the porch and headed out to the edge of the yard where he had gotten out of the car and spoke back to him in a burley voice; "Hey...wait just a minute. If you want to talk to me like that, let's me and you go off down here in these woods and you can do all the screaming and cussin' you want to 'cause I got some cussin' I want to do to. But I ain't goin' stand for you disrespecting my family or disrespecting me and this old lady sitting here in front of my family. Me and you can talk but we goin' have to do it somewhere else."

Daddy didn't say anything else he just started walking toward the patch of woods down the wagon road that lead from the house to the fields in the same direction toward where he had been sitting under the oak tree on the day before drinking out of that jug of moonshine whiskey. The young lawyer walked off in the same direction behind him. It must have been about fifteen minutes later that I heard a loud scream, "Ahhh!", come from those woods and I heard fast footsteps coming from that direction. In a minute I saw the young lawyer running as if he were sprinting a 100-yard dash. He was coming as fast as he could and I could see blood coming from his mouth. About twenty to thirty yards behind daddy was running as fast as he could with his pocketknife open in his right hand and using his left hand to create momentum. He was running and cursing at the young lawyer but there was no way he could catch him; lawyer was too fast.

The two of them came out of those woods like a hound dog chasing a rabbit. It all happened so fast that it seemed like the scene was over in a flash. Daddy was just a cursing: "Don't run, goddammit, wait till I catch you; you young dumb cracker son-of-a-bitch. I'll cut your goddamn head off if I get my hands on you, you no good sorry motherfucker. Don't run goddammit!!" But the young lawyer was running for his life. He ran back in the yard and jumped in his car and locked the door before daddy could get there. By the time daddy got in the yard he had the car cranked and the window on his side wound up. He hurried and backed the car out of the driveway and headed down the narrow road away from our house toward the main road.

By the time daddy got to the edge of the driveway the young lawyer was already half the way down the one-tenth mile of road from our house to the main road. As soon as he knew he was a safe distance away and daddy in his almost drunken state was in no shape to run any further, the young man stopped in the middle of the road and rolled down his window half-way and looked back at daddy and hollered: "Me and my daddy and the Klan will be back out here to take care of you nigger," and he sped away. Daddy was too tired to run any more, but he began to walk down the road as fast as he could and he began screaming some more although the young man had driven away. "Well you and your daddy and the goddamn Klan and whoever else you want to bring can come. I'll be here; I promise you I ain't going nowhere goddamn your soul. You and your daddy and the Klan be ready to go to hell 'cause I'm already ready and I ain't going by myself. Some of you son-of-a-bitches goin' wid me."

As a young child I was frightened out of my wits. I jumped up and ran in the house where my mother was getting ready to go to town and grabbed her hand and hugged her dress-tail. By that time my sisters had come to the front door to see what the commotion was about, and the brothers had come to the front of the barnyard and were looking over the fence. Cousin Mary Lou must have been frightened as much as I was. She didn't say a word she immediately got up and started to walk toward the same road where daddy was now standing and kind of mumbling to himself. She passed by daddy and headed home. Although she was an elderly lady in her late 60's she was moving hastily. Daddy didn't say a word to her he just turned and started to walk back toward the house and headed toward the barn.

Evidently daddy had hit the young white man in the mouth with his fist, which was the reason he was bleeding. But by the time he got to the car he had blood coming down both sides of his lips and there was blood on his shirt. I think everybody was scared that daddy had cut the man, but it seemed that he had hit him and went in his pocket to get his knife by which time the young man had turned and started running back toward the house.

Mama was scared to death, but she walked out toward the barn where daddy went and started to calling him. "Otha, come on in the house don't drink no more today." But just as sure as the sun was shining daddy had to hit that jug just one more time to cool himself down. He was in a rage he was so mad; he went into that barnyard just a cursing and swearing about what he would do to the goddamn Klan if they tried to come after him. Mama walked out to the fence and continued to call him. She told the older boys who were standing by the fence to go and see about their daddy and see if they could get him to come on inside the house.

Mama and the older boys decided not to go to town that afternoon. In fact, nobody left the house for the rest of the day. Daddy eventually came on back and went in the house and he and mama went into their bedroom to talk for a while. She had the girls fix him a washtub with some bath water in it and she got him to take a bath and change clothes. After daddy took his bath and changed from his overalls into some khaki pants and a khaki shirt he lay down across the bed and went to sleep. He slept for most of the rest of the afternoon. Everybody else went about doing the chores that they normally had to do on Saturday afternoons when they would have gotten back from town. Those chores were ironing the clothes for church on Sunday for the girls and washing the car, cleaning off the back of the truck for the boys and cleaning up the yard. The girls would also mop all the floors in the house and do whatever mending of garments needed to be done. Mama and the girls would begin to prepare the desserts for the Sunday dinner on Saturday afternoons and evenings so those would be ready for the big family dinner on Sunday.

When bedtime came that night we all went to bed as usual. We didn't sit around talking about what if the Klan was to come, or what we would do if they came. Daddy didn't seem worried at all, yet in his mind he must have been thinking about it. He didn't seem to have any fear and that is probably what gave us confidence and assured us that everything would be all right.

II. FROM OFF THE SOUIN LOVEY

We never knew much about daddy's life as he grew up as a child; he never talked much about his childhood or his early life. We do know that he was born in Jasper County and was brought up around the area of northeast Jasper County in between the small towns of Hero, Penantly and Rose Hill in the New Prospect-Tioch Community. Daddy was born on March 18, 1915 somewhere in that area. At the time, his daddy, Grandpa Richard Lang and his mother, Grandma Elvira lived on a farm they were buying or had bought somewhere in that area. Daddy never showed me exactly where he was raised or where that farm was located. We do know that Grandpa Richard owned some of the best farmland there was to be had in that part of the county. As far as I can discern, it was along the road from Penantly to Rose Hill through the Tioch Community going toward New Prospect Church. The Souin Lovey Creek ran through the land.

On that same road lived Mr. Charlie Salter's family who was one of daddy's contemporaries and one of his lifelong best friends, and the son of Mr. Sam Salter who was Grandpa Richard's contemporary. Mr. Johnson Davis who was also one of Grandpa Richard's contemporaries also owned a place on that road; he was slightly older than grandpa. Mr. Charlie Salter inherited his father's, Mr. Sam Salter's, place when his father died and lived there all of his life. I do know that it was along that road that daddy and mama got married, and they were on their way home when they did.

We never knew when or how Grandpa Richard came in possession of that land. In fact, although Grandpa Richard lived to be 97 years old when he died in 1978, we never knew much about his background either. We never knew his parents, where he was born, where he came from or where he had been during the early years of his life. His mother was named Caroline Lang but I am uncertain of the name of his father. We do know that his land was situated along the Souin Lovey Creek, which is a creek that runs through the northeast part of Jasper County where the hills are rolling and there are large expanses of open meadows where the grass grows tall in the summer time. The area is situated where the elevation is highest in Jasper County. When I was a child I can remember sometimes we would ride through that part of the county and daddy would talk about the Souin Lovey Creek and how he used to roam those hills hunting and fishing as a boy and teenager. But as far as I can remember he never pointed out exactly where Grandpa Richard's and Grandma Elvira's farm was located.

We did find out over the years that Grandpa Richard was the son of an Irish planter. After Grandpa died in 1978 I found out that he was born in 1881; we really thought he was older than he was, but his social security records showed that his birth year was 1881 which made him three years younger than Cousin John and about the same age as Cousin Mary Lou. The stories we did hear was that Grandpa was born somewhere in Georgia or South Carolina; his mother was a daughter of a tenant farmer on some plantation in South Carolina and she was impregnated by the white landowner.

After Grandpa was born and was around seven years old, his folks migrated to Mississippi and settled somewhere around Hero in southeast Newton County which joins Jasper County to the north. We never knew if Grandpa had any sisters and brothers; nor did we know who his father was. Grandpa never talked about any sisters or brothers and daddy never talked about any uncles or aunts on grandpa's side of the family. He did talk about uncles and aunts on grandma's side of the family.

I have heard daddy talk about Grandpa's mother's husband who was named Jesse Lang, but as far as he knew that was not grandpa's father. I once asked him if his grandfather's name was Jesse and his

Gone to Hell This Morning

reply was that was his grandmother's husband's name, but ole man Jesse was not Grandpa Richard's daddy. The conversation went no further.

In those days black folks did not talk about their ancestors, especially if their ancestors were mixed white and black. It was against the racial ethics for black folks to admittedly talk about the sins of white men with black women, which were just as prominent after slavery and during the Jim Crow era as they were during slavery. Grandpa was evidently the product of such sin. I never could understand how white men could sleep with and have sex with women of a race they supposedly hated so much; and especially since they believed that black folks were less than human which would have made such acts another form of bestiality.

Grandma Elvira was a Thigpen from Jasper County and the Thigpens, both white and black, in Jasper County are from the same stock. Her father was a Lewis Thigpen and her mother was Nancy (Willis) Thigpen. During slavery the white Thigpen family was a prominent plantation owning family in Jasper County. The black Thigpens of the county are the products of the intermixing during slavery and afterwards. The genealogy of the Thigpens in Jasper County is wrought with children of slave women bearing the Thigpen name and being found in the households of the Thigpen slave owners during that period.

The manuscript U.S. Census Records of that time document this clearly. I saw many instances of this when I was completing my doctoral dissertation on historic settlement and racial segregation in Jasper County during the 1970's. In fact, a publication I located in the Historic Archives of the State of Mississippi in the state library in Jackson gave a complete genealogy of the Thigpens and Alexanders of Jasper County that included many of our black Thigpen cousins from the late 1800's to the mid-1950's. There are clear resemblances of facial features and stature between the white and black Thigpens of the county. I remember one white man, Mr. S.F. Thigpen, who was mayor of Bay Springs for years who had features very similar to our Cousin Harvey and Cousin Will, both of whom lived to be almost 100 years old. Cousin Will was slightly over one hundred when he died and Cousin Harvey was ninety-nine, and just died in 1997. He was my dad's cousin.

When daddy grew up and became a teenager he lived and worked with Grandpa Richard after he dropped out of school. In those days young black men were expected to work. It was considered unnecessary by white folks and many black folks for black children to get a high school education, so black people did not push their sons, especially, to complete high school. The young women usually got married before they finished. Daddy, his oldest brother, Richard Jr., whom they called Bill Richard, and his other brothers Grover and Reedus all lived with Grandpa Richard and Grandma Elvira on the farm on the Souin Lovey.

Grandpa Richard and Grandma Elvira had seven children totally. Two of them died at young ages. The seven children were: Richard Jr. (Bill Richard), Reedus, Caroline, Purvis, Otha, Nancy, and Grover. Purvis and Nancy died at young ages during infancy. Uncle Bill Richard was killed as a young man in 1948 and Uncle Grover, the youngest, was killed in 1962 when he was gunned down on the streets of Laurel.

Uncle Bill Richard married Aunt Rosie who was a Kendrick from around Hero. Aunt Caroline (they called her Sister - "Sis") married early as was the custom for young women of those times. When Aunt Sis got married she went to live with her husband, Uncle Cap (Clarence McMillan was his real name) and they had two sons, Purvis and Clarence Jr. (C.L.); they also lived in the Tioch community as sharecroppers on a white family's place. Uncle Cap never did own a house or land, he was a sharecropper all of his days until he died in the 1970's.

When Uncle Bill got married he moved to Hero where Aunt Rosie's family lived and later moved to Laurel. But Uncle Reed and his wife, Aunt Ozzie, stayed on the place with Grandpa Richard and Grandma Elvira. Uncle Grover went off to the Army, married Aunt Ruth and moved to Laurel when he came out of the Army. Uncle Bill Richard became the east Jasper County badman. He was a drinker, carouser, and generally became known to many as the baddest motherfucker on the east side of the county until somebody caught him sleeping in his car one day with the window down and slipped up on him and killed him on the spot in 1948.

Grandpa Richard was doing good on the Souin Lovey as I was told. He had a fine place of about 130 acres of prime farm land and grew plenty of cotton and corn. He also raised fine saddle riding horses and he and each of his sons who lived on the place with him would ride the horses for sport on the weekends. Grandma Elvira, they say, was a proud woman who held a firm hand over her family and could take a switch to a youngun quicker than you could blink an eye. They say she always carried a seasoned switch under her apron-tail just in case some youngun needed a good whipping.

The Thigpens were always proud people and still are today, especially the black ones. I don't know much about the white ones because not many of them are left in the county and hadn't been for years. Ole man S.F. Thigpen was the only white Thigpen I ever really knew. He was Mayor of Bay Springs and owned and ran a feed and seed store on a prominent corner in town next to the railroad tracks for many years until he either retired or got too old to run it anymore. Anyway, after he retired and left the store it was soon torn down.

When the Great Depression hit in the early 1930's everybody was hit hard. White folks suffered and of course black folks did in Jasper County. I remember daddy talking about the only man in Jasper County who had any money when the depression hit was an old white man named Mr. Sam Russell who owned a big spread over near Rose Hill that stretched along Highway 18. This highway is the other main highway that runs through the town of Bay Springs from west to east and all the way across the county through Rose Hill. Ole man Russell owned land that had once been the center of a Choctaw Indian settlement before whites settled the county in 1833 after it was given over under the Treaty of Dancing Rabbit Creek in 1830. There had been a mission school on the place for the Choctaws for years and the place became known throughout the county as the "Old Missionary Place" and it stayed in the Russell family for years. It is probably still owned by Russells or their descendants. In 1971, I helped daddy build a house for one of the granddaughters of ole man Russell on the Old Missionary Place. A few years later daddy built a replica of the old Indian schoolhouse and cabin that were on the place in the late 1880's and early 1900's for some of the Russell descendants.

The historic fact is that the settlement that became known as the Missionary was the first white settlement to be formed in Jasper County after the Treaty of Dancing Rabbit Creek was signed in 1830. History records show that in 1825 a group of Irish missionaries led by a gentleman named Bardwell established the Six Towns Mission Station in Jasper County north of where the village of Paulding was later established. Historic evidence shows that the mission station was at approximately the same site as the historic settlement known as The Old Missionary. The missionaries erected a comfortable log house two stories high, a schoolhouse and a church. The missionaries left the area in the later part of 1833 and the mission station was discontinued. The Indians stayed on in the area and the land was later deeded to private owners as the county was homesteaded and settled.

Daddy always told the story that Ole Man Sam Russell had gone to the banks and taken his money out before the depression had set in really bad and all the banks had failed and closed. He said that ole man Russell would ride around with his money in a suitcase in the back seat of his car. He had a black man who drove him around while he rode in the passenger seat and drank whiskey all day long. Whenever he could make a deal he would buy land at a reduced price, he would pay off somebody's taxes to take over their land, or he would make whatever deals he could with those who were destitute and needed money in a hurry to bail out. But, he would only bail out other white folks.

When the depression came Grandpa Richard was in no better shape than anybody else. He had land but as far as I have heard it was mortgaged and the taxes had to be paid. Black folks had only been able to buy land because the federal government had set up the Farmers Home Administration specifically for the purpose of providing financial assistance for rural farmers and African Americans to be able to purchase homesteads and farms.

Grandpa Richard had taken advantage of this program and had borrowed against the land to finance its purchase. Every year farmers had to make additional loans to purchase seeds, fertilizer and equipment to plant a crop. These planting loans had to be repaid when the cotton crop was harvested and sold; the landowner only kept what was left after the yearly mortgage note and the planting loans were paid. Many years not much was left over for the farmers if the crops were not good or the rains didn't come at the right times which was more often the case than not in the South. The local banks were not about to loan money to the black farmers without the federal guarantee and a second mortgage against the entire farm for the amount of the planting loans.

Grandma Elvira, as I understand it, was really the pusher in the family and the brain behind Grandpa Richard's operation. The Thigpens loved land and still love land. They knew and understood the value of owning land, and even today every Thigpen family I know in Jasper County owns substantial amounts of land.

One cousin of daddy's, Cousin Chester Thigpen, who lives a few miles outside of the small town of Montrose in Jasper County owns thousands of acres and has been honored over the years as one of the most outstanding farmers in the state and the nation. Cousin Harvey, whom everybody always called "Bant" also owned a lot of land southwest of Rose Hill; so did Uncle Webb who was one of Grandma Elvira's brothers who lived in the same New Homer Community as Cousin Harvey. Thus, Grandma Elvira was the driving force behind Grandpa Richard coming to own land in the first place.

During those years that Grandpa Richard had bought his land, the 1920s, most of the African Americans in Jasper County were mostly sharecroppers and tenant farmers; living and working on white landowners' places. Their existence was not much different from that of slavery. Grandma Elvira, I was told, understood the value and the independence of owning land; she had come from a landowning heritage. She knew that the way to advancement for black people was through land ownership and economic independence.

At the height of the depression Grandpa Richard was in trouble like everybody else. He had land that was mortgaged, but he had no money. He had his sons living on his place with him - Reedus and his wife and Otha - to help him work the land, but he had no money. Uncle Grover was in the Army and Uncle Bill had married and moved away to Hero which was just a few miles north of the Tioch and Penantly communities. Without money he could not pay the mortgages and he could not pay the taxes. The first year Grandpa, daddy and Uncle Reed had managed to put together enough money by selling truck crops and vegetables along with whatever equipment they could to pay part of the debts; then they had to plant another crop for which they had no money to buy seed and fertilizer. Times were hard and things were getting dimmer and dimmer all the time. Without fertilizer the crop that year was virtually a failure. Plus, with all the gins closed and out of business they had not sold the cotton from the previous year.

By 1934, daddy was a fully grown man of 19 years old. As he recalls, he had no childhood because ever since he could remember he had to work like a grown man. During those times farming was the only livelihood black men had in the South beside logging and cutting and hauling pulpwood and timber. When they did go to school, it was only for four or five months a year; usually from November till March or early April. The other time was spent helping to make a living for the entire family. For most black folks during those times the only assets they had that they could count on were their children, so they had to get the most out of them and their labor that they could. Daddy told us that as far back as he could remember, to the age of six or seven years old, he always remembers working in the fields; helping to cut pulpwood and logs, and doing whatever else had to be done to maintain the farm and make a living.

In 1934, at nineteen years old and according to the standards of the times, daddy was fully grown and way past being ready to be married and start a family and a life of his own. Plus, his brother and best friend, Uncle Reed, had already married and had his wife, Ozzie, living with him on the place. In 1934, daddy had met mama, Hattie Denham, at a yearly church gathering known as "The Association." The Denham family had lived in the northern part of Newton County in a community known as Little Rock and close to another area around the Shiloh Church community.

Every year they would have these Association meetings in the fall of the year about the time that everybody had gathered their crops, usually in late October or early November. People would come from all around and all over Jasper County, and they would come from adjoining counties such as Clarke County, Newton County, Jones County, Scott County, and Smith County.

The Association would start on Wednesday or Thursday and would go on until Sunday. Everybody who was anybody or who wanted to be somebody would come to The Association. This was the place and the time to see and be seen, to meet and to be met. In addition to having an all day long church meeting with singing and preaching, there would also be a carnival atmosphere of activities going on outside the church and in the adjoining woods. There would be fish frying, box dinners being prepared, sold and served, bootleg whiskey, and every other goody one could imagine.

Of course off in the woods the rowdies would be drinking and gambling. Occasionally, somebody would either get shot at or cut in a bad fight that would break out. Rarely would anybody get killed. There would be heavy courting and men trying to entice women to do things they knew decent young women were not supposed to do. But there would be enough immoral ladies coming around to do what the moral ones wouldn't dare let it be known that the thoughts had crossed their minds. There was always plenty of side action going on at The Associations outside the church to more than justify the need for the preaching, praying, shouting and singing that was going on inside the church.

Daddy would tell the story of how Uncle Bill would come riding down the road on his shiny stallion and all the folks would start to scatter. Somebody would scream out, "Here comes Bill Richard" and everybody would start to take cover. Uncle Bill Richard was known as a mean man and would start a fight just for the hell of it to see whom he could whip. Daddy says Uncle Bill always carried a .44 caliber pistol and would come riding up and shooting in the air. People would take to the woods because they didn't want any trouble with Bill Richard. We never knew why Uncle Bill was such a rowdy.

It was at one of those Association meetings that daddy had met mama in the Fall of 1934. Daddy says that when he saw mama standing across that church yard, the minute he laid eyes on her and her eyes met his he knew she was the woman he wanted to marry.

She was tall and fair-skinned with high cheek bones and long black hair, and she had a tan complexion that reflected her half Choctaw heritage. At 24 years old, mama's dominant Choctaw features were glimmering; she was as pretty as any woman he had ever seen. Hattie Denham was a beautiful woman who was just mature enough to be fully developed and to look like a real woman, not a teenage girl.

Of course coming to The Association, everybody wore their finest homespun and hand-sewn fashions. Being in the fall and after the harvest season, usually the people who could afford to had bought new garments for the winter months, and the women had gotten fabrics and made new dresses. But in the years during the Great Depression times were hard and nobody was dressed as fine in 1934 as would have been the case in the mid to late 1920's when times were booming. By 1934, the hard times had fully set in and everybody was feeling the effects. Still, daddy and the other young men were pretty well decked out in their double-breasted suits and spit-shined leather high top shoes. The available young men were looking to meet the available young women and the young women were looking to be met and wooed by the men. Such was the case when daddy and mama met.

One of the events that would happen at The Association was what was called a "Box Supper." At the box supper the young women would have prepared a dinner which was brought in a box about the size of a shoe box, but have enough food prepared for two people. The idea was for the men to bid on the young women's box supper as they were auctioned off. The young man with the highest bid on a woman's box supper would get the privilege of eating the supper with the young woman whose supper he had bought. Daddy says at that evening's box supper on the day he met mama, he had made up his mind that he was buying her supper no matter how much it cost. He says he spent his last dollar and borrowed a few dollars from Uncle Reed to buy that supper that evening.

After daddy met mama that October at The Association he went to Hickory several times on his horse on Sunday afternoons to visit and to court her. When daddy met mama she was living with her sister, Aunt Annie and her husband Uncle Walter. Mama's mother had already deceased and she and her daddy, Grandpa John Denham, were living with Aunt Annie and Uncle Walter, since they did not own their own place and Grandpa John had gotten too old and sickly to take care of himself. By Christmas of 1934 daddy had proposed marriage to her and she had agreed. But the catch was he would have to bring her to live with him in the house with Grandpa Richard and Grandma Elvira because he had nowhere else to take her; and he had to get grandpa's and grandma's permission. The real hitch was getting Grandma Elvira's permission; he knew she would just as soon put a switch on his behind as to agree to his getting married.

Daddy says it was around Christmas time when he finally got up enough nerve to confront his mother. To his surprise she agreed without any fuss; but her edict was that the next time he went to see this woman he had better come back with her and be married. So daddy made arrangements with a white man, Rev. George Finch, who lived in Penantly and had a pair of horses and a wagon, to take him to Hickory and to Decatur on Saturday, January 15, 1935 to pick up his bride, take them to Decatur to get the license, and marry them. Reverend Finch was also a Constable or Justice of the Peace, and was also the postmaster and mail carrier at Penantly and could perform marriages for the county.

So on that Saturday daddy says he got up early and rode his horse over to Penantly to meet the man at Buggy J's Store which was the main general store in Penantly at the intersection of the road leading from New Prospect and the main road from Paulding to Hero, which is now Highway 503 that goes on to Hickory and Decatur. Daddy says he had maybe five to seven dollars in his pocket total, and that was all the money he had in the world on his way to getting married. Out of this money he had to pay the man for taking him to Decatur and back, and he had to pay for the marriage license.

On that Saturday morning when daddy was going to get married, when he got up it was snowing and snow had covered the ground with two to three inches. Mama said she was afraid he was not coming since it was snowing so badly. As Reverend Finch was the mail carrier they had to wait until after he had made his mail delivery that morning before they could get started to Hickory and then to Decatur. Mama had packed her lunch in a shoe box and had packed her clothes in a pillow case made from fertilizer sacks and she waited for her espoused husband to come, not knowing whether he would show up or not. That day mama wore a long blue dress that she had ordered from a catalog; the only bought dress she had which she had paid for from money she had earned that fall picking cotton on a white man's farm. Daddy had on his only blue double-breasted suit.

By the time they had gone to Hickory, then to Decatur to get the marriage license and back to Penantly, it was getting late in the day. They stopped in Penantly at Buggy J's Store to get his horse from where he had left him tied in Reverend Finch's barnyard and ate the picnic lunch mama had prepared and then headed home. By then the sun was going down and daddy knew he had better be home by dark; and he remembered that Grandma Elvira had told him he had better be married when he got back there. So on the way from Penantly to New Prospect daddy says he told Reverend Finch he had to marry them before they got home. They stopped in the middle of the road along near where there was a big oak tree on the side of the road and the man performed the marriage ceremony. That tree stood there beside that road for years and when we were growing up and would pass that tree on our way to New Prospect Church or to Aunt Sis' house to visit daddy would always point to that tree and remind us that was where he and mama had gotten married.

Daddy says that when they got home and he paid the man for transporting them and for marrying them he had one dime - ten cents - left to his name, and mama didn't have a penny. That's how they got started when they got married on January 15, 1935. When they did get home Grandma Elvira had a dinner cooked for them and they ate together with Grandpa Richard and Uncle Reed and Aunt Ozzie.

Surely 1935 was a tough year and was in fact the turning point of the depression for the Lang family. Uncle Bill had married to Aunt Rosie a few years earlier and was living somewhere close to Hero where her family lived. By 1935 Uncle Bill and Aunt Rosie had already had one child, Chester, and their second and last child, Emogene, was born in 1936. Grandpa Richard and Grandma Elvira, Uncle Reed and Aunt Ozzie, Otha and Hattie were living on the place in the New Prospect-Tioch community just east of Penantly. But without money to buy fertilizer and seeds for planting in the Spring of 1935 they were up the creek so to speak. The previous years crops of nearly thirty bales of cotton and several tons of corn were in the barns and sheds. The crop could not be sold in the Fall of 1934 because all the cotton gins had closed and nobody had any money to buy the farmers' crops. Just about all the businesses that supplied farmers and bought from farmers had long been closed and shut down.

The mortgage on the farm was already in arrears, and the planting loans from previous years, although they had been extended were long past due. All these loans and mortgage notes were being called for being in default. Grandpa Richard had already sold the horses he could sell and had traded other animals just to keep food on the table during the winter.

There was no doubt that times were tight; they were so tight until sometimes the food on the table would be fatback pork and a pot of young turnips and mustards and cornbread. At other times the meat would be wild game such as rabbits or possums and raccoons if there were shells for the gun, or if they could be run down by the men. Often times they would surround a rabbit and run him down and kill him with sticks rather than wasting shotgun shells to kill him. The shells would be saved to hunt raccoons at night and shoot them out of the trees if the lower limbs were too high for the men to climb up the trees and knock them down. The possums would be caught the same way by knocking them out of trees and killing them with sticks.

The only sweet to be had was the sorghum and ribbon cane syrups and molasses that were in cans in the storehouse. Molasses was used as the substitute for sugar. Thus, whatever had to be sweetened had to be sweetened with molasses. This was the origin of some interesting recipes; for example, molasses bread which became a prominent cake in the South and is now a family tradition that my mother used to make often when I was a child and teenager growing up. Sometimes ginger would be added to the same mixture and it would be called a gingerbread cake.

Molasses was also used during the depression years to sweeten tea and coffee; or for a dinner and supper drink molasses would be poured in a glass of water and stirred up to make a sweet drink. For years daddy would occasionally replicate this drink. To me it was horrible but to him it was a reminder of where he had come from and what he had come through. The molasses bread cake was always delicious. Molasses would also be poured over cornbread to make a substitute for cake. Parched corn would be ground up and boiled to make a substitute coffee.

The family stayed on the place on the Souin Lovey Creek as long as they could. As times were hard for everybody, nobody, not even the bankers and mortgagers were anxious to throw anybody off their places, for many of them had lost their places too and were just hanging on. In fact, during the next two years Uncle Reed and Aunt Ozzie had their first and only child, Clemertine, who was the first grandchild born on the place. She lives in Atlanta today. Otha and Hattie had their first two children on the place, Charles and Claude, who were born in February 1936 and July 1937 respectively. By the end of 1937 the eviction came and it was time to move.

Having done all they could to try and hold on to the place, there was nothing else that could be done. There was no money to be had and there was no way to raise any money. So in early 1938 the Langs had to find somewhere to go; they had to leave the Souin Lovey. The farm, land and the home were gone; it had been foreclosed on and there was nothing left to do but to find somewhere to live.

Ole Man Russell had the missionary place and had tenant farmers and tenant houses on the place that had been there for years. Some of the houses on the missionary place were slave quarters that had been converted to sharecropper and tenant farmer houses. From what I have heard the Russells were decent people, especially the old lady. I heard my mother talk over the years about how Mrs. Russell was so kind to the black women who lived on their place. Daddy also remarked that Ole Man Sam Russell was always a fair man. I know daddy thought well of his sons who were his contemporaries, one of whom was named Tom Russell and another owned a Western Auto Store in Bay Springs for years.

So the Langs packed their personal belongings, what furniture they had in the house, and other effects and moved to the Ole Missionary Place located just south of the intersection of what is now Highway 18 and Highway 503 about 5 miles southwest of the town of Rose Hill. From landowners to sharecropper/tenant farmers, that was where the Langs wound up in just a few short years and that was where they would be for a few years to come. Nevertheless, they were still a family and they had decided to stay together; Grandpa Richard and Grandma Elvira; Uncle Reed, Aunt Ozzie and Clemertine; Otha and Hattie and their two sons, Charles and Claude (who by this time was already nicknamed "Bubba" because Charles as a two-year-old could not say brother plainly and it sounded like "bubba" when he tried to call him brother).

They would stay and sharecrop on the Russell place for just over two years. The main reason for leaving was because there were other families who were there before the Langs arrived and they had the preferable positions in terms of choosing the acreage they wanted to farm. Because there were so many the pickings were slim and the shares were limited. But it was a respite in time of need and at a time when they could do no better. Being at the Ole Missionary Place gave them a few years to regroup and to make some acquaintances and lifelong friends who would be endeared for a lifetime and beyond.

Our brother, George Amos, was born in August of 1939 while the family was tenant farmers on the Ole Missionary Place. I can remember many times we passed along Highway 18 just as you pass over the last big hill before you can see the vast open land of the Russells nearing the missionary and brother George would show me about where the house used to sit where he was born. It was off the highway to the north near that last big hill before the big meadow coming up to the missionary.

One white family that had acreage nearby was the Tatums. When the Langs would finish the work they had to do on the Russell place they would hire themselves out to help the Tatums to carry out the work they had to do. One of the Tatums' sons was along the same age as daddy; they worked together and became lifelong friends also. The Tatums gave the family a cow to use for milk for baby George after he was born in 1939. If it had not been for that cow to provide milk the baby might not have had a chance. There certainly was no money to either buy milk or a cow. That cow and one mule were all the family had beside what household goods they had moved from off the Souin Lovey place. Mr. Tatum (the son) would later own concrete plants in Newton and Laurel, and during the 1960's and later daddy would be one of his best customers.

The men would also work as loggers and woodsmen during the non-farming season. Although it was still difficult to sell farm goods during the late 1930's, the big white landowners like Ole Man Sam Russell were beginning to regain their strength and were making the connections necessary to ship their goods to places like New Orleans. By this time the depression was beginning to cease as President Franklin Roosevelt had been elected and was instituting the New Deal Programs for recovery.

The election of President Roosevelt had brought new hope to the entire nation and all the people, both whites and blacks alike. The WPA Programs had come into existence and were providing supplemental income to the men as they would sign on to work in the CCC Camps. Also the logging business was picking up again as the New Deal had brought a building boom to the cities of the nation.

Just south of the Ole Missionary Place in 1917 a lumbering town had been established that was built by the Gilchrist-Fordney Lumber Company, the parent company of the famous Weyerhaeuser Company. The town was about 5 miles west of Paulding and was called Foulke after the name of the lumber company that started it. The Foulke mill town at its peak had about 1500 inhabitants. The big concrete mill stomp that was the seat of the biggest sawmill in the camp was still in place in the late 1970's when I was doing the research for my doctoral dissertation, and is probably still there today.

At its peak in the late 1930's Foulke was a boomtown. The company had built tenant houses throughout the camp; segregated housing of course, with houses for the white workers on one side of the camp and shanties for the colored workers on the other side of the camp. There were also school buildings for both races, stores, and all the other commercial and retail enterprises that were needed to run a company mill town. Even a spur line of the railroad was built from Paulding to Foulke.

Hauling logs for the Foulke Mill were three other men whom daddy and Grandpa Richard already knew and who would become lifelong friends; two of them would become long-time workers for daddy in the carpentry business in later years. Those men were Mr. Lawrence Moore and Mr. Bud Johnson. We used to call Mr. Lawrence Uncle Hank and Mr. Bud we always called Uncle Bud. Over the years as they worked with daddy they became just like uncles to us children. Even other younger men who worked with us would call them uncle as we would. The other man was Mr. George Clayton who was Lawrence Moore's brother-in-law, whom daddy already knew. His daddy was a long-time friend of Grandpa Richard's and Grandma Elvira's.

Mr. George Clayton's daddy along with Mr. Johnson Davis who lived in the Tioch community, Grandpa Richard and Grandma Elvira had gotten together during 1914 and formed the Rose Hill Union Vocal Singing Convention. Grandma Elvira could sing "Sefagio" or shape-note music. This music is sung by saying or singing the names of the notes (i.e., do, ra, me, fa, so, la, ti, do, etc.) instead of singing words of the song. Mr. George Clayton, Mr. Johnson Davis and Grandpa Richard could all sing as well as grandma. Grandma Elvira and her brother, Uncle Webb Thigpen, had learned music from the white folks she grew up with as a child. She taught grandpa and Mr. George Clayton to sing the shape-note music and they became the convention leaders, since women were not allowed to take leadership positions in the church in those days. They also were the main song leaders for the First Enterprise Association from which the singing convention was formed. It was from this beginning that they led the formation of shape-note vocal singing conventions throughout the southeastern part of Mississippi in Clarke, Newton, Wayne, Jasper, Smith, Covington, Scott and Jefferson Davis Counties. Even today every year in September there is a Southeast Mississippi State Singing Convention held somewhere in this area that was begun by those three.

Grandma Elvira and her brother, Uncle Webb, taught all of their nieces and nephews, their children and their grandchildren, as well as their brothers and sisters and in-laws to sing the shape-note music. Daddy told me that they used to hold singing clinics at different churches during the year where they would teach the music to young and old alike. All of the Thigpens were natural musicians and all of Uncle Webb's children even until this day can sing and play the piano. When I was a child and we used to visit Uncle Webb's house he had at least three pianos; he was a prolific pianist himself. The piano that is sitting in my daddy's living room even today was bought from Uncle Webb before he died in the 1960's. My brother Otha Jr. is a gifted pianist and daddy bought the piano for him to develop his playing. He can't read much music, but he can play anything you can sing.

In the 1940's after all the timber had been cut and cleared in the east Mississippi area the Foulke Company closed down the mill and moved to Seattle, Washington to become the Weyerhaeuser Company and left the town of Foulke high and dry. Today if you pass through that area and know where to look all you will see that is left of Foulke is the huge concrete stomp where the main mill blades once sat. The last time I was through that area, which has been quite a few years, everything else was a big open pasture.

After Grandpa Richard lost the land Grandma Elvira was never the same again. In a few years she became depressed and a recluse; eventually she would lose her mind. Her mind and her health began to fail after a few years. The idea of losing that land and the farm was too much for Grandma Elvira. At the same time they were trying to make a go of it on the Russells' place at the Old Missionary, but the chances there were too slim. The Foulke Mill was slowing down and getting ready to shut down as the logging business was playing out. The family had to make a move, so in early 1941 make a move was what they decided to do and they did.

III. ON THE EDDINS' PLACE

Early in 1941 the family moved onto the Eddins' place. The Eddins were a white family that lived in southwest Jasper County about five miles south of the town of Bay Springs and 3 miles north of the town of Stringer. When they moved onto the Eddins' place again the entire family moved together; Grandpa Richard and Grandma Elvira; Reedus and Ozzie and their daughter Clemertine; Otha and Hattie and their three sons. The Eddins' had two tenant houses on their place which was one of the reasons an agreement was made to move to the place. Uncle Reedus and Aunt Ozzie had a separate house for themselves and the others lived in the house with Grandpa Richard and Grandma Elvira. The Eddins' place was located along Highway 15 and just a few miles south of the road that leads from the highway into the Rock Hill Community.

When they moved to the Eddins' place, Aunt Ozzie who had finished high school applied for and was qualified to teach in one of the church/community schools. In those days colored teachers only had to have finished the eighth grade in order to teach, and if they had finished high school they were more than qualified to teach the colored children. So Aunt Ozzie began her teaching career. Later she would attend college in the summers and become a certified teacher, and she taught until she retired. She first began at the church school, which was at the Carlisle Missionary Baptist Church and was located not far from the Eddins' place, but was in Smith County.

Mr. Tom Eddins was a gentleman farmer and was a military man. When the family moved onto his place he was in the army and was stationed at Biloxi. He would come home once or twice a month. Therefore, the running of the farm was mainly left up to the Lang men. At the time that the Lang family moved to the Eddins' place the U.S. was on the verge of getting involved in World War II. Thus, Mr. Eddins commitment to the military service had precluded his being able to run a farm. His was a farm that was just being cleared and made ready for crop farming. Most of his acreage was in timber and stumps; hence one of the major chores the Lang men faced in moving to the place was clearing new ground acreage for planting.

The move from Rose Hill to the Eddins' place was a difficult one. It was a move to new territory and new circumstances. It was especially hard for Grandma Elvira. All the people the Langs knew and loved, all of their friends and kindred lived on the east side of Jasper County; from Hero to Penantly to Rose Hill and Twistwood, which was just south of Rose Hill. Although they only moved to the opposite end of the county it seemed like the other side of the world. They hardly knew anybody in the southwest part of the county and the land was rough; yet they had to make their way.

With the country heading into war there was much uncertainty as to whether the men would be called up for military service. With much of the land on the Eddins' place being uncleared for farming there was uncertainty about whether there would be enough cotton and corn raised to provide for the Eddins' and the Langs' needs. Some decisions had to be made in the midst of these uncertainties. After they moved Otha and Reedus went to work hauling timber and logging during the winter months. When the Spring of 1942 came they started clearing new ground to expand the planting acreage. Mr. Eddins had given them free rein to do what was necessary to make the place a productive farm. They realized that whatever they did would eventually be for his benefit and not for theirs.

The anxieties of frequent moving from place to place, the remembrance of the loss of the land on the Souin Lovey and the wear and tear was taking its toll on Grandma Elvira. She began to lose her mental faculties; her mind was going bad and she was becoming rebellious, resentful, hallucinatory and difficult to cope with. Grandpa Richard's resorting to drinking was not making things easier for the family. Not only were they having to monitor grandma's every move and action, they were also having to work long hours and keep grandpa from becoming an alcoholic and a problem drinker.

The situation was becoming grave for the family. It was especially complicated by what was happening to Grandma Elvira. Not only had she lost her mental faculties, her situation was making things unbearable for the rest of the family. To complicate matters even more, in late February 1942, Otha and Hattie had their fourth child, Walterene, who was their first girl. As ill as Grandma Elvira had become she still showed untiring devotion to that baby. She would stay up all night rocking and seeing after the baby; she would be talking to the baby; singing to the baby; and generally rambling on and on. In the process, though, nobody else could get any rest. There was great fear beginning to emanate because she had become so attached to the baby until she would not let anybody else do anything for her. She had become obsessed with caring for that child.

Grandma had begun to ramble not only in her mind but also in her actions. In a moment she could disappear into the woods or wander down a road, or just start walking and nobody would know where or which way she would be headed. There were often times during those months when the entire clan would have to search the woods and roads for her because she had gotten out of sight quicker than they would know she had gone. Sometimes Grandma Elvira would be just walking the road and singing; she loved to sing and even in her insanity she would still sing eloquently. The situation eventually became unbearable and they had to make the decision that they had dreaded having to make.

The State of Mississippi's main mental institution has always been located in a place known as Whitfield which is just southeast of Jackson and between Jackson and Brandon. In the Summer of 1942 the family had to commit Grandma Elvira to the facility. There was no other way; as much as the family dreaded doing this it had to be done for the sake of them all. It was either that or they would have had to restrain her at home which was impossible without causing her physical harm. She had become violent and almost totally uncontrollable. So for her safety and for their safety and in the best interest of the entire family they did what had to be done.

Having to commit Grandma Elvira to the mental hospital was a serious blow to the family but there was no other way. This was what had to be done. It was even more difficult because the family had no easy way of going back and forth to Whitfield to see about her. Not knowing many people in that part of the county also complicated the situation even more; and even worse was the fact that there was not much money available to hire anybody to transport them when it was convenient to go and see about her.

The first time they went to see about her Mr. Eddins had come home just before he was being shipped off to Europe to fight in the war and was to be home for a few weeks. Grandpa Richard hired him to carry them to see her and he was kind enough to oblige. Another time they went to see her Mr. Odis Duckworth who lived in the Rock Hill Community was hired to drive them. He had a big truck that he had bought to haul pulpwood and to haul cotton. The truck had a hauling body on it that could be taken off for hauling pulpwood. For the trip to see Grandma Elvira he had the hauling body and the family put chairs and stools in the body and sat on those for the trip. One other time they went to see her, Mr. Purgie Beavers who was Cousin John Beavers eldest son, was hired to carry them as he had a car of some make and vintage. The children were taken on the trip in the truck as it was the only vehicle that was capable of carrying the entire clan. On the other trips only the adults went with some being left behind to see after the children.

In April 1943, Otha and Hattie had their second daughter, Brenda Joyce. By this time they had settled into living on the Eddins' place and had been attending the church in the Rock Hill Community where they had met people and had begun to have association with them. They had come to know Cousin John and Cousin Mary Lou Beavers who were the patriarch and matriarch of the community, and were also the father and mother and father-in-law and mother-in-law of many of those who lived in the community and attended the church. As Grandpa Richard and Cousin John were of the same age and generation they had hit it off very well and their acquaintance proved valuable.

Not long after Brenda was born in 1943, Grandma Elvira died at Whitfield. They brought her back to Jasper County and buried her in the cemetery at the Hopewell/Wesley Chapel Methodist Church, which is located in the Tioch Community about a mile south of Penantly. Other members of the family - Grandpa Richard, Uncle Bill Richard, Uncle Grover - would be buried in this same cemetery over the years as had been the other siblings who had died in infancy; but none of their graves were marked the last time I visited the cemetery in 1999 as their markers had been removed or deteriorated badly over the years.

After Grandma Elvira died, Otha made it his mission to own a farm again. His mother's passion for land ownership had been his inspiration for both ownership and independence. Realizing how important owning land had been to her, it became his inspiration to seek to own land of his own. Daddy and Grandpa Richard decided to seek out and buy another place of their own as a joint venture. Since Grandpa Richard had been foreclosed on before when he lost the place on the Souin Lovey, his reputation would not allow a place to be bought in his name. So daddy had to be the sole proprietor.

The family stayed on the Eddins' place a few more years until 1946, when they got the house built on the place in Rock Hill. Shortly after Grandma Elvira died in 1942, Otha made a deal to buy 120 acres from Cousin John Beavers in the Rock Hill Community. In 1943, he bought the farm from Cousin John for $1200, which was financed by the Farmers Home Administration. A home had to be built on the place, so daddy and Grandpa Richard found a barn that was being torn down and was for sale. They bought the lumber from the barn and used it to build a small 5-room house. In late 1946, Otha and his family and Grandpa Richard moved into the house on the farmstead in the Rock Hill Community. Reedus and his family would stay on at the Eddins' place for another year and then he bought a place just north of the Rock Hill Community and moved there.

Once again the Langs were landowners and full-time independent farmers. Mama didn't mind moving away from the Eddins' place at all. In fact, she was rather happy to finally be moving into a house of her own. Mama and Mrs. Eddins had never gotten along very well; Mrs. Eddins would tend to exert her authority and would help herself the to belongings of the tenants as if they were all her own. She would just go into the Langs personal gardens and help herself to their vegetables and not think anything about it. That would upset mama. Daddy often joked about how the worms would start on one end of the rows of greens or peas and Mrs. Eddins would start on the other end. By the time the worms and she got through picking there wouldn't be any left for anybody else.

IV. GRANDPA RICHARD AND MAMA LELA

Although Grandpa Richard had lived with the family until they moved to the Rock Hill Community, I didn't get to know him or really come to know and recognize who he was until I was eight or nine years old in the late 1950's. I had seen him before then as a little child and had admired him so that I had proclaimed my own nickname – Richard - after him. From the time I could remember all my brothers and sisters, as well as mom and dad and the aunts and uncles have called me "Richard". Even my closest friends from high school still call me by that name. At some point in my early years, before I can even remember, I had met Grandpa Richard when he came to visit at our house and had declared that I wanted to be called Richard after his name.

Right after the family moved to Rock Hill Community Grandpa Richard met and married our step-grandma Lela Chapman, whom we all called Mama Lela. She was a proud woman from a prominent family that lived in the area close to Hero in a community known as the Mt. Moriah Community after the church located there to which they belonged. Mama Lela had been a schoolteacher at one of the church schools in the community and had a high school diploma, which was more than the certification needed to teach at the colored schools in those days. Her previous husband by whom she had several grown children had been killed in the war; thus, she had inherited the farm they owned and his veteran's pension. So she had money coming in every month and a fairly decent house to live in. Grandpa Richard didn't have much of anything.

Ever since I knew Grandpa Richard from the time I can first remember him, he always wore a suit and necktie. In fact, Mama Lela insisted that he always wore a suit and necktie. Every time we saw them, as far back as I can remember, he was wearing a suit coat, dress trousers and a white shirt and necktie. It didn't matter whether he was going anywhere special or not, he wore his suit and necktie wherever he went. Why Grandpa Richard was always dressed to kill I never really knew, but every time we saw him he was suited up. It was probably because Mama Lela had been a teacher, and in those days teachers were somebody special. Thus, it was a status symbol for her husband to be dressed up wherever they went.

I never really knew what Grandpa Richard did or had done for a living until I was older. When I became old enough to know and remember him he was already an old man in his seventies and had a bald head. He was a dumpy, short man of about five feet and six or seven inches tall. He was always a pleasant fellow, but also a stern man. I never remember him working the farm he and Mama Lela lived on or raising any crops though he must have raised corn and cotton. But later on their farm was all turned into pasture and was growing up in seedlings, and he never had more than one mule and one or two cows. He must have used the mule to plow the garden because there was a rather decent garden that was next to their house on the west side.

Undoubtedly Grandpa Richard had worked hard over the years. I remember him having a study build and his body was solid as a rock. He loved to rock us little children on his knees. He would sit us on his knees and bounce us as if we were riding a horse. His frame reflected his Irish ancestry. Being a relatively short man his hands were disproportionately large. It seemed he had the largest hands of any man I ever saw, and all the men in our family have similarly large hands.

Grandpa Richard never did have much money and he and Mama Lela never did own a really good car. He always had old cars that could hardly make a trip to town and back without having a breakdown. He was one of the few people in the county to ever own a Studebaker. He had an old Studebaker Lark that would hardly run most of the time and for which it was almost impossible to find parts when it needed repairs. Plus, Grandpa Richard hardly ever kept enough gas in his cars to make it to town and back without running out of gas.

There would be times when Grandpa Richard would be on his way to town or somewhere else and would call daddy from wherever he was to come and get him because he had run out of gas. It didn't matter to him that he lived on the other side of the county. There was one time just around Christmas that he called late in the night for daddy to come and get him. Mama Lela had a daughter, Flora, who lived in Los Angeles, California and she was going to visit her for Christmas. In order to catch the train for California she had to go to Hattiesburg, which was south of Laurel and Bay Springs and probably 70 miles from where they lived close to Hero. It must have been on a Saturday night that grandpa was on his way to Hattiesburg to take Mama Lela to catch the train.

Anyway, Grandpa Richard had gotten somewhere between Bay Springs and Laurel when he ran out of gas. This must have been around Christmas of 1954 because Charles was still at home. So grandpa had gone to some white family's house close by the road where his car stalled and gotten the man of the house to bring him to our house for daddy to come and get him some gas. It was a cold night and daddy hated to get out of bed, but he woke up the older sons and they got up to go with him. As there was nowhere to buy gas that time of night, and daddy didn't have any in a can there at home he decided to take the truck and car so that the boys could pull grandpa's car back to our house as he brought grandpa and Mama Lela in the car.

As it turned out, when they got to where grandpa's car had stopped, he didn't have any money in his pocket at all and had only had a quarter tank of gas in his tank when he started out. Daddy scolded him for doing such a stupid thing in the cold of winter, but that did no good. Daddy ended up taking Mama Lela to Hattiesburg to catch the train and buying grandpa gas to get back home.

Mama Lela made it to California all right. But when she got out there she had no money to make it back home. She had gone out there with no money in her pocket thinking that her daughter would have money to send her back home. However, her daughter was just making enough to sustain herself and could not afford to send her home. Grandpa Richard of course had no money to send her for a train ticket home so she was stuck.

She stayed in California all that winter and until the summer. In fact, Grandpa Richard had planted his crop before she eventually made it back home. One day that summer somebody who lived close by Grandpa got the word to daddy and told him he needed to come and see about his daddy; something was wrong because Grandpa Richard had been acting strange. It was in the middle of the summer, but when daddy arrived at Grandpa Richard's house that evening he was sitting by the fireplace with a big fire roaring and wrapped in his overcoat and a blanket.

Grandpa Richard had concocted a scheme to get the money to get Mama Lela back from California. He was planning on setting the house on fire and burning it down to collect the insurance and using some of the money to send to Mama Lela to pay her train fare back home. He was going to pretend to have gone insane and not know what had happened or how the house had caught on fire. That was why he was burning a fire in the fireplace for a few evenings and walking around in the dead of summer with an overcoat and scarf on everyday. He was trying to convince people who lived close to him that he was losing his mind. Daddy scolded Grandpa Richard severely this time, but again it did no good. Daddy ended up sending Mama Lela the money to come back from California and Grandpa Richard was supposed to pay him back after he had gathered his crop and sold his cotton. Of course daddy never did get a cent of his money from grandpa, and neither he nor Mama Lela ever mentioned the money owed daddy again.

They said Grandpa Richard was receiving a pension of some kind, but nobody ever said and I never knew what kind of pension or what it was from. Evidently he must have been drawing a pension from Social Security in his later years. The only work I can ever remember daddy talking about him ever doing was building barns and doing carpentry remodeling work. I know that he was known for his barn building skills because when we would ride through the eastern part of Jasper County and the southern part of Newton County at times daddy would point out to us barns that Grandpa Richard had built.

Up until Mama Lela died in 1977, every now and then, she and grandpa would come and spend a weekend or a few days with us once or twice a year or so. They would always come on the weekend in the summer when we were having the revival at Blue Mountain. Grandpa enjoyed that because he would get a chance to see Cousin John and Cousin Mary Lou when they were living, and all the other people in the community whom he had gotten to know when he had lived in Rock Hill and when they had lived on the Eddins' Place before.

Every Christmas we would go to Grandpa Richard's and Mama Lela's for Christmas dinner. Mama Lela and her daughter, Mae Lou, who lived next door to her and Grandpa Richard would cook up a big Christmas dinner of all of their favorite dishes. They would have either roast chicken or turkey and dressing, collard greens and several other vegetables, fried corn, candied sweet potatoes, potato salad and all kinds of relishes and deserts galore. They would always have way too much food cooked up. Before the meal was served, Mama Lela would have everybody gather around the dinner table and she would have us to sing two or three songs and she would pray a prayer and have grandpa to pray a prayer. Then she would read a scripture or two and make a big ceremony. We children would be anxious to eat and we hated going through all of that pomp and ceremony before we could dig into the food.

Although they lived in a decent house, it was not a luxury mansion, and it was heated mainly by the big fireplace in the living room and a heater in the sitting room between the kitchen and the living room. The formal dining room was off from the main portion of the house and had no heater in it. Thus, at Christmas time it was fairly cold in the dining room. By the time we got to eat the food would have gotten cold and would need to be heated again which caused another wait.

We used to always joke about how Mama Lela would pray and sing so long until the food would have gotten cold, and how the collard greens would have about a half inch of solid grease frozen over them by the time we got a chance to eat any of them. It was painful for us young children to have to wait so long to eat Christmas dinner at Mama Lela's house, but she had to go through her ritual. We thought we would freeze to death waiting to eat in that cold dining room while she sang and prayed and read scriptures. Each year as siblings got older and could make their own decisions, more and more they would decide to stay home rather than go to Mama Lela's Christmas dinners. However, as we got older and in college, we came to look forward to visiting Grandpa Richard and Mama Lela at Christmas time. It became a family ritual that we came to enjoy.

As we got older and Grandpa Richard got older it became a joy to visit him because he was always so grateful whenever somebody came to visit him. He dipped snuff, and would sit in his rocking chair in the sitting room where the fireplace was and would dip his snuff and spit the snuff juice into the fireplace. It was so funny to us because he would sit about eight to ten feet from the fireplace and would spit into the fireplace from there. He would make such a big deal of his spitting; he would rear back in his chair and make a big heave toward the fireplace leaving a stream of snuff juice all the way from his chair to the fire along the floor. Somebody would always have to be cleaning up his trail of snuff juice.

In the summer time he would sit on the porch and dip his snuff and spit into the yard off to the side of the porch. When the fire was roaring in the fireplace in the winter, Grandpa Richard would almost drown out the fire with his snuff juice. He would wait until he couldn't hold it any longer because he would have so much in his mouth, then he would spit a long stream into the fire. The fire would make this roaring noise as if somebody had poured water on it.

Whenever Grandpa Richard came to visit us and went to church with us he would always borrow a dip of snuff from Cousin Mary Lou, Cousin John, or Cousin Rosie, who was Cousin John's and Cousin Mary Lou's daughter. He would have his own but he just wanted to have a taste of theirs. He would always say to one of them, "Let me have a dip of your snuff, yours might taste a little better than mine." We would be cracking up laughing at grandpa borrowing a dip of snuff. Snuff dippers had a bond just like smokers; one snuff dipper could always bum a dip of snuff from another.

Grandpa Richard also liked to take a swig of whiskey now and then when he got older. He had been a real whiskey drinker in his young days but as he got older he could only take a sip because his steps had gotten slower and because of his arthritis in his knees he had to walk with a walking stick. Whenever the older boys would go to visit him they would always take him a taste of whiskey. They would only take him a half-pint bottle of bourbon which was his favorite and he could slip the half-pint into the inside pocket of his suit coat where Mama Lela wouldn't see it. Daddy used to always laugh about how grandpa would take a swig of the whiskey and lick his lips with his tongue before he would wipe his mouth with his arm and the sleeve of his shirt. Every time grandpa would take a drink of whiskey he would go through that motion; lick his lips, and wipe his mouth with his arm.

After a few minutes he would say, "I believe I'd better take another drink of this whiskey; I believe this tastes better than the last I had." Although he would always have the same brand, after that second drink he would declare, "You know, I believe this is some of the best whiskey I ever had." It was so funny to us because no matter when grandpa had a drink of whiskey it was always better than the last whiskey he had, and would end up being the best he ever had.

Daddy used to laugh many times when he would tell the story of how grandpa had come to church once and had had too much whiskey before he came, so he was about half drunk. They were having a singing convention so they had called on grandpa to lead and direct a song. The choir was singing with him, but grandpa got lost in the song and lost his timing. The choir had gotten ahead of him and gone on with the song. Grandpa had stopped the choir and declared, "Y'all wait, dammit, y'all don' got ahead of me. Don't run-off wid my song. Wait on me." Everybody had broken out laughing at grandpa because they knew he was a bit tipsy. But the people took it in good humor and replied, "Uncle Richard you know you don' got lost."

For some reason Aunt Sis never did get along with Mama Lela and never did like her at all. Everybody else in the family would call her Mama Lela, but Aunt Sis always called her Miss Lela. She never did approve of grandpa marrying her in the first place and she always thought that Mama Lela was too uppity. We never did understand her resentment of Mama Lela, but we knew she didn't take kindly to her. It would be Aunt Sis who would wind up looking after Grandpa Richard during the last year of his life after Mama Lela had passed away in 1977.

V. ROCK HILL COMMUNITY

Not everybody who participated in the Civil Rights Movement marched in the streets, sat-in at restaurants and lunch counters, rode on freedom rides, or participated in voter registration drives. Not all of the civil rights fighters of the 1960's and 1970's were beaten by police, bitten by police dogs, drenched with fire hoses and hauled off to jail. Some who were advocates of civil rights chose to fight their own fights, and kept their own faith; they stood on what they believed, defied the racial ethics of the times and lived to fight another day. My father, Otha Lang, Sr., was one of those people who chose to go it alone. Yet, he fought a good fight and won the victory; and he did it his own way.

I was about four or five years old when I first remember anything about my family and myself. Yes, it was in the Spring of 1954 that I have my first recollections of my life and my family. It was around the time of my birthday, early April 1954, that I came to first remember anything about my life. It was also around the same time that my oldest brother, Charles, was graduating from high school.

I was born on April 2, 1949 and for my birthday in 1954, Cousin Mary Lou Beavers had killed a duck and fixed a special dinner for my birthday. Cousin Mary Lou and Cousin John Beavers were the elderly couple who lived on the farm next to ours, but their house was only about a good tenth of a mile from our house; just about a good four or five minutes walk. As a child I could easily run it in three minutes flat.

In 1954, we lived in a little green five-room house on a farmstead of 120 acres in the community of Rock Hill which was a rural neighborhood of mostly African American owned farmsteads. The Rock Hill Community is located about five miles south of the town of Bay Springs, Mississippi, and west of Highway 15. Bay Springs is one of the county seats of Jasper County in the east central portion of the state. Paulding, which is a town on the east side of the county, is the other county seat. There were 15 to 20 or so African American families who owned farmsteads and lived in the Rock Hill community. There was one white family, the Jernigans, who also lived in the community, and two other whites that owned land in the community but did not live there; they were Mr. Buddy Foster and Mr. Robert Abney. Most of the families in the community owned 60 to 120 acre farmsteads; a few maybe had more and a few had less. But everybody mostly farmed as their main source of livelihood.

Almost all of the men in the neighborhood who owned land were farmers, but they also did something else after the farming season had passed. For example, the men who had teenage children would usually work at other jobs or trades during part of the year and even during the farming season if the children were old enough to do most of the farm work. Almost every family had four or more children, for children were an asset on the farms as they were the main source of labor; except perhaps during harvest time when neighbors and neighbors' children would be hired by each other to help especially with the cotton picking.

My daddy farmed and he also was a carpenter. By the mid-1950's he had become highly skilled and widely known for his expertise as a house builder. He had learned the carpentry business by trial and error, and by teaching himself the trade. His daddy, Grandpa Richard Lang, had also done some carpentry work over the years, but not like my daddy. Otha Lang had set out to become a master of the trade from the time he had begun, for in it he saw a way out of the life of poverty and the living hand-to-mouth of a dirt farmer. Daddy often told us the story of how the only pay he received for the first house he contracted to build was one window sash unit, which was an extra one he ordered for the house but didn't use. After he paid all of his labor and material bills that was all he had left; he knew then he either had to learn the business or get out. He decided to learn the business.

So in 1954 with all of his children still at home, and the oldest just finishing high school, daddy was almost at the height of his farming and was beginning to make the carpentry business his main priority because the oldest three sons were doing most of the farming. This allowed daddy to concentrate on his carpentry business. Rather than just doing repairs and rehab jobs, daddy had taken on a crew of four or five men, some of whom had some experience in carpentry and some who were young men in their twenties with young families whom daddy had taken under his wings to train and teach them a trade.

Throughout his career as a carpenter daddy often took young men under his tutelage who were just starting out in life and allowed them to learn some aspect of the building trade. Some became carpenters, others became brick and stonemasons, still others became roofers or concrete finishers. Many of them and their sons and grandsons still practice the trade they initially learned by beginning working with daddy who paid them and gave them the opportunity to learn the trade that would sustain them for a lifetime. That was daddy's method of community development and freedom fighting. He believed that a man who had a trade and skill could go anywhere and command a job to make an honest living for himself without being dependent on anybody else. He believed if you had a skill it didn't matter what color you were, you were an individual of worth and the world would recognize you and give you a chance.

Thus, each of his five sons was skilled and qualified in some aspect of the carpentry trade. The only brother who had absolutely no interest in the trade, Otha Jr., still learned to be an expert painter and as he grew up to own his own home wished he had taken a greater interest in learning more of the trade.

In 1954, as I remember, we were farming about 80 acres of the 120 acres daddy owned and the other 40 acres were in pasture and timber. He needed the pasture for grazing for the four mules he owned and the twenty or so herd of cattle. Cotton was the main cash crop, and corn took up the largest portion of the remaining cropland. Daddy was probably planting close to 50 acres of cotton and 25 acres of corn. The other cropped acres were in vegetables for consumption and subsistence such as sweet potatoes, peas and beans, peanuts, sugar cane for molasses, beets, and greens.

I never shall forget that Spring of 1954. It seems that everything in life came to me crystal clear and it is as vivid in my mind today as it was then and has been over all these years. On my birthday I remember going up the road to Cousin Mary Lou's and Cousin John's house for the mid-day meal, which was called dinner instead of lunch. Cousin Mary Lou had prepared the roast duck and dressing (stuffing), which was made from cornbread, onions, green peppers, and spices like sage and garlic, and the broth from the duck. Dressing was always served with baked chicken, duck, turkey and other fowls. She also had a pot of butter beans, hot corn bread, candied yams and lemon pie. Cousin Mary Lou always had a jelly cake and a caramel cake which she baked on the weekends for the Sunday dinner. It was always a pleasure to go to her house to eat because she was the best cook in the community and she loved to feed the children who came to her house to visit. One of the greatest joys as a child was going to Cousin Mary Lou's and Cousin John's house anytime during the week.

Cousin Mary Lou and Cousin John were the oldest people in the community, in fact they were the ones who founded the Rock Hill Community. Cousin John had been born in the 1870's as the son of a white man and a black woman. You could obviously tell that he was half-white because his hair was long and black and naturally straight. I remember as children my sisters loved to go to Cousin John's house and comb his hair. They would get his hairbrush and comb and they would comb and brush his hair as long as he would let them. Each one would take a turn combing and styling his hair; then the next one would mess it all up and re-comb and style it. It was a joy to them and he didn't mind one bit.

It was fascinating to see a black man with such "good" hair. At the time we had no idea Cousin John was half-white. We just knew him as the kindest old man, and Cousin Mary Lou was the kindest old lady. She was the closest I had to a grandmother because I never knew either of my real grandmothers; I only knew my step grandmother whom Grandpa Richard married after Grandma Elvira died. My mother's mother and father were dead long before I was even born. Cousin Mary Lou would always make a big pan of biscuits in the morning for breakfast because she knew that as soon as the mailman came and brought the mail my sisters and brothers would get the mail and bring it to their house and she would fix each one a biscuit with something special in it. My favorite was a biscuit with jelly in it; we called it a "jelly biscuit." My brother, Otha, who was almost two years older than me, would get a biscuit with a piece of ham or fried fatback in it; we called his a "meat biscuit." Everyday around 10 o'clock we would get the mail and head to Cousin Mary Lou's and Cousin John's house to get our biscuits, especially in the summer time when the other sisters and brothers were out of school and we had all the farm work done.

The mailboxes were located at the church, about three-tenths of a mile from our house in the opposite direction from Cousin John's house. It was our pleasure as children to go and get our mail and their mail and bring it for them because we knew we were going to get a treat from Cousin Mary Lou. We could hardly wait for the mailman to come and bring the mail. Sometimes we would listen for his car and we knew the sound of his engine distinctly from anybody else. Many times we would race to be the first to get to the mailbox so we could carry the mail. Other times we would do chores for Cousin John like carrying in firewood, drawing water from the well and filling his water buckets, helping to pick vegetables and shelling or preparing vegetables for canning and cooking. Many times we would get a chance to stay and eat with Cousin Mary Lou and Cousin John; the food at their house just tasted better than it did at anybody else's house.

Cousin John had inherited around 2500 acres of land from his white father sometime in the early 1920's. He had used this land wisely to found a community and to accumulate enough wealth to support himself for a lifetime. What Cousin John did was to sell the land to other African American families and thus create a community. As I recall, Cousin John never had to work for anybody else during the time I was growing up, and by the time I became a teenager he had long been drawing a pension. I never knew what his pension was from. It was probably a Social Security check.

Moreover, it is very likely that he grossed a small fortune from selling off most of his 2500 acres over the years.

There was another man who had come into a considerable amount of land adjoining Cousin John's. This man was Mr. Wash Moffett who had divided his land between his sons, Ezra, Moten, Booker T., and Harvey who had started their own farms and raised their families in the community. This man was a contemporary of Cousin John and was deceased by the time I was a child. Most of the children, except for Mr. Ezra's were grown and had moved away by the time I was old enough to remember. Mr. Ezra's children were along the same age as me and my siblings, except for some who were older than my oldest brothers.

Mr. Wash Moffett was also a preacher and had started the first church in the community on his land which was called Rock Hill Missionary Baptist Church. It was later moved from its original spot onto another plot of land which he donated for the church and the community built another church. It was named Blue Mountain Missionary Baptist Church which is still in existence and on that same plot of land in the central part of the community where the two main roads in the community come together. The building, which is now the church, was started in 1956 and completed and added onto over the years.

In 1954, every family in the community farmed, hunted, fished, gathered berries and other wild fruits in the summer and fall, and some of the men did other types of work to make a living. Seems like every household had a number of children, and each seemed to have a child the same age as everybody else's child; so every child had playmates and schoolmates the same age as they were. Every week you would see your playmates and schoolmates at school and you would see them at church on Sunday and be in the same Sunday School class with them. It was like the whole community was an extended family. And except for the Langs, it very much was because everybody else was related to the Beavers and Moffetts and the Agees. Plus, all of these families had intermarried so they were all related to each other either by blood or marriage or both except for us Langs. We were the outsiders who had been the last ones to move into Rock Hill.

Daddy moved his family to Rock Hill in 1946 after he bought the 120 acres from Cousin John and Cousin Mary Lou. We never really figured out whether or not Cousin John and Cousin Mary Lou were really daddy's cousins. We just always called them cousins. Anyway, Cousin Mary Lou had some relationship to the Thigpens in Jasper County, and daddy's mother, Grandma Elvira was a Thigpen.

It was presumed that they were distant cousins since all the Thigpens in Jasper County, both blacks and whites, were related from the intermixing that took place during slavery and the period immediately following. That is how the kinship of Cousin Mary Lou and Cousin John came about; it was more claimed than real. During those days it was customary to call people cousin if they were remotely related, or even out of courtesy.

When daddy and his family moved to Rock Hill, he was the last to buy land from Cousin John, so he got probably the last section of land that Cousin John was selling, which was located right next to his 120 acres that he was keeping for himself. You see, by the 1940's Cousin John was already an elderly man in his late 60's or early 70's. Thus, he was looking to reduce his farming since all of his children were already grown except his last son, Lemon, whom everybody called Tamp. He was fourteen or fifteen at the time. Cousin John was aiming toward retiring from farming; so it was feasible for him to reduce his landholding to a more manageable size for his maintenance. Daddy got the last portion that he would sell.

The Rock Hill community extended along a gravel road from Highway 15 all the way to the Jasper/Smith county line, and even about a mile beyond the county line into Smith County for a total of about four miles. The road was actually built through Cousin John's land to connect his farmstead home to the main highway. In fact, I heard the old men tell stories of how they helped to build the road using their mules and horses and their plows and slip-disks to grade the dirt and move it to form the road. During most of my childhood and even until I was in college in the late 1960's the road through the community was dirt and gravel. It was only in the late 1960's and 1970's that the roads in the black communities were asphalted and paved. You could tell the white communities from the black communities in the South during the segregation and Jim

Crow eras depending on whether or not the roads were paved and the conditions of and the types of houses.

The Rock Hill Community began, as I said, about a mile into Smith County where Cousin Louis and Cousin Annie Ceal Moffett lived. Cousin Annie Ceal was one of Cousin John's and Cousin Mary Lou's daughters who had married to her husband, Cousin Louis Moffett, when she was early in her teenage years. In those days, the 1930's when they were married, it was customary for farm girls to marry in their early teens and for farm boys to marry by the time they were 17 or 18 years old. Cousin Annie Ceal and Cousin Louis had 16 children during their married years. They had more children than any family in the community. Some of their children were grown and married and had children of their own before their last children who are younger than me were born. Some of their children still live within the community.

Anyway, we considered Cousin Louis' farm as the west boundary of the community although Mr. Wash Moffett owned land beyond this boundary and for years Mr. Ezra Moffett farmed this land after Mr. Wash had died. Coming east from Cousin Louis' farm toward our house was about a mile of emptiness which was timber land owned by Mr. Robert Abney and Mr. Buddy Foster who were white men who just owned the timber land but had no houses in the community. Cousin John and Cousin Mary Lou had the next farm which joined ours. Then, there was Mr. Ezra Moffett's farmstead and house that was on both sides of the road and adjoined our land. Next to Mr. Ezra's land was the church, Blue Mountain, and its cemetery which was across a road that went down behind the church over to Cousin Rosie's and her husband's farm. Uncle Sun Milsap was her husband at this time. Uncle Sun was actually her second husband. Her first husband and the father of her children was Mr. Harvey Moffett who was Mr. Ezra's brother and Mr. Wash's son who had died in 1944. Cousin Rosie later married Uncle Sun whose real name was Holiday Milsap. Mr. Harvey donated the land for the church's cemetery and the site next to it for the community schoolhouse.

Next to our land on the east and off the main road was the farmstead and the home of Mr. Hargie Campbell and his wife, Mrs. Maggie. Mr. Hargie was always somewhat disabled and could only work certain periods because of an injury he had received fighting in World War II. Thus, he farmed and also drew a disability pension. But when he worked, he worked as hard and harder than any man in the community. He always prided himself in competing in work, it was his way of showing that he was capable and although he was disabled, that he was just as good a man as anybody else. He was the healthiest man in the whole community, for he never owned a car and walked almost every place he went. He often walked the five miles to town unless somebody would pass by and offer him a ride.

The Agees were the next families who lived in the community and their land adjoined the church's land and Mr. Ezra's land going east. Mr. Rice Agee was the patriarch of the Agee clan. All of his sons had married and built houses on his land along the road joining his house and land. There was Junie who built a house next to Mr. Rice's, then Bill (whose real name was Rice Jr.) had built his house next to Junie's. Across the road was T.W. Nixon's house who had married one of Mr. Rice's daughters, Martha Ruth. Further down the road was another son, R.J. (Robert James) the oldest son and his wife Kathleen who was Cousin Rosie's daughter. In later years others of the Agee descendants, sons and daughters, grand children and great grandchildren would marry or start families and build houses along this stretch of the road. But in 1954 these were the ones who were already there as I can remember.

Joining the property of R.J. and Kathleen was the house and property of Shorty and Mary Everett. Shorty, whose real name was Houston Everett, was another implant in the community. He was called "Shorty" for an obvious reason, he was only about four feet tall, but Shorty was one hell of a man. He could out cuss the best of men and he could fight with the best of them as well. As short as he was, no one, black or white, dared fuck with Shorty; if they did they were definitely aiming for a good ass whipping. Shorty didn't take shit off anybody. His wife, Mary, was the daughter of one of Cousin John's sons, Purgie, who was married to Cousin Dorothy, although everybody called her Draughthy.

Cousin Purgie originally owned the land next to Shorty and Mary and lived and farmed there until he moved to Gulfport on the Gulf Coast and sold the place to Mr. Eli Ingram and his wife Mrs. May.

Cousin Draughthy was the sister of Cousin Purgie's brother Sank's wife, Cousin Delia. Thus, Cousin Sank was also one of Cousin John's and Cousin Mary Lou's sons. They lived off of another road that went west off the other main road in the community that split and went northwest from the church.

But further east on the main road heading toward Highway 15 and adjoining Cousin Purgie's land lived Mr. Odis Duckworth and his wife Mrs. Roena and their family. They probably owned more land that anyone in the whole community and much of their land is still in the Duckworth estate now. However, half of the land belonged to Mrs. Roena as part of her family's estate, the Barlow Family inheritance. Their land extended up the entire west side of the main road of the community from the church and adjoining T.W. Nixon's place all the way to across the road from where Mr. Odis Duckworth had his house and adjoining the only white family that lived in the community, the Jernigans, who were considered poor white trash and lived in the worst house in the entire community. After Mr. Jernigan died, his family was the first in the entire community to live in a trailer house. What a reversal of circumstances, especially in that era. I never knew until I was much older why the Jernigans were so poor, especially being white. I believe it was because the ole man laid on the bottle and wouldn't work; at least I never remember him holding a steady job anywhere. His place was always the disgrace of the entire community.

At the end of the east boundary of the community and joining Mr. Odis Duckworth on the west side and the white family that lived along side the Highway 15 and at the end of the main road to Rock Hill was Mr. Abraham Quince and his wife Mrs. Margaret and their children. These were the families along the main road into Rock Hill. The Quinces were the only family in the community that didn't belong to Blue Mountain Church, but they were very much a part of the community.

Going west from the church and away from the main road were other families who belonged to the community. The Duckworth's land ran along the east side of this road for about three-quarters of a mile until it joined the land of Mr. Wash Quince. On the west side of the road passing the church cemetery was more of Cousin

Rosie's land. At the end of her land about a half-mile past the church was a road that led to Cousin Sank's house and farmstead. Mr. Wilk Ingram and Mrs. Elzie Ingram, his wife, owned the land and lived adjoining Cousin Sank and going further northwest along that road. Mr. Wilk was the brother of Mr. Eli Ingram.

The next family whose land joined Mr. Wilk's was Mr. Virgil Duckworth who was the brother of Mr. Odis Duckworth. His land was just across the road from Mr. Wash Quince's place. Further to the west of Mr. Virgil was Mr. Delbert Moffett and his wife Mrs. Leona. Their land had actually belonged to Mrs. Leona which she had acquired with her first husband, Mr. Laster. Mr. Delbert was the next oldest man in the community after Cousin John. As a matter of fact, Mr. Delbert may have been a little older than Cousin John. He had fought in World War I and had almost frozen to death in Germany during the war. He too was disabled and was bent over as part of his disability. He always walked humped over and could never fully straighten up his back. Also his voice was very low, he could only talk above a whisper. His property was considered the further most northwest boundary of the community in that direction. Adjoining his property and that of Mr. Wash Quince was the property of another white man who had bought a place once owned by my daddy's brother, Uncle Reed, who had bought that place about the same time as daddy bought his place, but had decided he did not want to be a farmer. Or rather Aunt Ozzie had decided she did not want to be a farmer. So he had moved to Laurel and became a barber after working in the Masonite Plant, Laurel's largest industry, for a number of years.

Mr. Wash Quince moved away to Beloit, Wisconsin in 1956 and left his property vacant. He, Mr. Booker T. Moffett, Mr. G.B. Moffett and Uncle Reed were the first to move away from the Rock Hill Community area, although Mr. Wash Quince was the last to go during that period. In 1955 or 1956, Lawrence Page who was married to Cousin Rosie's daughter, Earleen, built a two-room house in between R.J.'s and Bill Agee's houses and moved into the community. In earlier years, Mr. Ezra's oldest son, E.Z., had lived in a house on the land that was owned by Mr. Robert Abney. That land had belonged to one of Mr. Ezra's brothers who had sold it to

Mr. Abney. Mr. Wash Moffett had lived on property that adjoined Mr. Ezra's to the west but was in Smith County. That property had been bought by Mr. Buddy Foster, and was also west of Cousin Rosie's and Mr. Ezra's property and was where the original Rock Hill Church was located.

This was the situation of Rock Hill Community in 1954. I have probably not included some families that should be included, but if I have not they were the sons and daughters or the sisters and brothers of some who are mentioned. There are two that come to mind already: Mr. G.B Moffett, Cousin Louis' brother, had once owned land and lived somewhere west of Cousin Louis; Mrs. Isabella who was Mr. Odis Duckworth's mother had a house she had lived in before she died which was located across the road from Mr. Wilk Ingram's place on the road that went northwest from the church. There was also a house that was vacant located across the road and west of Mr. Odis Duckworth's house that he had built for his oldest son when he had first gotten married. In 1954 that house was vacant.

In 1954, the Rock Hill Community was a typical African American rural neighborhood in the South; and there were thousands of similar communities where blacks were segregated socially and spatially throughout the rural South from Texas to Virginia. The exceptions were where blacks were sharecroppers and tenant farmers. In these instances black families who were either tenant farmers or sharecroppers would live in substandard houses located on the white landlord farmers' lands, usually but not always in a location remote from the landowners dwelling. Or, the tenant farmer families might have lived in a dwelling located on a separate holding of the landowner's but totally apart from their dwelling and maybe even in another community.

Nevertheless, in the Rock Hill Community as in other similarly situated communities all the families were two-parent families; that is, both the mother and father were present in the household unless one parent had died. Every father worked and supported his family and every mother, except in rare instances, stayed home and raised the children and ran the household. The mothers and teenage daughters prepared the meals, did the washing and ironing, canned and preserved the fruits and vegetables for the family's winter bounty. The fathers and teenage sons plowed the fields, raised and harvested the crops, cut the wood for the stove to cook the meals and for the winter's use in heating the home, mended the fences, cleared the land for cultivation, and did all of the repairs to the house, barns and sheds on the farmstead. They also hunted and fished to supplement the family's subsistence in summer and winter. Moreover, the women and children picked berries, plums, and other fruits and gathered nuts in season as well.

In rural Mississippi in the mid-1950's life for blacks was simple and seemingly easy as long as they knew their place and stayed in their places socially, economically and politically and didn't run afoul of white folks. Often times when the black men and their sons had finished plowing and harvesting their crops, or even before they had finished with theirs, they would hire themselves out to work for and help the white men in surrounding and adjoining communities to plow and harvest theirs. The whites expected the blacks to help them even if their own work had to go undone until the whites' work was completed. The black men, even though they were not obliged to do so usually did because it was expected and was the norm. A black man and his sons would be looked upon with disdain and considered uppity by whites if they turned down a request from a white man for their help, especially if it were someone they knew and lived close by.

Only on rare occasions would a white man and his sons help a black man to accomplish his work. It was considered beneath a white man's dignity to help blacks on their farms, even for hire. But once in a while it would happen, especially in instances of baling hay. Usually the whites were the ones who could afford to own hay-baling machinery and equipment; thus, they would hire themselves and their equipment to blacks. Hay-baling was a lucrative business and there was money to be made. One thing I learned early in life even in the South, when it came to making money off blacks nothing was below white folks dignity and pride. Whites have always been able to find some way to profit and benefit off black folks.

Mississippi in the mid-1950's was the scorn of the nation in race relations, discrimination and prejudice. People in Alabama,

Arkansas, Georgia and Louisiana were glad there was Mississippi. Since Mississippi was the poorest state in the nation, which it still is, and since it was hailed as the most racist, inhabitants of the other southern states could always look down their noses at Mississippi and feel proud that there was a place worse than their own states. But the same things that were going on in Mississippi were going on throughout the South. There were no safe havens in the South during those times.

But we felt secure in the Rock Hill Community just as others felt secure in their rural communities. Everybody knew everybody else and if a family needed help they could feel assured that the people of the church who were also their neighbors, friends and people of the same community would come to their rescue. It was sure that no family was going to starve or that their children would be without clothes. The women of the church and community would make sure that those less fortunate or destitute were fed and clothed, and if families needed help they were sure to get it from their neighbors.

Rarely was there ever an instance of anybody going to jail or getting in trouble with the law. The men would drink bootleg whiskey on the weekends and get drunk, but as long as they were in Rock Hill and stayed in Rock Hill they were safe. Sometimes they would get drunk and raise hell with cousins, brothers or kindred, but usually nobody got hurt and by Sunday morning, and certainly by Monday morning when it was time to go back to work everything was back to normal. Such incidents provided the fuel for the weekly gossip and ridicule. Usually the culprits would be so ashamed that they would be fearful of showing up at church because they knew everybody else would be talking about and ridiculing them.

In those days it was almost unheard of for a black man to take off and leave his wife and children without support. It was almost unheard of for children to be unruly and disrespectful of their parents, or any other adults in the community. If a man did leave his wife and children, the men of the church and the community would take it upon themselves to see to it that the family was provided for. That man when he did show himself back in the community would be expected to give account of himself to the church and community as to his intentions before he would be accepted back into good graces and fellowship in the community.

It was also just as rare that a young girl or single woman got pregnant out of wedlock. I remember when the first incident of that kind happened; it was a public scandal of unequaled magnitude. It was the custom for the young woman to come before the church body and make a public apology to the community for having committed such a sin. Plus, she was ostracized and the other young women of her age would no longer be allowed to socialize with her. The consequences for a young man who impregnated a young woman were not as severe, but he too was looked upon with disdain, especially if he did not marry the woman and support the child.

It could well have been that 1954 was the best of times and the worst of times for the families in Rock Hill. At any rate, it was to be the beginning of a new era in the South. However, being a young child then it seemed like heaven to me. I had four older brothers and three sisters to look after me and a mother and father who seemed to love us more than it was possible to love in those days. Plus, I had Cousin Mary Lou and Cousin John next door who were surrogate grandparents and they loved us just like their own grandchildren in the community. What more could I have asked for in rural segregated Mississippi in the mid-1950's?

Going to church and going to a hog-killing seemed like two of the greatest pleasures that anybody could have ever had in life because usually you could see almost all the people of the community at either. And, at either event on most occasions you got the chance to eat all you could hold, especially at the revival meetings they would have in the summertime at the churches in every community throughout the county. They were called "protractor meetings" and until this day nobody has ever been able to tell me why. But each year starting in late June through early September, on every Sunday during that time there would be one at some church. And just about every Sunday during that time we would go to a revival somewhere.

Although there would be two or three sermons preached on those days, the big attraction was the eating. The mothers would cook and bring a big box of the best foods they knew how to cook. Usually they would have baked chickens, hams and dressing, ham hocks and the best greens, beans and peas, dumplings, potato salads, cakes and pies and cobblers of every kind and all the other kinds of good food you could imagine, and everybody could eat as much as they could stand. Often relatives from the northern cities like Chicago and Detroit and other places would come back home and spend that whole week of the revival. It was like a homecoming celebration. These were the joyous events of the summer. Yes, it was the best of times and the worst of times.

Usually somebody in the community would slaughter a young yearling cow and would sell shares of the meat to any other family that wanted to buy some. Or, two or three men would go together and buy a young yearling and slaughter it and divide the meat among them. So there would be plenty of good fresh beef in the box dinners and there would be plenty to eat off all week long. People in the community probably ate more beef during that week than they would all year long. Back then there was really no way to preserve beef for long periods of time as nobody had refrigerators or freezers in which to store frozen foods. The cold storage they had was iceboxes that were not powered, but were insulated storage bins. People would buy ice from the icehouse in town or off the ice trucks that would come through the community every so often selling blocks of ice in 25 or 50 pound blocks that would be wrapped in blankets and stored in the ice boxes. Sometimes these blocks would last almost all week depending on how hot it was and how well insulated the icebox was. At mealtimes, ice would be chipped off the block to fill the glasses of drink being served with the meal. It was a real luxury to have ice-cold drinks for dinner and other meals.

I can remember that during the revival and at Christmas daddy would always make a banana cake that was his favorite. Daddy was an excellent cook and every now and then on the weekend he would fix some flapjacks that he loved also. His flapjacks were the best in the world, and he could fix two different kinds. One kind was made mostly from corn meal and the other was made from flour. When daddy fixed flapjacks and salmon patties we were delighted because we knew we were eating high on the hog.

Also, when the women were serving the dinner on the grounds during the Sunday afternoon of the revival, daddy and the other men would always stand around and hold their wives purses while they served the meals. This was the only time you would ever see the men of the community holding a woman's purse under any circumstances. Holding a woman's purse was something that a man would not normally be caught doing except at this special time of the year.

Like the annual revival, hog-killings in the community were special times. Usually people would start to kill hogs and cure their winter meat around Thanksgiving when the weather began to turn cool. Prior to that time for about a month the hogs that were going to be killed and cured would be put in a special pen and fattened up by feeding them on corn and other grains. This was done so that the hogs would put on as much fat as possible; the hogs were not only for meat but also for lard, which was the fat produced from cooking out the fat meat of the hogs. The lean meats were preserved for eating.

At hog-killing time neighbors would come and help with the process which would take all day and into the early evening. Usually a family would kill three or four hogs at a time, and if it were a large family like ours, there would usually be two hog-killings during the year. One would be around Thanksgiving and the other in late January or February. The process would start early in the morning before day with the boiling of several pots of water in big wash pots outside. This hot water would be used to scald the hogs after they were shot and bled so that the hair could be scraped off.

Hog-killings were a ritual and ceremony that also was a social gathering. Men and women would gather to help and to socialize; others who may not have time or could not spend the day would stop by just to visit with those who were helping and to eat some of the fresh meat and cracklings. On those days the women would be cooking samples of all the different kinds of meats from the hogs and that in itself would be a feast. From December until the end of February there would usually be at least one hog-killing a week going on in the community.

It was around 1954 that the schools in Jasper County were first consolidated, and the same year that my oldest brother, Charles, finished high school. Prior to that time black children attended church schools that were subsidized by the county, but were held in the churches throughout the black communities. The county would provide so much money to pay the teachers and the community (churches) would make up the rest to support the schools. In Rock Hill the men had gotten together and built a one-room school out back of the church where the cemetery is now located. I remember that school vividly although I never attended because when I became old enough to attend school in 1955 the schools had been consolidated into a central school, Bay Springs Vocational High School in Bay Springs. The big school, as people called it, had first started around 1948 and was first a school for students in the ninth through twelfth grades. The elementary and junior high students were still attending the church/community schools until 1954.

During those days if the teachers who taught at the church/community schools were from out of town or from another community they roomed with families in the community where they taught and went home on weekends. Usually as a supplement to their salaries they were roomed and boarded by families in the community for free or for a nominal fee. In those days automobiles were still a scarce commodity for blacks, so transportation was still mainly by mule and wagon. A few men had pick-up trucks and some men still rode horses. I can remember daddy hitching up the mules and wagon to go to town on Saturdays to buy groceries and do shopping. That must be a flashback for me to earlier years, because by 1954 daddy had owned at least two cars. In 1954 he owned a 1949 or 1950 black and white Pontiac four-door sedan. He had previously owned a blue four-door Buick that had a sloped back end that we children called a "fish-tail Buick."

Many times the men of the community would have to provide transportation for the teachers at the church schools to get them back and forth from their homes on weekends. When they built the big school in Bay Springs the county did not provide buses for the black children to get to school. Instead, men of the community bought old buses or converted their pulpwood hauling trucks into buses and the county would pay them to provide transportation for the black children.

I never shall forget that Mr. Odis Duckworth was the first man who owned and drove the school bus from the Rock Hill Community. His first bus, which was number 13, was an old long-bed pick-up truck that he had installed a school bus body on the back. The school bus body was separated from the cab of the truck where he sat to drive and the seats were wooden benches that he had built and installed in the bus body. Sometimes he would even borrow benches from the church or the community school and set them in the bus for seats, especially if he had to haul more students than usual like to a field-day event or a ball game at another school some distance away. I remember going on the bus to some of those events with my older brothers and sisters even before I began going to school.

Yes, when I recall my first remembrances of 1954 life for me couldn't have been better. As a young child I had everything I could imagine right there in Rock Hill. It was very unlikely that anybody would consider such a quaint place to look for or hope to find a civil rights hero. Who from such a humble setting would have the courage or the wit to lead a civil rights movement, or to fight a civil rights fight? Everybody, both whites and blacks, knew that to stand up and defy the code of racial ethics of the times would mean certain death in the backwoods of Mississippi in 1954.

The Rock Hill community in rural Jasper County in the piney woods of southeastern Mississippi was neither the logical place nor the likely place to look for or even think about finding a civil rights hero in 1954. It was a humble community of simple African American men and their families struggling to make a living out of not even the best land in the county. Black folks were always relegated to the poorest land wherever they lived in the South during the post-Reconstruction period. Black folks were allowed to own land only in those areas designated for them, which had to be separate locations from where the white folks lived. The historic patterns of settlement and land ownership during the early 1900's shows a clear pattern of racial segregation which was as distinct in the rural South as it has been in the major cities over the years.

The Rock Hill community gets its name from the prevalence of sandstone rock that is the bedrock of the area's geomorphology.

Throughout the community along the hillsides there is always an outcropping of white sandstone; it is always lurking not far beneath the topsoil and the uppermost layers of the surface. It was this rock outcropping along the hills that gave the community its name - Rock Hill.

Whenever the men would attempt to dig a well, or whenever there was new ground to be cleared, the rocks were always present and presented an obstacle to the easy accomplishment of either task. But somehow the men with their strong wills and determination were always able to overcome the layer of rock, which was always there at 10 to 30 feet beneath the soil.

The men of Rock Hill for the most part were not men of high intelligence. Hardly any of them had a high school education; my daddy had probably more formal schooling than any, and he had only completed the 10th grade. But once he started to work in the carpentry business he had tried to avail himself of every book on carpentry he could find and afford; and every other high school textbook he could get his hands on. Often times he would have the teachers at the church school get him a copy of the geometry books, math books, science books and any others they could spare. In the evenings when he would come home from work he would complete all of his chores outside the house, eat his supper, and then he would retire to his easy chair and grab a book. Being an avid reader, daddy came to appreciate the opportunity to expand his base of knowledge by reading. It was this thirst for knowledge that inspired his children to excel and seek to be top students; that plus the sure assurance that a strapping was awaiting if we did not excel.

Daddy would sit and read and nod for a while; then, if it was during the school year, he would give attention to every child's homework to make sure they were doing their assignments. Those were a must and had to be done by the time the children's bedtime, which was no later than 10 p.m. on school nights. Every night after supper was finished and the dishes were done and all the outside chores were completed, the dining room table was cleared and all us children would gather at the table with our books and assignments to do our homework. By the time we were finishing up, daddy would have completed his reading and nodding. He would come to the table to check everybody's work.

Daddy didn't tolerate any more than one "B" on a report card for a grading period; no excuses. More than one "B" was an automatic strapping with his belt, no questions asked and no toleration granted. He meant for every child to be an excellent student; and surely enough each of us except one finished high school as either the valedictorian or salutatorian of our classes.

VI. MOVING TOWARD INDEPENDENCE

When daddy and Grandpa Richard and the family moved to the Rock Hill Community there was already a cadre of men in the community and there was already a strong community in place. Cousin John Beavers and Mr. Wash Moffett had been the founders and the patriarchs of the community and there was no doubt that they had been the stalwarts of leadership. Why shouldn't they have been; after all, everybody in the community was either their descendants or were married to their descendants, except for the Duckworths and the Quinces. There was already a strong sense of community and community unity. There was also a strong value system and belief system in place as well.

Mr. Wash Moffett was a preacher and was the founder of the original Rock Hill Church, which became Blue Mountain Missionary Baptist. I'm not sure as to whether he had already passed on when the Langs moved to Rock Hill. Nevertheless, by 1954, John Beavers was clearly the senior patriarch in the community and was the recognized leader in most regards. The roles and dominance of those in the community were so obviously defined until almost every adult who attended church on Sunday had a usual seat where they sat. If someone was not there you would easily recognize their absence by the vacancy of their place on the pew. And, if a visitor or someone else unknowingly sat in one of the elders' recognized seat, they might even be politely asked to move and yield the seat when the elder came in.

Most of the men were farmers and were satisfied to just be farmers and hunters. Uncle Sun Milsap worked for the railroads and was the only exception among the men of the community during that time. He was an exception to the community also as he was not related to anybody except through his marriage to Cousin Rosie, who was also Cousin John's daughter, after her husband and the father of her children had died.

When daddy arrived in Rock Hill as a permanent resident, he had already had experiences and exposures that most of the men in the community had not experienced. He had been through the trauma of losing land and a home place with his father and mother. He had already experienced the loss of his mother both through her death and earlier through her losing her mind and being confined to the state mental hospital. He had also had the experience of his Uncle Webb, who was his role model, having attended Tougaloo College and receiving a college degree in music and becoming a teacher and principal as well as a successful farmer and landowner. Daddy had also been a sharecropper and tenant farmer at the Old Missionary Plantation that had become a sharecropper place and on the Eddins' place. He knew he didn't want to be either of those again. He also had been instilled with greater aspirations by his mother and his Uncle Webb to become something more than just a farmer who depended on the land. He sought a higher sense of independence; he wanted to be his own man.

Grandpa Richard had been a barn-builder over the years. He had built and helped to build barns all across east Jasper County and the adjoining counties of Clark and Newton. Thus, he had learned the basics of carpentry and he had exposed his sons to that skill. Otha Lang knew there was money to be made in building and he knew that he had the ability to build. But he wanted to build more than just barns; he wanted to build houses. When he landed in Rock Hill he met other men, especially Purgie Beavers and the Beavers' cousin, June Beavers, who lived in Soso, a small town and community in Jones County. Both of these men were venturing out and working occasionally as carpenter's helpers with some of the white carpenters and builders who needed helpers and would give them a chance once in a while to work with them. Rice Agee was another man in the community who was also joining this legion of men who were looking for other work outside of farming.

Daddy began to join with these men and to accompany them on some of the side jobs they would do for other black families. Daddy saw in this venture the opportunity to develop a skill that would make him employable and would also create a demand for his service among both blacks and whites. He wanted to become a master carpenter, not just a carpenter's helper. He knew that in order to do this he had to learn every aspect of the carpentry business. His Uncle Webb, in addition to being a teacher and farmer, was also a painter. He had gained a reputation as an excellent painter and was becoming widely known throughout the area. His encouragement to his nephew, Otha, inspired him to become a master carpenter and a mentor for other men. Uncle Webb had learned a lot in his education at Tougaloo College. He was the one and only member of the family to hold a college degree at the time. What he had learned that would inspire his nephew was that there was a world of knowledge out there beyond one's immediate environment and surroundings that could be had simply by reading.

Independence became the aim of Otha Lang and his driving force. Not only did he want to be independent himself, he also wanted to see other men become independent as well. He began to study the carpentry business to learn as much as he could about contracting and building. Uncle Webb managed to get him a set of books on one of his trips to Jackson about basic building techniques, structure and design. Daddy also began to seek out opportunities to get small jobs. He and Grandpa Richard first started to do jobs on their own, then daddy began to get other men in the community to come and work with him.

At first there was a lot of hesitation on the part of the men of the community to work with him. Most of them had never done any work independently; they had always worked with and under the supervision of white men in their carpentry experiences. And, in order to be an independent carpenter, one needed a truck to operate in order to haul supplies and materials to and from the jobs. In 1948, daddy bought a truck from Mr. James B. McBay, Sr. who was a white man whose property adjoined daddy's property on the east side. Mr. McBay also lived not too far from the Eddins' place; in fact his place was along side of Highway 15 south between the Eddins' place and Rock Hill Community. With the truck, which daddy bought for a price of $1000 and Mr. McBay loaned him the down payment, daddy could haul pulpwood, short logs, farm materials and supplies, and he could use it to do carpentry work.

Daddy has always been a risk taker, and a black man buying a truck for $1000 in 1948 was certainly a big risk. Hardly any of the men in the community had vehicles during that time. Mr. Odis Duckworth had a truck, and Purgie Beavers had a car; G.B. Moffett, Cousin Lewis' brother also bought a car during that time. But daddy was thinking ahead of his time and ahead of the men in the community. For he knew that these men were hardworking men who had the potential to become much more than what they saw themselves becoming. He knew that they could also help him to become what he wanted to become - independent.

With his truck and the skills that he already had, daddy set out to find and contract building, remodeling and whatever other kinds of carpentry jobs he could find. At first, Purgie Beavers and June Beavers were the only ones who would come along and work with him, later others would join. The men had their reasons for not wholeheartedly coming along. These men were farmers and sharecroppers, that was what they knew and that was what they had been until John Beavers came into possession of his land and decided to build a community and a small fortune for his own livelihood by selling that land. They knew they did not have the skills to be full-time carpenters and builders on their own, nor did they have the knowledge to manage any kind of independent business on their own. Most of them could read and write but only at a grade school level for most of them had only completed grade school. Even Mr. Ezra Moffett who had been a teacher at the church schools in the Carlisle Community and Shady Grove Community schools in Smith County had only finished the eighth grade, which was all that was required to be a Negro school teacher in those days.

Another reason the men were hesitant was because their elder leader whom they knew and trusted, namely Cousin John Beavers, did not totally sanction the idea. But his own son, Cousin Purgie and his cousin, June Beavers, saw it as an opportunity to gain independence as Otha Lang also saw it. They were willing to join the idea as long as somebody else would assume the risk of both providing the skills and knowledge and the financial risk of making the agreements which daddy was willing to do.

Daddy believed that if the men of Rock Hill Community could gain the skills to make themselves employable outside of farming they could pass these skills on to their sons and build a generation of black men who would be able to make a living anywhere in the country. He saw this as a way out of dependence on the land and on the whims of white men; he saw this as a way to compete with white men on an equal basis. For if black men could build houses and build them as good or better than whites, and if they could build them faster and cheaper than whites, then they would be able to compete with the whites in the building business.

He knew also that he had to be able to do every part of the building business, from the foundation to the roof. That meant he had to learn every aspect of the business; how to estimate the costs; how to design the buildings; how to frame and finish the buildings; how to do the concrete and masonry work; how to lay the bricks and blocks; how to design and build the roofs; how to do the flooring including the tiling and other work. He set his mind to learning everything there was to know about building and he would teach any other black man who wanted a chance what he learned if they were willing to work with him and learn from him.

In 1948, daddy, along with June Beavers, Purgie Beavers and Rice Agee, set out on his own. June Beavers had heard about a project that was up for bids in Laurel which was four or five houses in one block that were to be built. June was scared to go after the job on his own, but he believed that a black could get the job if he put in a bid for it and his bid was low enough to get the job. Again, daddy decided to take the risk and put in a bid with the agreement that the other men would come along and work with him to complete the job if they got it.

Sure enough, they got the job and daddy had his first building contract to build four houses on the north side of Laurel, and in a predominantly white neighborhood. He and other men went to work along with Grandpa Richard and daddy's three oldest sons. They built the houses and when they were completed, all the bills paid and all the men paid, daddy's profit was one complete window sash unit that had been ordered extra. Although they did a splendid job on the houses which are still standing in Laurel, daddy knew that he had much more to learn about the building business if he were to be a profitable builder. But he knew that he could learn what he needed to know, and he knew he wanted to and would learn what he needed to know. He was on his way to becoming independent.

After daddy and the men finished the project in Laurel in 1948, he was looked upon differently by the men of Rock Hill. And he was different in some respects. He was a risk taker and he was an independent thinker and actor. He acted on his own and in his own best interest. He acted without approval and many times he acted alone. Yet, he was looked upon as a leader in his own way but as a leader without any acknowledged followers. Nobody in the community was about to recognize him for his boldness or his independence or even for his foresight or knowledge. To do so would be to acknowledge that he was more intelligent, wiser, and somehow above them. So in their own ways they followed him, but did not acknowledge his leadership.

Nevertheless, the men of Rock Hill came to accept that Otha Lang had something to offer that they could use and that would be beneficial to them and the community. Even though he had begun by working with them, now they were willing to work with him and to learn from him. For they saw that he was bold and willing to take risks and to allow them to learn from him and to gain from his risk taking. Thus, they would become joiners and take advantage of his skills and the opportunities he would provide for them to expand their horizons by coming along with him and working with him. From then on, Otha Lang always had a cadre of men he could employ when he needed to, and that he did over many years.

Over the years daddy mentored many a young man from the Rock Hill Community in the carpentry and building business and trades. Starting with Rice Agee's sons, R.J., Junie, and Bill (Rice Jr.), all of them became master masons who worked many years as bricklayers, but who could also do many other parts of the building trades. In fact, through the years they were able to build beautiful homes in the community that still stand as monuments to their skill. Not only the Agee men, but others also gained and learned from daddy's mentoring. There were Lemon (Tamp) Beavers and Sank Beavers, Cousin John's sons, and Carey Beavers and King Beavers, Cousin Sank's sons, who also taught their sons to be builders, carpenters and masons. There were other men who married into the community who also worked with him over the years and learned from him and were able to support their families and to build their homes.

Daddy became a mentor of men and a leader of men without even intending to do so, more by chance than by design or intention. There were also those in the community with whom he did not manage to cooperate very well and with whom he never managed to have endearing relationships. Early on he had conflicts with one of his neighbor. Daddy had learned from his mother and his father to be a strict disciplinarian with not only his children, but also anybody's children. He did not and would not tolerate anything but the greatest respect from his children or the children of anybody else. He believed that children should know their place with adults and that they should stay in that place. In other words, children should have respect for adults at all times and in all places.

It was sometime during 1948 that the men of the community were working on the road. Although a wagon trail had been built from the main highway through the community in the early 1930's, in the late 1940's the men were using their mules, horses and tools to widen and improve the road since the county did not put many resources into the building and improvement of roads in the black communities during those times. It was while they were working on the roads that daddy and one of his neighbour had an altercation. It seems that one of the neighbour's sons, Joe Louis, either said or did something out of order. I believe that he and Charles, Otha's oldest son, got into an argument or maybe even a fight. Daddy separated them and attempted to chastise the both of them when the neighbour stepped in and drew his kaiser-blade on daddy because he did not want him to chastise his child or any of his children.

Not having his pistol with him and seeing that the man had the drop on him, daddy backed down and let the matter go. However, he vowed then and there that never again in his life would another man catch him unprepared to defend himself, and never again would any man in that community get the drop on him. He realized then as no man in the crew (and there must have been at least ten other men present) came to his defense, that he was alone and that he would have to stand alone.

He also realized as it was to be shown over the years that he had no real friends in the community and that he could never really depend on the other men to either defend him or to stand up for him or with him. He was an outsider and they would always view him as an outsider. But that was alright because he never intended after that day to ever need to depend on any of them to either defend or to stand up either for him or with him in his life ever again. From then on, he realized that when dealing with them and any other men he would have to stand by himself and for himself. Two things he would never do again; he would never be unprepared to defend himself, and, he would never again not defend himself.

Some years later after the neighbour's son had spent time in the state penitentiary he came to daddy and apologized for disrespecting him. He also told him that he wished that somebody had disciplined him as a child, maybe he would have turned out to be a better man and a man who respected his mother and daddy as Otha Lang's children respected him and as they respected other peoples= parents. After serving several stints in jails and prison, the son died a young man under suspicious circumstances; it was believed that somebody had run over him and left him dead somewhere in one of the towns on the Gulf Coast.

Over the years daddy's interaction with the men of Rock Hill was cordial but guarded and distant. He never really fit in with them, but that was partially because they never really allowed him to fit in with them. They, more than he, saw him as different; maybe they even saw him as trying to be more than them or trying more to emulate white men than black men in the risks that he took. Daddy was venturesome and he always sought to reach far greater than his grasp. He wanted to excel, he had been inspired to excel by his mother and by his Uncle Webb who was his idol. He didn't have a formal high school education, but he educated himself by buying books and reading and exposing himself to people from other parts of the country and the state from whom he could learn.

The other men of Rock Hill were completely satisfied to live within the confines of their community and limit themselves to what it had to offer. Daddy, on the other hand, loved to travel and he sought out opportunities to travel if it was no farther than to the other side of the county to visit old friends and relatives where he had grown up; or even to Meridian to visit his mother's sisters and their husbands for the weekend. He loved to learn new things and he sought out opportunities to learn new things from whomever he could. He felt he could accomplish anything he set his mind to, and he would not be limited by what other men, either white or black, thought of him and his ideas. He was his own man.

Because daddy was his own man and had his own ideas and chose not to live by the dictates of Cousin John or any of the others, they saw him as attempting to take over as the leader of the community. In actuality, daddy only sought to share what he knew and what he had learned with the other men in hopes that they could improve their lots in life as he sought to improve his. Daddy bought his first vehicle in 1948 when he bought the truck from Mr. McBay. A few years later in 1951 he bought a car, and almost every three years after that he bought a new car until into the 1960's. He bought more new cars than most of the whites in Jasper County during those years. That act alone brought much ire from both whites and blacks. Since it bothered the whites, it also bothered the blacks even more and caused the black men of the community and the county to shy away from him. They obviously felt that if the whites had concern about a black man overstepping the racial bounds of prosperity and brought the wrath of the Ku Klux Klan against himself, while the Klan was in the community they might decide to visit wrath on others as well. Thus, it was the safe thing to do to keep distance between themselves and Otha Lang.

Many times the men of the community would get together and go hunting or fishing, but they never invited daddy and his boys to go along. The only men who would ever invite my brothers to go hunting with them were Uncle Sun Milsap and Mr. Hargie Campbell. In fact, the only men in the community with whom daddy ever had meaningful relationships were Cousin John Beavers, Lewis Moffett and Uncle Sun. When he was a drinking man Mr. Rice Agee and Mr. Abraham Quince were two good drinking buddies. R.J. Agee and Herman Moffett were two that always looked up to daddy and thought a lot of him. After Cousin Lewis Moffett died, his two sons, Ulen and Johnny, looked up to daddy as their surrogate father; and their brother-in-law, Early McCullum, still considers daddy one of his best friends and sees himself almost like one of daddy's sons.

No matter how others saw him, Otha Lang was a trailblazer in many ways; and as he blazed a different trail for himself he also opened a way for others to follow and made it easier for them to follow the trail because he took the risks. In doing so he produced sons and daughters of his own who became just as independent; but he also produced a community of men who knew skilled trades and who could make a living for themselves. He taught a whole community of men and men beyond that community from all over Jasper County to build houses and gave them skills that nobody could ever take away from them. They in turn taught their sons the same skills and others so that at least three generations of men from that community and across the county are carpenters, bricklayers and stonemasons, concrete finishers, roofers, painters, electricians and plumbers. Many of them would never have had the chance to learn those skills anywhere else because nobody else would have given them the chance to practice and make mistakes the way that daddy did. Yet, many of the sons of those men who learned their skills working with daddy don't even know the role that Otha Lang played in them being who they are, what they are, and why they are where they are today.

VII. STRUGGLING

As a child I could not have realized what was the significance of my daddy's actions. I didn't realize at the age of five in 1954 what were the meanings of the Jim Crow system of the South, or the reasons for the separation of blacks and whites. I just knew that white folks were different and that they held a place of privilege in society that blacks did not hold and could not hold. It soon became clear to me what all of this meant as soon as we got our first television which must have been either late in 1954 or early 1955.

Television exposed us to a larger world outside our immediate surroundings and brought us to the reality of the racism and prejudices that we knew already existed toward blacks in American society. We knew about the separate and unequal treatment that African Americans and other minorities experienced in the South, for it was obviously a reality every time we ventured outside the boundaries of the Rock Hill Community no further than to the town of Bay Springs. In all the public places there were signs with "whites only" and "colored" with the second-rate facilities reserved for the "coloreds" if there were facilities for us at all.

In Bay Springs, as in other small towns throughout the South in the 1950's, blacks were expected to know their place and to stay in their place, which most of them did. Segregation was the way of life, yet, the prominent white families depended on blacks as cooks and domestic workers in their homes. Black women cooked their meals and cared for their children, usually spending more time nurturing their children and teaching them than the parents themselves. Yet, when black folks came to town to shop in Bay Springs racism was so rampant until the blacks had certain areas of town where they would park, which was off the main street in an alley next to a feed and seed store owned by the mayor of the town, Mr. S.F. Thigpen, who was the distant cousin of the same black Thigpens who were my daddy's mother's ancestors. They all came off the same Thigpen plantation.

We had been elated to see the "Amos 'N Andy Show" on television and the "Little Rascals" for no matter how denigrating they were at least we saw some black faces we could relate to. During those early days of watching television, it was so uncommon to see a black face or a minority person on television until when one did come on everybody in the household would stop what they were doing and rush to the television. Whoever was watching would usually call-out to the others and we would all drop whatever we were doing and come running.

I knew it was frightening to see my daddy chasing that young lawyer from the woods that Saturday afternoon in May 1954. I don't remember much else about that Summer of 1954. I can't remember whether daddy worked on other houses or not that summer. It seems that after he left the lawyer's job, later in the summer he started on a house for Mr. Jimmy Pittman who was the newly elected Sheriff of Jasper County. I do know that we were all excited because our oldest brother, Charles, was going off to Jackson College in the fall.

I do remember that on the next morning, that Sunday morning, after the incident with the young Lawyer I was sitting on the porch waiting for the rest of the family to get ready to go to Sunday school. The girls always got me ready first so I would be out of the way while everybody else was getting dressed. Daddy was also sitting on the porch, but he was not waiting to go to Sunday School. He was sitting there waiting for us to go to church so that he could sneak back in the woods and find his whiskey jug and get him another swig or two before he quit for the weekend. During those times daddy didn't go to church too often at Blue Mountain except for the business meetings on the fourth Saturday afternoons and occasionally for the preaching on the fourth Sundays. Although daddy was the elected church clerk during those years he didn't have too much to do with going to church on a regular basis.

Daddy's lack of involvement and his not having enthusiasm for regular church attendance probably stemmed from the distant relationship he had with most of the people in the community. He had tried to be involved but they resented him and his progressive ideas. This was the situation not only with the people in the church and community but in other instances as well. For example, in 1948 the county had built a big school for the colored children in the West Jasper County School District in the black community known as "The Quarters" in the town of Bay Springs. A principal from Jackson, Mr. B.J. Norman, had been brought in to be the principal of the new school. Daddy had been elected the president of the PTA during that first year. Some incident happened whereby daddy and some of the other officers were falsely accused of mishandling the PTA's funds. Daddy resigned as the president, quit the PTA and never got involved in school activities again. In fact, he would only go to school for graduations of his children and maybe to see a play or other event or activity in which one of his children was participating. Otherwise, he was not an organization man and stayed away from any kind of organizational activity until later years when he became a preacher.

On that Sunday morning in 1954 as daddy and I were sitting there on the porch waiting, a car came driving into the driveway. I could see as the car approached that the driver was a white man, but this time it was an older white man and he drove very slowly and cautiously. As the car approached the front yard, daddy sat up erect in the chair where he was sitting on the far end of the porch away from where the car was approaching. When the car came to a stop daddy recognized the man as the young lawyer's daddy, the old man. He hollered out to him, "Get out and come in." My heart was beating fast because I felt something terrible was fixing to happen, but I didn't know what. I wanted to get up and run in the house, but even as a young child I didn't want to leave my daddy out there by himself.

The older white man answered daddy, "Otha, can you and me talk?" He didn't say good morning, hello, or any other usual greeting. It was the Jim Crow custom in those days that white folks never directly greeted blacks. To do so would put them on an equal status and acknowledge their humanness, which white folks never intended to do. Daddy was not conceding, but he was cordial when he replied. "It depends on what you want to talk about." He replied, "I understand you and my boy had a run-in yesterday." Daddy got up from his seat and headed out toward the car which was parked about 50 feet from the front of the porch. As he walked toward the car he kept talking, but he had his right hand in his pocket on his pocketknife. "Well, your son came to me in the wrong way and I had to straighten him out. I don't know how you expect me to build a house if you gon' cut off the materials. I ain't intending to build a house and pay for it too. But your boy came down here cursing and disrespecting me and my family on my place. I won't stand for him cursing me and my family and I won't stand for you doin' it either; so if that's what you came to do you'd better turn that car around a git out'a my yard right now caus' I ain't gon' stand for that from you, him and nobody else."

The old man had a very solemn and sorrowful look on his face. But daddy continued. "Another thing; your boy threatened me that you and him and the Ku Klux Klan would be back out here to take care of me. I want to tell you just like I told him. I ain't afraid of you, or him, or the Klan, or whoever else y'all want to bring. Y'all can come to try to kill me if you want to. But let me assure you that I'm ready to go to hell this morning; y'all better have your minds made up to go with me 'cause I don't intend to go by myself. I intend to take somebody with me. It just might be you and him if you show up out here with the Klan. Make no mistake about it, I will kill the first somebody who shows up here wrong."

By this time daddy had gotten out to the car where he was and he leaned against the front fender next to where the man was sitting. I sat there on the porch and overheard most of the rest of their conversation. He explained to daddy how he had gotten tired of his son and his daughter-in-law, especially the daughter-in-law, not being able to make up her mind and decide what she wanted in the house and sticking to it. The costs were mounting way beyond what he had intended to spend on building the house and he had to cut them off. Daddy let him know how frustrating it was for him to continue to build and tear out what was being put in, but also let him know that he had tried to be patient and work with them, to which Mr. Ulmer agreed. However, daddy told him in no uncertain words that cutting off the materials without at least talking to him was the last straw and he would not stand for that kind of disrespect.

I heard daddy tell the old man that morning something that I heard him repeat many times during my life. He told him: "There are two things that when I leave them I'm through with them one way or another and that is a job and a woman. Under whatever circumstances I happen to leave either one of them, I'm finished and I won't be going back." Daddy further told him, "You can pay me for the time you owe me for me and my men or you can keep it and I'll figure out some way to pay my men. But I won't be coming back to finish that job. You can figure on getting somebody else to finish that if you want to, or whatever you want to do with it is up to you. But I'm through with it."

They talked some more. Daddy got out his pencil and had some paper brought to him so he could figure what he owed him for the week's labor and the old man wrote him a check for that amount I presume since I saw him give daddy a check. As I recall, daddy did agree to let his two oldest sons go back and put in the moldings and paint the rooms that were already finished in the house, and they did that next week. But daddy did not go back. That next Monday morning he went looking for other work and let the rest of us finish the planting and get started on the cotton chopping. May passed without incident and we headed into the Summer of 1954.

Later that summer I believe daddy and the older boys started building a house for Mr. Jimmy Pittman who had recently been elected Sheriff of Jasper County. Mr. Pittman was a prominent man about the same age as daddy, and from a prominent family in the county. He owned land and lived on the main road from Bay Springs going east into the Lake Como settlement. The Pittmans, like most of the prominent white families that lived outside of town, owned a lot of land and cattle. He had contacted daddy to build his house because he had seen his work and knew that he was one of the best builders in the area. Plus, he knew that daddy would give him a good price and quality work. So late in the summer of 1954, daddy and his crew including Claude and George, his second and third sons, and several men from the Rock Hill Community went to work on the Jimmy Pittman house.

Over the few years that daddy had been building he had, by this time, learned a lot about the building business and had become proficient at one of the trademarks of his building career, which was figuring out and developing an estimate of the cost of a building. Ever since daddy almost lost his shirt on the first houses he contracted, he had set his goal to be able to figure the estimated cost of a building almost to the last dollar and cents. Daddy would do all of his figuring by pencil and paper, there were no hand-held calculators or computers in those days, and only a few storeowners and prominent white business owners had possession of adding machines. So when daddy had to prepare and estimate for a bid on a house he would spend hours figuring the costs of materials.

He became proficient at figuring these costs to the extent that he would know the prices of certain pieces of lumber by their size and grade and could recall this information from memory. Daddy learned this information by diligently studying the billings and receipts he would receive from the lumberyard whenever he purchased materials. He even knew the costs of items such as pounds of nails by different sizes, and kept abreast of the prices whenever they changed. He would figure out exactly the numbers of the different pieces of lumber of certain sizes that would be needed in the building and he would make a schedule of each type and the numbers of pieces that would be needed. He would then figure out the estimated costs of all the materials that would be needed to build the house from the foundation to the roof. He became so good over the years until he could determine the dimensions of the house, and knowing what kinds of finishes that would be required he could estimate the costs within a few hundreds of dollars just from the dimensions alone.

In his later years of building, he would prepare the bid estimates on a per square foot basis relying on his years of experience and knowing the going costs of materials. Daddy specialized in the building cost estimation and he passed this skill on to his sons who wanted to learn it. I remember either helping him do cost estimates or doing them for him during my high school years. Sometimes daddy would be doing estimates for several jobs at a time, especially during the early 1970's when the low-income housing business was booming in Mississippi.

While things were at a lull during the early part of the Summer of 1954 before daddy started the Jimmy Pittman house, Charles, the oldest son had taken a job with the Alexander Hardware Lumberyard as a delivery driver and helper. Since he was planning on enrolling at Jackson College (now Jackson State University) in Jackson, he needed to earn some money to pay for his schooling. He had a burning desire to go to college but there was no money to pay for it. As it was, the oldest boys had to use some of the money they made working to help support the family. But perhaps if Charles could make enough money he would have a chance of attending college in the fall.

At that time the Lumberyard was only paying its helpers about $15.00 per week and Charles had six or seven weeks to work before he went to Jackson College in early September. During those times there were no federal student loan programs or grant programs. The only way black students went to college was only if their families could afford to pay their way, or they worked and paid their own way, or if they were on the GI Bill or some kind of scholarships which were few at black colleges. In fact, during those days even the black athletes had to either work their way through or work for their scholarships; there were no free scholarships in those days.

Several of Charles' schoolmates who had played basketball with him at Bay Springs had already gone to Jackson College to play basketball. They were Billy McDonald and Houston Cooke. Charles wanted so much to join them at Jackson College since he had heard so much about college life from them during their visits home. It was his dream to get to Jackson College, and the family wanted him to go. Nobody knew how it would be paid for, however. Daddy and mama both knew that the family could not afford to send him, money was too tight, but they were determined to let him give it a try anyway.

As fate would have it, in the Fall of 1954 Charles went off to college. Since he had no scholarship and could not afford to live in the campus housing, which was limited anyway since Jackson College only had one men's dormitory at the time which was used mainly to house athletes, he had to be housed off campus. Mama's half brother, Uncle Lester Wells, who owned a laundry and dry cleaning business in Bay Springs, one of the only black owned businesses in town for a number of years, his wife, Aunt Lillie, had a cousin who lived in Jackson. Mrs. Emma Huddleston lived at 1107 Isaiah Montgomery Street in Jackson which was several blocks away from the campus. She had what was considered a big house for the times with several spare bedrooms. Through Aunt Lillie, mama was able to arrange for Charles to room with Mrs. Huddleston for $20 per month.

Twenty dollars per month, or five dollars per week does not seem like much money to pay for housing in this day and time, but in 1954 when the going wage rate, even for a black housing contractor, was $0.75 to $1.50 per hour, $20 dollars per month was a considerable amount of money. Plus, tuition had to be paid. Nevertheless, since Charles wanted to pursue college, and it was a good thing to do, he gave it a try.

When he arrived at Jackson College, Cousin Clemertine was there for her second year, and another distant cousin, John Emmett Lang from Newton was also there. John Emmett was the son of one of Grandpa Richard's cousins, Will Lang. Cousin Will and his sons had a majority of white and Indian blood, for they looked more white than black. They were very light complexioned and had long and straight black hair. If one did not know them, it could easily be assumed that they were white.

The same year that Charles and Cousin Clemertine were at Jackson College, Cousin Chester, Uncle Bill Richard's oldest son was sent to the penitentiary from Laurel for stealing. Chester had finished high school a year or two prior to Charles and Clemertine and had been mostly bumming around Laurel with what would have been considered gangs during this time. He wound up in jail for a stint. When he was released on probation a year or so later daddy was assigned as his guardian by the probation officer. Chester's sister, Emogene also finished high school the same year as Charles and Clemertine but she did not attempt to go to college; within a year or two she got married.

Charles stayed in college a year but it was difficult financially. At the end of that first year he had decided that he would have to do something different because the financial burden was too much on him and on the family. He wound up having to work long hours at whatever jobs he could find which took away from his studying time. Thus, his grades suffered. He would work weekends as either a busboy or waiter at the King Edward Hotel in downtown Jackson, or at whatever else he could find. With the wages and tips he made he tried to pay his rent and tuition, but often times he would send a few dollars home to mama to help her to buy things for the other children and for herself. The money daddy could send him was just not enough to cover everything that needed to be covered and pay his room and board and tuition for college.

When Charles came home for Christmas he had run into Joe Nell Quince, Mr. Wash Quince's son, who was living in Beloit, Wisconsin and was visiting for the holidays. In his conversations with Joe Nell he had extended Charles the invitation to come to Beloit if he decided he wanted to leave the South, and if college did not pan out for him. The factories, especially the Fairbanks Morse factory in Beloit, were hiring and there were ample opportunities for jobs. When the school year was over Charles had saved enough money for a train ticket to Beloit. Mama fixed him a hefty lunch and gave him a few dollars to have in his pocket; Charles boarded the train in Jackson headed for Chicago and on to Beloit.

Although daddy would rather have had him stay and work with him, he wished him well and saw him off to Wisconsin. He knew his chances were better there than in Mississippi at the time. Work was slim anyway in the Spring of 1955 and did not look promising for that summer. In the Spring of 1955 daddy was finishing up the house for Mr. Jimmy Pittman, and the only other prospect he had for the summer was going to Mobile, Alabama to do just the foundation and the frame-up on a house for Mr. Pittman's brother who lived there. He would not try to dissuade Charles from going to Wisconsin since he had nothing better to offer him.

Neither he nor Charles particularly cared for the idea of Charles going back to work for the lumberyard in Bay Springs on a permanent basis. Everything looked like the best bet for Charles was to go to Wisconsin.

So in May 1955 when school was out, Charles headed to Beloit, Wisconsin; daddy, Claude and George headed to Mobile, Alabama; and the girls, brother Otha and I headed to the hot cotton fields and truck crop patches one more time as had become routine for us and as would be our routine for all the years until we finished high school in the 1960's. There was nothing so dreadful in our lives as either chopping or picking cotton. Those were the two most dreaded jobs on the farm. All the other tasks were relatively easier; nobody enjoyed chopping cotton or picking cotton. I believe that's why the adults had so many children so they would have somebody to do those two jobs for them.

It seemed that 1955 was a tougher year for everybody in Rock Hill than 1954 had been. I know that school year had been different for me because I had started school, and instead of attending the church school in Rock Hill as my other brothers and sisters had done when they began school, I had to go to the big school in Bay Springs. The reason was the schools had been consolidated by the county which meant that all the local community church schools that had been run mostly out of churches in the black communities were closed. I never shall forget that first day that it was announced that the church schools would no longer be operating. I remember my brother Otha and sister Bobbie coming home about lunchtime and telling mama they had been sent home because the school had been closed. The other brothers and sisters were already going to the school in Bay Springs.

Anyway, in the Spring of 1955, about a month before school was to be out for the summer, the local church schools were closed and everybody started riding the bus to the big school in Bay Springs. When they made the shift, mama just sent me along with the others since I had turned six years old on April 2. For some reason they took me and allowed me into the first grade. Since my mother had been teaching me at home across the years anyway, they allowed me to complete the first grade in that one month left in the school year.

Because I was already so far ahead of the other children who were in the first grade and who had been in school all the year, the teachers and the principal decided not to hold me back. So it was decided that when I returned the next fall I would go to the third grade instead of the second grade. I was reading on about a fourth grade level anyway and could do all the arithmetic at about the third grade level also. That is how I got my jump start ahead of the other children my age in the community and I stayed ahead of them from then on. As we grew older and those who were my same age realized I had been put ahead of them from the outset, they resented me for that. But as most of my brothers and sisters were the smartest in their classes and everybody knew it, and the teachers generally made a big deal about it, we were somewhat resented by most of our peers anyway; so we kind of got used to being treated special and being resented.

None of that made any difference to us because our self-esteem was super high anyway. Mama and daddy kept us pumped up by encouraging and supporting us to do good, and would not permit us to do otherwise. Both of them were strict disciplinarians; they demanded good grades and good discipline from their children. We had to respect everybody, especially other adults, regardless of who they were, black or white. We knew that if we got a bad report card, or if a teacher ran into mama or daddy anywhere in town or at church and told them we had been acting up in school, or that we were not paying attention or following the rules, we had a whipping coming. The last thing you wanted in life was for either mama or daddy to whip you, especially daddy. We would beg mama to whip us if we needed or deserved a whipping for something rather than for her to tell daddy and for him to whip us. Our parents loved us dearly and did the best they could to provide for our livelihood, but when it came to discipline, respect and obedience, neither mama nor daddy would take any mess.

VIII. THE CITY-WIDE USHER BOARD

It was in the summer of 1954 that mama and daddy along with Mr. Dessie B. Young would initiate an effort that would be an historical monument in Jasper County and most of the surrounding counties throughout east central and south Mississippi. I shall never forget that on a Sunday afternoon in late June of that year my brother, Otha, and I were playing cars in the front yard when Mr. Young drove up in his 1952 green Chevrolet car. Mr. Dessie B. as we always called him affectionately, worked as a mechanic at the E. Martin Jr. Chevrolet dealership in Bay Springs. Although the dealership has long been gone, the building still stands in Bay Springs near the intersection of Highways 15 and 18, the major intersection in town. It now houses a feed store and nursery.

Anyway, Mr. Dessie B. came to visit with mama and daddy, but his visit was not entirely social. The three of them had been talking along about what they would eventually come up with that afternoon. My brother and I were on our knees playing with our bottle cars. We never had many real toys to play with so we had to be innovative in creating our own. One of our favorites was to take empty flat bottles and pretend they were cars. Empty bottles of Syrup of Black Draught, which was a popular laxative during those times, made the best bottle cars because the bottles were about an inch thick, six inches long, two and a half inches wide, and had about an inch and a half long neck. They were excellent for pretending to be toy cars.

We were busy on our knees in our short pants playing bottle cars as daddy and mama and Mr. Dessie B. sat on the porch and talked. What they talked about was the condition of the black churches throughout the county and the need for the churches to build new buildings and to properly train ushers. Another need was for some kind of program that would allow the young people to develop their talents for working in the church. I remember them talking about a program that would rotate from church to church and would bring a number of churches together and have a talent program of singing, but not for preaching. This way whatever monies were raised could be left with the host church, and every month the program would be held at a different church, thus during the year each church in the area would host the program at least once.

The reason they decided to exclude preaching was because if they had preaching it would create conflict about which preachers would be allowed to preach. And, even worse, the preacher would expect to get paid whatever money was raised. This would defeat the purpose of helping to raise funds to build new church buildings and improve the conditions of the churches. At that time, all of the black churches in Jasper County were small wood frame buildings and most of them were deteriorating, some badly. The idea they came up with was to start a program that they would call the "City-Wide Usher Board."

The way the program would work was laid out that afternoon. I never shall forget the excitement the three of them shared and exhibited about coming up with this idea. The way they decided to form the organization was to invite and recruit churches to join and agree to host the program when it was their turn to do so. The initial plan was to have twelve churches to become members, but as it turned out only nine churches eventually joined. Those churches were: Blue Mountain, First Baptist Bay Springs (the black First Baptist, not the white one, of course) Bethlehem Methodist, Phalti Baptist, New Zion Baptist, Jerusalem Baptist Lake Como, Nazareth Baptist, John Divine Baptist, and Gavin Chapel Presbyterian. Morning Star Baptist in Bay Springs and First Baptist in Stringer were invited but did not join at first. First Baptist Stringer became a member in later years, but Morning Star never joined.

Mama and daddy and Mr. Dessie B. sat there all afternoon that day discussing how they perceived the program would operate while Otha Jr. (Pap as we always called him) and me played with our bottle cars in the yard. Little did we know that we were witness to an event that would have great impact all across east and south Mississippi for years to come. In a few months the City-Wide Usher Board would be up and rolling. It was either in September or October of 1954 that the first program was held at First Baptist Bay Springs which was Mr. Dessie B. Young's home church. The program was scheduled for the fourth Sunday evenings at 6:00 p.m. sharp, and beginning in that September and from then on, every fourth Sunday evening we would find ourselves going to the Usher Board Meeting.

They decided that Mr. Dessie B. would be the president and presiding officer; mama was the recording secretary. There would be no other officers except matrons who were the elder ladies of the organization and who were in charge of the female ushers; and the head ushers who were the adult men in charge of the male ushers. Mrs. Argell Falls and Mrs. Ruby Pierce who were teachers in the school districts, and who had been teachers at the community church schools before the consolidation took place, were selected to be the head matrons. Mr. J.C. Milsap and Mr. Mose Clayton were the head ushers.

Evidently the City-Wide Usher Board must have been divinely inspired. After it was started it became the biggest church gathering ever. During those early years the crowds would be so big until most of the churches could not accommodate the people. If you wanted to get in the church for the program you had to be there early. Consequently, people would start gathering at the church where the program was going to be held around 3 o'clock in the afternoon and just wait until the church opened so they could get in and get a good seat. It was a big thing to go to the Usher Board and people were coming from all over the county and from surrounding counties. The programs were raising big money for the host churches and the churches started to developing building funds and making plans to build new churches and renovate their existing buildings.

A few years after its beginning, the idea of similar programs in other areas of the county and the state was spreading like wildfire.

From all parts of southeast Mississippi people were coming to learn about how the program had gotten started and how they could start similar programs in their areas. Everybody was elated and excited about the program except the black preachers and pastors. Since there was no money to be made by them, and since they were not given the notoriety for having founded the program and for the progress it was bringing to the churches and to the young people who were given a chance to develop their talents and abilities, the preachers and pastors for the most part were not embracing of the City-Wide Usher Board, although they were not overtly against it since it was raising money and leaving the money for the churches' benefit. What made the Usher Board unique and more beneficial to the churches than any other programs both then and now in the area was no officers were getting paid; no preachers were getting paid; all the money raised at a church was being left for that church; large sums of money were being raised for the churches; and, at least once a year each church that was a member would get a chance to host the program and reap the benefits.

By 1956, there were Usher Board programs in a number of areas around southeast and central Mississippi. The next one to be started after the one in west Jasper County which was called the Bay Springs Area, was on the east side of the county which was started by Mr. George Clayton with the help of Mr. Dessie B. and mama, and was called the Heidelberg Area City-Wide Usher Board. Following that was the one around the town of Louin and north Jasper County with a Mr. Martin Madison as President, then Rose Hill, and Raleigh and Smith County, followed by Jones County, and Scott County around the towns of Forest and Lake. From there it spread to Newton County, and Wayne County, then to Leake County, and Clarke County, to Covington County and to Taylorsville in Smith County, to Simpson County and to other parts. Within two to three years the idea of this program had spread throughout all of these areas and was having great impacts.

After a few years it was forgotten by most that mama and daddy were co-founders of the Usher Board, and that the concept of the program was the main idea of daddy. He relinquished the leadership of the organization to Mr. Dessie B. because at the time daddy was not an avid churchgoer; he would go on occasion but he did not make it a point to be there every time there was something going on at church as mama did. Still, he demanded and insisted that we children would be there with mama every time she went both to Sunday School, to the worship services, and to the Usher Board meetings. With Mr. Dessie B. at the helm, the Usher Board exploded on the scene and spread like wildfire.

The Usher Board began in 1954 at about the same time that black communities throughout that part of Mississippi were getting electric power. In 1954, the Rural Electric Power Associations were also spreading throughout the South, and one result of their spreading was that electric power lines were being installed through the black communities. Cousin John Beavers was the first in Rock Hill to have the power installed in his house and daddy was the second. When we got the electric power, not long after daddy began to buy electric appliances including a washing machine, a refrigerator, a deep freezer and a television. The Ed Sullivan Show was an early favorite that came on every Sunday night at 7:00 o'clock following Disney World. The Ed Sullivan Show was the model upon which the program for the City-Wide Usher Board program was designed.

The City-Wide Usher Board program would begin at 6:00 p.m. promptly when it was held on the fourth Sunday evenings. The program would begin with deacons from several churches having a prayer service and devotional. Usually they would sing three long-meter hymns and have a prayer after each hymn. After the devotional, the program would be turned over to Mr. Dessie B., the president, who would preside over the remainder of the program. The program would usually last until about 9 o'clock. Mr. Dessie B. tried to pattern himself after Ed Sullivan, he would do some kind of monologue for maybe ten minutes, and then he would call on each church represented to render a song. Then, intermittently, young people would be called on to sing special renditions; visiting churches from outside the area would be allowed to sing as well.

After five or six of the member churches had rendered their songs there would be an inspirational prayer given by one of the ministers who were present with all the ushers and elders gathered around the altar at the front of the church. The matrons would be given a time on the program to give their inspirational speeches to encourage the ushers to perform well and to learn the procedures being taught to them. Usually these turned into mini gossip sessions since the matrons didn't have much to talk about in the way of instruction, they took this as an opportunity to chitchat about whatever.

At the end of the Usher Board program there would be a grand march during the time that the offering was being collected. During this time all the ushers would line up on the outside of the front of the church and they would march around the table to pay their offering while singing was going on. This grand march was the highlight of the program and nobody wanted to miss it. Everybody who was anybody wanted to participate in the grand march. It was an exciting event because the ushers would all be dressed in similar uniforms; usually the women ushers would wear a seasonal uniform, blue and white in winter, white in summer, and gray and white in spring and fall. The men would wear black suits with white shirts and black ties in the winter and black coats and white pants in the spring and summer. The grand march was something to see because all the ushers would be marching in perfect step and would make a grand turn each time they reached a corner. You didn't want to miss the grand march. At the Homecomings sometimes there would be as many as two or three hundred ushers marching in the grand march all in their usher uniforms.

After it had been in existence for about two years, in 1956 it was decided to have an annual Usher Board Homecoming. This was an annual event that was scheduled for the second Sunday weekend in June. This was a big fund-raising event that brought together all the Usher Boards from all across the state that had been formed. After the first one, it was decided to hold it every year and the money raised would be divided among all the churches in the area. By 1958, each area, each county, and each local organization of nine or ten churches started hosting their own Usher Board Homecoming. These events grew so large until they had to be held in school gymnasiums and large city auditoriums in order to hold all of the people who wanted to attend. They eventually outgrew their usefulness and they began to fizzle in the mid to late 1970's. The City-Wide Usher Board still exists to this day although it is attended by just a handful of people who are still around and who were there from the beginning and can remember how valuable it was to the building of the black churches and communities in the area during those early times.

IX. INTO THE CIVIL RIGHTS MOVEMENT

If 1954 was the year of my awakening, 1955 was a pivotal year for our family, our community, and certainly for the nation.

It was the year that the Civil Rights Movement began. I shall never forget that it was just after my daddy and brothers returned from working in Mobile, Alabama during that summer of 1955 that the mutilated body of Emmett Till was pulled from the river in the Mississippi Delta. Although I was just a child, I can remember the pictures and the news of his death and discovery vividly. We had just gotten a television during the Spring of 1955. In fact, we had just gotten electricity installed in our house during the Fall of l954.

Emmett Till was a young black boy who was brutally murdered and his body mutilated in the town of Money, Mississippi in the Delta during the Summer of 1955. He was visiting with his grandparents during the summer, but he lived with his single-parent mother in Chicago during the rest of the year.

While visiting with his grandparents in Mississippi that summer, he and another cousin had gone into a store in the small town to purchase candy. Upon leaving the store, Emmett Till had made the grave error of speaking to, whistling at or saying something to a white woman from the town. She in turn had told her husband that a nigger boy had made a pass at her. The husband and some of his cronies had gone to Emmett Till's grandparents' home in the middle of the night and dragged the thirteen-year-old boy from their house. They took him out and killed him; mutilated his body by cutting off his genitals; cutting out his tongue; gouging out his eyes; and chaining concrete boulders to his body and dumping him in the river.

In a mockery of justice that was not uncommon in the South during the 1950's, the husband was brought to trial. Of course he was found innocent and released. The spectacle of that incident and the trial that followed will forever be seen as one of the lowest points in the history of racial injustice in Mississippi. The state's reputation and image will forever be linked to the Emmett Till saga and the travesty of justice in the face of overwhelming evidence that was allowed to happen in that case. Even the governor of Mississippi showed up to congratulate the murderers and spoke favorably on their behalf. It seems unimaginable that whistling at a white woman would exact such a harsh penalty that would go unpunished in the United States of America, even in 1954.

The news of Emmett Till's death had sent a shock wave and wave of fear throughout the black community of Mississippi and the entire South. Both black adults and children alike felt the fear and trepidation of his death. It was especially hard on our family because the men were away. You could sense the fear; every time the news came on everybody in the family would gather around the radio or television, whichever was on, to hear what the latest was concerning what was going on in the Mississippi Delta. As a little boy, I was scared to death. I could see myself having the same thing happen to me, which in those days and in that time was not a far-fetched impossibility. In fact, it was probably more a possibility than impossibility. It was certainly a situation that would cause sleepless nights, and as I remember, since daddy was away, Charles was home, and the other two brothers were with daddy, I made it my business to sleep in the bed with mama as many nights as she would allow me to.

Daddy and the older brothers must have returned from Mobile around the first week of August, about the time that Emmett Till's body was discovered. Even in their own community and among themselves, black folks didn't talk too openly about what was going on. To talk openly would be taken as a sign of insolence by white folks. Also, the black folks could never tell who among them would be brazen enough to go and tell some white person who among them had said what. Most blacks who did work on paying jobs worked either as domestics or as laborers for whites, and many of them would dare to tell the whites what certain blacks might have said to gain more favor for themselves or just to make some conversation. No doubt about it, the Summer of 1955 was hot in Mississippi in more ways than just the summer heat. Black folks, men, women and children were scared to death.

When daddy returned from Mobile it seems he had just a little more work to do on Mr. Jimmy Pittman's house, and also on a Mr. Sims' house, who was another white farmer who lived just down the road from Mr. Pittman. Daddy was not too aroused about Emmett Till's death as many of the other people in the community had been. He more or less saw the situation as none of his business and felt that if the young boy had stayed in his place and not done something to put himself in a dangerous situation he would have still been alive and everything for everybody would have been all right. Daddy's attitude was not vastly different from those of many other people, blacks and whites. Several incidents that happened within a few days and weeks after he returned would prove crucial for daddy and would awaken him to the serious reality of what Emmitt Till's death had meant to Mississippi and to the nation.

A few days after daddy had returned home from Mobile, my brother Otha and I were playing in the main road that went through Rock Hill, just at the curve where the road turned between our house and Cousin John's house where the driveway road from our house met the main road. We were playing with old car tires which was one of our summertime pleasures. We would roll the old tires down the road and pretend we were driving cars. On this particular day Mr. Robert Abney came driving down the road on his way to his farm on the other side of Cousin John's house. We saw his car coming down the road and moved out of the road into the ditch as we had been taught to do when we saw cars coming down the road. Although we were safely out of his way, Mr. Abney stopped his car when he got there next to us and blurted out, "If you little nigger boys don't get out of this road the next time I come through here I'm going to take you to jail," and he drove away.

Scared out of our wits we ran to the house as fast as lightning. I mean we ran with all the strength we could muster. When we got home we fell on the porch and crawled into the house because we were out of breath. Although we had only ran a good two hundred yards or less, you would have thought we had run several miles. Mama saw us fall on the porch and came to the door and asked us in a panic, "What's the matter with you children? What happened to y'all?" We could hardly talk, but I managed to get a few words out, "Mama that white man say he goin' take us to jail." "Take you to jail for what" she asked. By then both of us were in tears, just bawling our hearts out, we couldn't talk any more.

It took a while for mama to calm us down so that we could tell here the whole story about what happened. We did our best to convince her that we had gotten out of the road in plenty of time as we had been taught. The way we were crying evidently she believed us, otherwise we would have been due a whipping. But being aware of the times and what was going on, mama realized that we probably had not done anything to provoke this insult so she comforted us and took us in the house and took a wash cloth and some warm water and soap and washed our faces and cleaned us up. Cleaning-up our faces didn't do much for clearing out the fear that the incident had put in our hearts. I think it was that incident that first caused me to start hating white men. Before that I had never thought much about them at all except from the incident with the lawyer, and from that incident I probably felt more concern for his welfare than anything else, especially since I knew the hurt daddy would have put on him if he had gotten his hands on him.

Sometime during the night after all of us children had gone to sleep, evidently mama must have told daddy about the incident that happened that day. I don't know what or how she told him. Mama and daddy always had their private conversations after they figured all the children were asleep at night. But that night daddy woke up the whole house with his anger. I mean he was as mad as a wet setting hen when the dogs were trying to attack her brood of chicks. He was cursing and ranting as if he would raise the roof on the house about what he would do to that sorry-assed white son-of-a-bitch if he harmed one of his children. He swore that when he saw the motherfucker again he was going to give him a piece of his mind and let him take him to jail. Mama was pleading with him to calm down and to let it go; not to cause any trouble or to get himself in no trouble because his family needed him out of jail more than he needed to be in jail. But as mad as daddy was, he couldn't see it that way. He was ready to go to hell.

All of us children just lay in our beds and let the whole scene play out before us as if we were fast asleep. We didn't dare grunt or make a sound, because we were supposed to be asleep anyway. If daddy had even thought one of us were not asleep he probably would have grabbed us out of the bed and made sausage out of us with a belt or a switch.

The next morning you could tell that everybody had heard what had gone on and what had been said. The whole house was tense and daddy was still just as mad as ever. If it had not been a workday he would have probably gone somewhere and gotten him a jug of whiskey and started drinking. But since it was a workday, daddy was just angry and upset. Nobody knew what daddy was thinking that morning, nobody knew what he was going to do, and nobody, not even mama dared to ask him or even attempt to have a conversation with him. But we all knew he was not to be pestered with, so we all walked lightly until he left for work.

After daddy and the older brothers left for work the girls tried to get mama to talk about what had gone on the night before, but mama wasn't about to betray daddy's trust. Plus, she never would divulge the content of her and daddy's private conversations anyway. So it was a futile effort.

It must have been early in the week when the incident with Mr. Abney had taken place, perhaps on Monday or Tuesday. It was not until that Saturday morning that I remember seeing his car pass the road again. I was so scared all week until I never would look toward the road when cars would pass in fear that it would be his car. Around the house things had been calm and cautious. When daddy had returned home from work that particular evening of the next day when mama had told him about the incident he was his usual self, but you could tell that inside him he was studying the situation.

After dinner every evening he would just go out on the porch and kind of sit and watch the road for a while until darkness would start to set in. We would all gather around the television after our chores had been done and watch the evening shows. By this time in the summer we had been watching television long enough to know exactly what was coming on and when; we had our favorite shows already and we were not about to miss them.

Whatever daddy wanted to watch of course took preference over what anybody else wanted to watch; so we were enjoying his being pre-occupied with other things. That gave us the opportunity to fuss over what we got to watch in our quiet way. We were not about to let daddy hear us fussing or arguing over what we were going to watch; that would mean the television would be turned off and everybody would find something else to do like find a book to read or go do an extra chore.

At first when we had gotten the television we were the first household in the whole neighborhood to have one. The people in the community would come in the evenings around dusk to watch television for a while. It was a novelty beyond all imagination to most of the families in the community and they wanted to see a television up close. Some of them had never been close enough to a television to even touch one, so it was something to behold. They would talk about whether what was being seen was real or imaginary; whether the people were actually inside the television; and speculate about how the thing actually worked. Having a television was a history-making event for us in the Rock Hill Community and it caused quite a stir. Of course, it caused a lot of jealously among the children of other families and some resentment. We just considered ourselves fortunate to have one because it served to broaden our horizons and exposure. As it was we could only receive two or three channels anyway; the two from Jackson and the one from Meridian. Once in a while late at night we could pick-up the channels from New Orleans or Mobile.

It was early the next Saturday morning when daddy was sitting on the porch after breakfast picking his teeth and humming a tune that he saw Mr. Robert Abney's car pass along the road heading toward his farm. He would usually come and check his cows several times a week and on the weekends. When daddy saw his car pass he jumped with excitement and said in a subtle voice to himself, "I'm gonna catch that peckerwood son-of-a-bitch this morning." Daddy jumped up from where he was sitting and checked his pants pocket to make sure he had his pocket knife and just started walking toward the road in a hurry.

Only me and Pap (Otha, Jr.) were sitting there on the porch with him since mama and the girls were in the house washing the dishes and making the beds, and doing whatever other chores they had to do. I don't know whether George and Claude were out at the barn or had already gone to the woods or to the fields to pick peas or beans; probably the latter. Anyway, when daddy headed down the road, Pap and I got up and curiously began to ease our way out that way behind him. We stayed far enough away so as not to make it seem that we were following daddy, but we wanted to see what was about to go on. We felt safe since daddy was in front of us, but we did not want to see that white man up close. It would have been like our looking on the devil himself. So we made it seem like we were only interested in playing in the ditch and bushes along the driveway road that led to our house.

Daddy made his way all the way out to the main road and found him a comfortable spot to wait and look. It was obvious to us that he was waiting for Mr. Abney to come back by the curve. So he waited, and we waited while pretending to play. After about a half hour or so you could hear a car coming along the road back toward our house. As it topped the hill in front of Cousin John's house we could see that it was Mr. Abney and daddy had spotted it also. When daddy recognized the car he started waving in an up and down motion that signaled for the car to stop.

When Mr. Abney saw daddy there beside the road waving for him to stop, he began to slow down and eventually came to stop right beside where daddy was standing there beside the road. Daddy hurriedly walked around to the left side of the car next to the driver's side and just reached and grabbed the handle and opened the car door before he said anything. By this time Pap and I had gotten a little closer so we could hear since daddy's attention was no longer focused on what was going on in our direction. We could hear him clearly as he began to talk to Mr. Abney. "I understand you said something to my boys the other day when you came along Mr. Abney." Before the man could respond daddy cut him off and kept on talking. "I heard you said something to them about taking them to jail. Well, I just want to tell you one goddamn thing, if anybody is going to jail around here I want you to take me. But let me tell you one goddamn thing, don't you ever say another goddamn word to one of my children, and best don't you even stop your damn car along this road by my house when you pass here. I want you to know that I ain't involved in that Emmett Till shit that's going on, I'm just a man trying to make a living and provide for my family as best I can. But I ain't goin' to take no shit off you and no other peckerwood, so don't start no shit. Now I'm ready to go to hell this morning, I don't know if you got your mind made up to go or not, but if you ain't then you better get it made up in a hurry 'cause me and you both can go in a minute. And, another thing, if you and the Klan decide to come visit me, I'll be here 'cause I ain't planning on going no where. But when you git here be ready do die if you thinking 'bout killing me 'cause I intend to kill somebody too."

Daddy slammed the man's door as if he would tear the door off the car. Mr. Abney seemed as if he didn't know what had happened, but he didn't say a word to daddy. I believe he was too scared to say anything. He slowly drove away without saying a word and daddy just stood there in the road looking in the direction that the car had gone. But we could see that daddy had turned mad. Oh was he mad as he walked back toward the house. He was so mad that he was cursing to himself every step he took; and he hadn't even had a drink of whiskey.

By the time daddy started to walk back toward the house, Pap and I had long since ran back and were sitting on the porch as if we had been there all the time. We didn't want daddy to think that we had heard what had gone on, that probably would have meant we would have gotten our rear ends tanned. So we pretended we were playing on the porch. But as daddy got closer to the house we decided in unison without saying a word that we had better find us another place to hang out for a while, so we headed inside the house and crawled under a bed.

If the murder of Emmett Till had not been enough source of fear in us little kids, the incident with Mr. Abney had sure enough given all of us the ultimate fear. We children just knew that any night the Ku Klux Klan was coming to kill us all. There weren't many whites that passed by on the Rock Hill road, but there were enough that we would see several during the day and early evening. Now every time Pap and I saw a white man's car pass along the road we would run and hide. We just knew it was the Klan coming to get us and murder us. Daddy never showed a moment's fear and he never missed a meal or a night's sleep. He would go about his business as if nothing had happened. He would go to work everyday, come home in the evenings, eat his meals and get in his easy chair and nod while watching television with the rest of us until it was time to take his bath and go to bed. He would get up and go to bed and sleep as sound as a bear in hibernation. Why he was not afraid I could never figure out.

From that day of the confrontation with Mr. Abney forward, for as long as he lived and owned that farm on the other side of Cousin John's house, as many times as he passed along that road and as long as I lived at home until I finished college, he would pass that road and he never so much as looked at one of us again. If we were walking along the road, or playing along the road or whatever and he passed by he would speed up and go his way as if we were not even there. If we waved at him he ignored us; it was as if we were invisible to him. But he never insulted or tried to intimidate us again either.

It was a long time until I grew out of the fear of white men, it was probably in the early 1960's after the Civil Rights Movement had come full circle that I began to see them as what many of them really were, cowards who were only brave under the darkness of night and the cover of sheets and hoods. Other incidents of my daddy's courage as I grew up served to assure me that this was the case for many whites in the South who had the law and the sentiment of their kind on their side.

During the Summer of 1955 following the murder of Emmett Till it seemed that every where you turned some white man was threatening and intimidating blacks all over Mississippi and even in Jasper County. Another incident occurred just a few weeks after daddy's confrontation with Mr. Abney that provoked his wrath and caused him to have to put himself on the line. In late August daddy and the boys were working on Mr. Sims' house in the Lake Como Community. One morning daddy was on his way to work but had to go by the lumberyard to pick up a bill of materials before he could go to work. As usual, he had to wait until all the white contractors and carpenters had gotten their orders filled before he could order and receive his materials. That never seemed to be a problem for daddy because he was accustomed to this practice.

On this particular morning, however, daddy had gotten his load of materials and was heading across town to the job. As he left the lumberyard he had to go right through town which required him to cross the railroad tracks that ran along the north side of the lumberyard and up a fairly steep hill to the center of town. Loaded to the hilt as he was with the short-bed 1953 Chevrolet pick-up he was driving, daddy had to take it slow because he had quite a few sixteen to twenty-feet pieces of lumber on the truck. As he slowed to cross the railroad tracks and head up the hill a white fellow in a pick-up passed him and slowed down to yell out the window at daddy; "Git that goddamn piece of shit out of the road nigger, can't you see I'm trying to git by." The man slammed on his gas and sped up the hill. Daddy could see that he pulled into a parking space at the top of the hill in the center of town, but didn't get out of his truck.

Daddy wanted to hurry up, but he couldn't for two reasons. He was loaded so heavily that his pick-up was getting all the power it could, and if he had sped up he probably would have emptied his load right there in the middle of town. So he had to just ease along until he made it to the top of the hill which was probably two-tenths of a mile. When he got to the top of the hill he saw the fellow still sitting in his truck right at the stop sign in the middle of town. Daddy pulled his truck to the side of the street as much as he could just behind the fellow's truck.

Before he knew what was happening, daddy had gotten out of his truck and rushed over to the fellow's truck, opened the door and reached in and grabbed him in the collar and pulled him out of his truck. Before the fellow could say a word daddy had him on the ground with his foot in his chest and his knife around his neck. "What did you say to me back there when you passed me?" Goddamn your soul, if you so much as grunt I'll cut your goddamned head off and throw it out in the middle of this goddamn street to the dogs son-of-bitch. I mean just grunt, bat your eyes, fart, do something to give me an excuse to cut your motherfucking throat. You don't know me peckerwood but you're fixin' to learn me this morning. I ain't bothering nobody; I'm just trying to make a living as best I can. But you peckerwoods ain't goin' run over me just 'cause I'm black. Now I'm ready to go to hell this morning; if you ain't ready you better git ready in a hurry 'cause if you fuck with me again, me and you both going. If I let you git up and don't kill you, if you ever see me again you better act like you don't see me."

The whole scene happened so fast until it seemed as if it didn't happen at all. Pap and me were in the truck with daddy that morning for some ungodly reason. He had decided that we were going to work with him to pick up the scrap wood and clean up all the trash around the job. Even at six and seven years old daddy believed that every able body should work so here we were witnesses to another horrifying episode in a matter of weeks. By the time daddy turned the man loose he was crying like a baby, but he hadn't said a word. When daddy turned him loose, he put his knife back in his pocket and walked back to the truck, got in and proceeded to head to work. By the grace of God, there was nobody nearby who paid attention to what had happened.

It seemed mighty strange that the streets were virtually empty that morning. But as mad as daddy was it probably would have made him no difference. Whenever he got that upset and angry he was literally ready to go to hell if it happened to be his time. It soon became apparent to us, even as little boys that daddy was not about to be a man that would be intimidated or pushed around. He had a firm resolve that he would either live like a man or he would die like one; either way didn't seem to make him much difference. But he was determined to stand up for himself even if he had to stand alone or die trying.

Obviously the word got around about the two incidents, or at least about the one in town. As I grew older, I came to doubt seriously whether Mr. Abney had told anybody about his confrontation with daddy. But it was probably certain that this other fellow had told people about what had happened. Anyway, later in 1955 the Civil Rights Movement would take a full swing with the Rosa Parks incident in Montgomery and the bus boycott that followed. That incident coupled with the Emmett Till murder had brought a wave of fear to the entire South for black people. You could sense the mood and the tensions between blacks and whites everywhere you went and at every turn. You could sense it when you went to town and went in the stores, when you traveled along the roads when whites passed blacks on the roads they would make obscene gestures. All sorts of things were happening to make life miserable for blacks. Those were tense times and they would only become tenser throughout the remainder of the 1950's and well into the 1960's.

After daddy finished the work for Mr. Sims there was no more work for him to be had for months. In fact, all of the black carpenters were idle except for small remodeling and piddling jobs that they could get from the few blacks who had some money to do repairs on their houses. As I look back now, I don't know how we made it through that year. I was too small to really understand all of what was going on and the impacts, but I know times got tight and it looked like the black folks in Jasper County would be starved out. Many blacks that worked for whites were laid off, even some of the women who worked as domestics were let go in retaliation for what was going on in Montgomery.

Martin Luther King, Jr. became synonymous with the troubles that were rising in the South and was pictured as the devil himself by whites. He was blamed for all the troubles that were taking place in the South. You could hear whites talking in the stores and on the streets; "If that uppity nigger would mind his own business and stop stirring up the good Negras everything would be all right and everybody could get back to normal." Little did they know that normal as they had known it would never be normal again. Even many blacks openly criticized him and wished that he would just go away and leave everybody to their business.

Daddy didn't embrace the Civil Rights Movement. He also saw Martin Luther King, Jr. as a troublemaker, but that was his business. He didn't see where he should be concerned about changing the social system in the South. He just wanted to be left alone to make a living as best he knew how and not be bothered with civil rights. But there was no way of escaping the impacts of the movement because everybody would eventually be caught up in it whether they chose to participate actively or not.

If the Summer of 1955 had been an intense one, the Summer of 1956 was even more intense, especially for the Lang family. Early that summer one of daddy's cousins, Thelda Lang, the son of Will Lang and the brother to John Emmett who had been in Jackson College with Charles, had been accused of raping a white woman in Laurel where he lived. He was working as a gardener for a white family on the north side of Laurel where the white aristocracy of the town lived. Evidently he was having an on-going affair with the mistress of the house. On a certain day in May or June of that year the man of the house had come home unexpectedly and found Thelda and his wife engaged in the sex act. Although the mistress admitted to having an on-going affair with Thelda, he was locked up on charges of rape.

The woman was declared mentally deranged and hospitalized.

Meanwhile, Thelda Lang was locked up in jail without bail. That incident brought a lot of attention to the Lang name and brought much consternation to everybody associated with the name. At the time daddy had two brothers, Uncle Reedus and Uncle Grover, who were living in Laurel. Thelda had a wife and three or four children who were all younger than ten years old. One of his sons, Mitchell, would play the same instrument as I played, bass tuba, in the marching band at Jackson State University with me in the late 1960's when we were both students there.

As it turned out, Thelda was brought to trial sometime during the fall or winter of that year. Somehow he was declared mentally insane and sent to the insane asylum at Whitfield rather than found guilty and sent to prison at Parchman. He stayed in Whitfield for years, at least until the late 1970's when he was finally released. Mitchell and I visited him several times when we were students at Jackson State in the late 1960's. He was just as sane as we were from what I could tell, and a whole lot smarter because he had spent his time educating himself while locked up. He would ask us about books we were reading in college and quote passages from some of the authors eloquently.

One thing that daddy did in the Spring of 1956 to help ease his financial situation was to sell the back sixty acres of his land to Mr. James McBay, the white man whose land joined ours on the back side. Mr. McBay was a full-time farmer and had wanted the land in order to expand his cattle pasture. Cotton was on the decline and daddy was decreasing the amount of cotton he was planting anyhow because the prices had dropped so low. So he made a deal with Mr. McBay and sold him the sixty acres.

Selling the sixty acres served another purpose. On the backside of our property also lived a real and racist redneck, a white man named, a stuanch racist who had publicly threatened to kill any nigger who belonged to the NAACP. Some times our cows would go through the fence and get in his pastures. Other times he would let our bulls into his pastures to breed his cattle. Since we always had a better stock of bull than he did this was his way of upgrading his herd without getting permission which would have been denigrating for him. Anyway, daddy figured that as things were developing eventually he would have a run-in with the man and one of them would end up dead. If he got Mr. McBay owning the land in between them, this would provide the buffer needed so that he would never have to deal with him.

Some years later, Mr. Hub Darby, a known NACCP life member Lewis Moffett, would be found dead; shot through the window of his house. He lived just across the Smith County line, probably five miles from our house in the Carlisle Community. His property also joined the white racist to the west. It was known by some that Mr. Darby was a life member of the NAACP. Anyway, a young black man from Smith County was sentenced to life in prison for his death on purely unsubstantiated evidence and a coerced confession. It seems the young man had been caught by Mr. Darby a few months prior bestializing his cows. That was the main evidence against him. Nevertheless, some years later on his deathbed it was alleged that the white racist confessed to killing Mr. Darby, but the young black man was never released from prison as far as I know.

Selling the land to Mr. McBay provided daddy the financial cushion he needed to survive until he could get a crop planted in the Spring of 1956. Charles had gotten settled into a job at the Fairbanks Morse Plant in Beloit, Wisconsin and was making a decent wage there and working part-time with Joe Quince during the days in his wrecking and hauling business. He was able to send money home every other week or so to help out the family. As it appeared things would only get worse before they would get any better in Mississippi, especially for those blacks who depended on whites to make a living which was the majority of blacks in Jasper County.

In the Spring of 1956 the second oldest brother, Claude, was graduating from high school. He had no real aspirations about going to college; in fact, all Bubba, as we all called him, wanted to do was to just get out of high school. In the spring, a few weeks before he was to graduate from high school he was driving the family car, a black 1954 Pontiac Sedan, to work one day or either on a social trip and was involved in a horrible accident. Although no one was seriously injured, the car was totaled. Daddy took the proceeds from the insurance payoff and put some of his own money with it to make a down payment on a brand spanking new 1956 Pontiac Star Chief with an extended bumper continental spare kit on the back. It was undoubtedly the prettiest car in the county, and was probably one of the most expensive. About the same time daddy bought that car, Mr. Will H. Alexander, one of the sons of the Alexanders who owned and operated the major hardware store and lumberyard in Bay Springs, had bought an identical car but without the fancy continental kit.

Needless to say, a black man owning and driving such a fancy car, and one that rivaled that of one of the richest white men in town did not set well with either the white folks or the black folks. It was especially troublesome considering the civil rights struggle that was taking off in Mississippi and across the South. But daddy didn't care, it was what he wanted and what he figured he could afford, or ill-afford considering how slow work had become during that time. The car, the confrontations and the word getting around that Otha Lang was a crazy nigger going around pulling a knife on white men made for intense and fearful times for him and for the family. Although it didn't seem to bother daddy that much, mama was petrified with fear. She didn't talk about it much, but we children could tell that she feared for daddy's life and for the safety of the family. She did the best she could to put on the best front, but we children could see the agony in her face.

It probably intensified things for other black families and the other black men in the community and the county. But as daddy saw it every man had to stand on his own and on his own ground. He was not trying to lead any other men to take any particular stand one way or the other, he just knew what he had to do to protect himself and what he stood for. If other men opposed his stand and his actions it was their prerogatives and their lives.

X. AWAY FROM MISSISSIPPI

By the time Bubba graduated from high school he had made up his mind that he was going to leave Mississippi. Uncle Emmitt Armstrong, mama's sister Aunt Dessie's husband in Meridian, had brothers who lived in Sandusky, Ohio who were carpenters and masonry workers. Bubba had become a skilled bricklayer working with daddy during the summers and across the years, so he figured he had the skills to make it on his own. With daddy's help Bubba was able to buy a year-old 1955 Pontiac Super Chief Sedan, which was a step down from Pontiac's top-of-the-line Star Chief which daddy now owned. It was a nice car and would serve Bubba's needs for a few years. With his new car and a few dollars in his pocket, by the end of the Summer of 1956 Bubba headed to Ohio to make it on his own.

By the end of that summer, it had become obvious to daddy that there would be no substantial work for him in Mississippi for a while. He had to make a decision. Several things happened that summer that helped him to make that decision. Charles had come home to visit sometime during the summer. He had bought himself a nice 1955 Pontiac Star Chief two-door coupe; it was a deep brown and white with lots of chrome and it was a sharp car. He had told daddy that there were opportunities for carpenters in the Beloit area and there was lots of building going on. The white contractors in the area didn't seem to mind hiring black men as long as they could carry their loads and do the work.

Joe Quince, Mr. Wash Quince's son with whom Charles had connected in Beloit had also come for a visit that summer. In fact, he and Charles may have come together. Anyway, Mr. Wash Quince had made the decision that after he gathered his crop that fall and sold it, he was getting out of farming and moving to Beloit for good. He had decided that farming was no longer a profitable way to make a living, so he was closing down his farm and moving north to make a go of it.

Mr. Wash Quince was a different kind of man than the other men in the Rock Hill Community. He was a man who would speak his mind and say what he thought to whomever would question him or challenge him. He was daddy's only supporter and encourager. He had admired the way daddy had stood up for himself and defended himself. As the Civil Rights Movement was shaping up it was probably apparent to him that he would find himself in trouble soon with the white folks in Jasper County, so it was best for him to head north. He had made the decision to do so in the Fall of 1956.

Meanwhile, beginning in the early spring and across the summer, the people of the community had decided to build a new church at Blue Mountain. In fact, during that spring they had leveled off a plot next to the old wooden church and had broken ground and started the foundation of the new church that would be built of cinder blocks and wood. Although the church did not have enough money to build a new building entirely it had been decided to make a start. Part of the reason was because other churches in the area had begun to build new buildings to replace their old wooden frame ones. The people of Rock Hill believed they needed and could build a new church, especially since there were now a number of men in the community who were working in the building business.

As had become the custom among rural African American congregations in the South, when they needed to raise money the church would ask each family to give so much over a period of time. This is what had happened at Blue Mountain that year, each family was asked to give $200 on the new building fund in order to start building the church. Of course not all the families were able or willing to give that amount of money, but enough had given that there were two or three thousand dollars raised.

Gone to Hell This Morning

Reverend Wilmer Carter, probably one of the best and most progressive pastors that ever served the church was eager to make his mark in the community and in the larger area. Building a new church was just what he wanted to do. So with his strong leadership, and the challenge presented by other churches in the area starting to build new buildings, a new church at Blue Mountain was underway, at least a new foundation got underway. I never shall forget that when they started the excavating, the men of the community came with their horses and mules and their grading equipment and did most of the ground leveling themselves.

To this day Reverend Carter still rates as one of the most progressive and most involved pastors that Blue Mountain Church ever had. He was a full-time pastor in a sense although at that time we only had preaching at the church one Sunday out of the month. Before he became pastor, that Sunday was always the first Sunday of the month. But because he also had other churches that he was already pastoring, the pastoral Sunday at Blue Mountain was changed to the fourth Sunday to accommodate him and it stayed on the fourth Sunday until the 1980's when the church started having two pastoral Sundays a month. Now Blue Mountain has a worship service every Sunday. Back in those days the churches only had preaching one Sunday of the month.

What made Reverend Carter outstanding was that he started having special programs to involve the youth of the community, and involved them in activities to develop and enhance their talents. For example, on Sunday evenings after the preaching services we would have what was called a Baptist Young Peoples Union (BYPU) which was a training program. It was a great fun program, but it was also a great learning experience. Every month Reverend Carter would give us certain scriptures to learn and recite, and we would have contests to see who could best recite the scriptures. He would always give prizes to the top three contestants. We would also have drills to see who could find certain bible verses and passages first. These programs did a lot to involve the young people in the church and gave us children real incentives for coming to church.

Reverend Carter would also visit the homes of church members during the week, and got to know every family and every child by name and face in that community. He would come on the Saturday afternoon prior to the pastoral Sunday for the church business meeting, and he would stay over night at one family's house as was the custom of the times for African American preachers in that area. Most of the pastors of churches were from places some miles away. Reverend Carter was from Beaumont, a town in Perry County in southeast Mississippi, which must have been at least 75 miles away. But with the road conditions and for what our church was able to pay him, it was to his advantage to stay over night.

Reverend Carter would stay with any family in the community who invited him. It didn't matter to him what condition their houses were in or how much they had or didn't have; if they invited him he would accept the invitation. He loved to visit our house and stay with us and we loved to have him. He and daddy became good friends although daddy sometimes would miss church, especially if he had had too much to drink on Saturday night. But he made sure we were there every Sunday and we were most of the choir anyway.

Many times on Saturday evenings daddy would get us all together and we would have to practice the songs we were going to sing on the Sunday for him so he could direct us on the parts. That is how we learned to sing in harmony, and because there were eight of us he had us all singing different parts. The girls would sing soprano, alto and contralto; the boys would sing first and second tenor, baritone and bass. Whoever was not singing one of these parts was the person who was leading the song. When daddy was around you didn't sing out of key and you sang your part exactly as it was supposed to be sung. George was the main leader along with Walterene and Brenda. When the Lang children showed up at a church everybody knew we were always ready to sing; and we would out-sing just about anybody else who showed up.

Reverend Carter loved to hear us sing; that was one of the reasons he loved to stay at our house. The other reason was the girls admired him and treated him like a king. But he was a great inspiration to us children and we looked up to him because he took so much interest in the children of the church. Whenever he stayed at our house he always wanted us to sing a few songs for him during the evening. We loved the special attention he gave us. He thought Brother George was the best vocalist he had ever heard.

On Saturdays and some evenings that summer during the week the men and their sons would come together and work to get the foundation dug and put in for the new church. By the early fall they had the foundation completed. That was as far as they could go that summer because the money they had raised ran out. It would be a number of years before they would complete the new church.

When the crops were gathered in the Fall of 1956 around the end of October, daddy, Mr. Wash Quince and his wife, Mrs. Anna, packed up daddy's 1956 Pontiac and headed to Wisconsin. Daddy was in hope of finding profitable work and Mr. Wash and his wife were in hope of starting a new life totally. They would never return to live full-time in Mississippi again.

Daddy left and George was the oldest son left at home with mama, the three girls, Pap and me. George was in his senior year in high school and was about eighteen years old. Since daddy had taken the car the family was left with the pick-up truck as the main source of transportation. It was the first time and the only time in our lives that I could remember there not being a car for us to ride in. We children had become accustomed to riding in a car, and now to have to ride on the back of a pick-up truck somehow seemed to lower our dignity. Plus, it was getting cold as winter was approaching. Our saving grace was the fact that George and daddy had built high sideboards to haul cotton to the gin on the truck. We left those on the truck so that when we had to ride on the back of the truck to town or to other churches for a distance the high side boards would serve to shield us from the wind.

What hurt us most was that mama had to ride in a pick-up to town and to church; but mama didn't seem to mind at all. In fact, she seemed rather to enjoy riding in the truck rather than having to drive that fancy car and have people staring at her every time she went somewhere as if she was a rich woman or somebody extra special. Mama was always modest that way; she liked simple things and never was one for much fancy stuff. She never wanted people to think of us as a family of means, or to misconstrue that our family had more than anybody else. That was just the way she was. It had to do with the way she was brought up; her parents had been sharecroppers and had never even owned their own home. Just to have a home of her own, even a simple wooden frame house was all she ever hoped for. As fate would have it in the years to come she would have much more.

When daddy left for Wisconsin there was definitely a void in our household and in the family. Although Charles had left two years before for college and then a year before for Wisconsin, and Claude had left earlier that spring for Ohio, daddy's leaving seemed the most relentless of all. Although we revered him and looked up to him, when he left there seemed to be a sigh of relief that came over us, especially at this time. Yet, there was still an unconscious fear in our lives considering the times and what was happening in the South.

We pretty much went about our business as usual; going to school every day, doing our chores, looking after the farm, gathering firewood, tending the animals. All of these things we children were now responsible for seeing that they got done with George's supervision and mama's urging. The last thing we wanted was for daddy to come home and find something not done properly. Not so much that we feared a whipping, which we certainly did, but more so because we wanted daddy to be proud of us and that we could carry on in his absence.

While daddy was gone, he would write mama a letter just about every week and send her money. By this time we had a telephone installed, so he would call at least every two weeks. Before the weather got really bad up north, daddy drove home at least once a month. He might not have come home in the dead of winter in January and February, but during the other months he would make that trip every month which must have been at least 18 to 20 hours during those days without interstate highways. How he could do that is beyond my imagination, but he did. It was at that time that I came to realize how daddy loved his family and what we all meant to him. He spent more time talking and interacting with us children during those weekend visits home than he had ever spent during the early years as we were growing up. Of course he had spent a considerable

Gone to Hell This Morning

amount of time with the older three brothers who were closer to him, but now he spent time with us younger ones which we cherished.

Before this time I had never really gotten to know daddy because he never really spent any time with me. As a little child Charles had always taken care of and looked after Pap and me. In fact, until Charles finished high school, I thought he was actually my daddy and that daddy was my granddad. That was until I met Grandpa Richard and came to know and remember him. It was a precious moment in my life to finally have daddy spend time actually talking to me rather than disciplining me. Pap and me began to look forward to those visits from daddy and couldn't wait for him to come home.

When daddy would come home from Wisconsin he would always get there about midnight. The trips took a long time and he would leave Wisconsin usually before day in the morning on Fridays and arrive at home late on Friday night. He would leave going back some time by midday on Sunday so he could be back in time for work on Monday morning. We would beg mama to let us stay up until daddy came when she knew he was coming home. She would let us know if she knew definitely that he was coming. Sometimes she would know but wouldn't tell us so that it would be a surprise when we woke the next morning and daddy was home.

Daddy stayed in Wisconsin working until the Fall of 1957. Although the money was good, daddy absolutely hated the cold weather and being away from home. Of all the bad things that Mississippi represented, he has always sworn that there is no better place to live in the world. He couldn't wait to get back home. By the time daddy returned home George had graduated from high school in the Spring of 1957 and with his supervision, we had planted and cultivated the crop for that year.

George was an excellent big brother, for he had patience and a kind and nurturing spirit. He got along with everybody and people all over the county just loved him. He was an accomplished vocalist and idolized Sam Cooke and the Soul Stirrers who were one of the hottest gospel groups of the 1950's before Sam Cooke stopped leading the group and began singing pop music. In fact, by 1957 Sam Cooke was already a top pop singer with such hits as "You Send Me," "Only Sixteen," and others already making the charts.

George loved anything he sang, either gospel or pop, and the Dixie Hummingbirds, another gospel group who were rising to the top and would become his all-time favorites for years.

Even back then, George was an accomplished vocalist and everywhere he went to church he had to sing. People just loved to hear him sing and he could certainly raise the hair on your head when he was in church. He was one of the favorites at the City-Wide Usher Board, and when he had his sisters and two older brothers singing with him was when he really would shine.

When George finished high school and had finished getting the crop planted that summer, Charles came to Mississippi for a visit and George went back to Wisconsin with him. In fact, Charles had come in October of 1957 after he had gotten married to bring mama back home and to bring his bride for the rest of the family to meet her. Mama had caught the train to Wisconsin to be there for their wedding.

By that time daddy had returned to Mississippi. Just about the time George got to Wisconsin and got settled, a recession set in and work got slow. He and Charles had joined the men that daddy had worked for when he was in Wisconsin and were full-time carpenters. Charles had met his bride, Phyllis Edwards, who was from a family of eight girls, and they had gotten married in October 1957.

During the year that George was in Wisconsin he had attended night school at a business college in Beloit and had learned to type extremely well. He attended classes several times a week at night. He had wanted to go to college badly, and would have been a great college student; he was smart and had finished at the top of his class. But the money was just not available at that time and he remembered how difficult it was for Charles that one year he had spent at Jackson College. And, although he was a top-notch basketball player, being from such a small town as Bay Springs he had not gotten any notice from any of the colleges in the state for an offer of a basketball scholarship. So attending college was for all practical purposes out of the question.

Somehow Charles and his bride and George managed to stay in Wisconsin during the Winter of 1957-58. Although work was slow, they had managed to make it somehow. George had gotten a job working at the Fairbanks-Morse Plant while Charles continued to carpenter as long as there was a little work going on. He also continued to work with Joe Quince whenever there was no carpentering work going on. With Phyllis working at one of the downtown department stores they made it through that long and arduous winter.

By late Spring of 1958 daddy had managed somehow to land two houses to build, both for whites. One house was in the Lake Como community and the other was in the Antioch community which was just northwest of Lake Como. The house in Antioch was for a Mr. Fletcher Evans who worked at the Alexander Hardware Store. It slips my memory now who the other house was for; it was not too far from the Jimmy Pittman house and was along the same road. Both houses were to be brick veneer and were fairly large houses.

Although daddy had gotten a reputation as a radical and rebellious Negro, he was also recognized as a superb builder; his prices were cheaper than the white contractors (they had to be in order for him to bid against them and get the jobs). Thus he had to work harder and build houses faster than they did. As long as he had the good labor of his sons he had been able to do just that. In the Summer of 1958 the sons came to his rescue. Since building construction had slowed to a halt in Wisconsin, Charles and George were willing to come. Things were no better in Sandusky, Ohio and soon Bubba was back in Mississippi working with daddy again that summer.

George came home early in the Summer of 1958, but Charles didn't come until early that fall. Phyllis was pregnant and was expecting the baby that summer, so Charles stayed in Wisconsin until the baby was born. In early September Charles came to Mississippi and went to work with daddy. Once again the entire family was back together. Only this time there was an addition. Charles now had a wife, Phyllis, and on July 23, 1958 she gave birth to their first child and the family's first grandchild and nephew, Charles E. Lang, Jr., who was from birth affectionately nicknamed Chucky. But Phyllis and the baby wouldn't join us until after Thanksgiving 1958 when Charles, George and me would return to Wisconsin in Charles' car to pick them up over that weekend.

It was truly miraculous that all of us had been able to live in our little five-room, two bedroom house during all those years when we were growing up. It was even more miraculous that we were able to do it again now with three grown sons and teenage daughters; but during those times no black families in rural Mississippi lived in luxurious homes. So being overcrowded and cramped was an accepted way of life. People did what that had to do in order to survive, and families could always make room for one or two more family members when the need arose. That was exactly what we had to do in the Fall and Winter of 1958.

Actually, as we would come realize soon in the Fall of 1958 things were not so bad with all of the family at home and living in our small wood frame house. Things would get even tighter before that summer was over. On the first Sunday of August all of us had gone to the home church where mama had grown up as a girl for the annual revival meeting. All mama's sisters who were in Mississippi and their children were there also. The church was the Little Rock Baptist Church which was a few miles out from the town of Decatur, Mississippi. Mama's sisters, Aunt Addie Blackwell from Meridian and her husband Uncle George, Aunt Dessie and Uncle Emmitt and their children, Aunt Annie who lived out from Hickory, and Aunt Fannie who lived in Hickory were all there along with mama's brother, Uncle Monk and some of his family. It had become a custom that every year they would all meet either at Little Rock or at another church they had attended as teenagers, Shiloh Baptist, which was a few miles east of Newton.

On this particular Sunday everybody was so excited because mama's sister, Aunt Euralea whom they called Beabo, and her family were coming from California. It was probably the first time they had made the trip from California in five or six years, so everybody had gathered there to meet and greet them when they arrived. They had planned to arrive that day while everybody was at the revival at Little Rock.

Aunt Beabo and her family made it to Mississippi that afternoon, but they never made it to Little Rock for the revival. When they were just outside the town of Brandon, which is about 15 miles east of Jackson, they had a head-on collision with a drunk driver. Aunt Beabo's husband, Uncle Joshua, was killed instantly and Aunt Beabo was critically injured. She was driving at the time of the accident and had gotten behind a slow-moving truck on the two-lane Highway 80 which was the major route from west to east in central Mississippi at the time. In haste to get to their destination, Uncle Joshua had urged her to pass the truck on a section of the highway that did not allow her enough sight distance. Before she could get in front of the truck the speeding drunk driver, who was white, came dashing over the hill and around the curve driving way beyond the legal speed limit.

Aunt Beabo suffered two broken legs, a broken hip and severe internal injuries along with damage to one eye. Her children who were with them, Linda, Walter and Bobby suffered minor injuries. Within a few days the children were released from the hospital, but Aunt Beabo was hospitalized for the better part of two months. A few days after the wreck, Uncle Joshua's body was shipped back to Los Angeles where his family buried him.

When the children were released from the hospital they came to live with us, and later when Aunt Beabo was released from the hospital she initially came to live with us also. I can't remember exactly how we all managed to live in that small house but somehow we did. I can remember that almost every evening daddy and mama and some of the other family members would make the trip to Jackson to see about Aunt Beabo in the hospital, the University of Mississippi Medical Center. In fact, daddy insisted that somebody would go and see about her just as he insisted that she could come and live with us until she recovered. I know some of us had to sleep on blankets on the floor, and we slept all over the house wherever there was room enough to put a blanket down; but somehow we made it.

Aunt Beabo and her children stayed with us until sometime around Christmas, then they went to Meridian to stay with Aunt Addie and Uncle George Blackwell. They had a fairly big house in Meridian and there was nobody there but the two of them. But Aunt Addie was somewhat older, she was mama's oldest sister, and her health was not the best. Thus, she was not fully capable of seeing after Aunt Beabo when she first came out of the hospital. Aunt Dessie with her four children and the house they were living in actually had less room than we did in our house.

Aunt Beabo and her children stayed in Mississippi until the Summer of 1959 and then they returned to California. I think she may have visited Mississippi once again before she died in the late 1970's or early 1980's. Her children never came to Mississippi again. But while she was there, daddy treated her just like she was his own sister rather than his sister-in-law. Even when she moved to Meridian with Aunt Addie, every other weekend or so he and mama would go to Meridian to see about her.

In those times, the late 1950's, black folks had to look out for each other. Family and community were all they had. They couldn't depend on anybody or anything for their safety and security. Certainly, they could not count on the justice system and the social welfare system was mainly for the benefit of poor whites, especially in the South. So if family and the black community did not look after one another nobody else would or even cared. Those were the times we lived in and lived through.

XI. OPPORTUNITY DENIED

In 1958, it seemed that things were happening so fast that we could hardly keep up with the times. It seemed that everybody in the family was moving somewhere, going somewhere, or just moving around. I remember that during the Summer of 1958 the girls had taken a trip to Wisconsin with daddy and George, but us younger children had to stay home. That was one reason that Charles had let me go to Wisconsin with him and George when they went to pick up Phyllis and the baby that Thanksgiving. I can still remember how excited I was to have the chance to go outside Mississippi. What I remember most was that when we crossed over into Illinois and came into the town of Cairo, Illinois sometime around one o'clock in the morning, some convenience stores and nightclubs were still open. Charles stopped at one of the stores to get a beer, and I got a hamburger from a cafe next door. I remember he went right into the front door of the cafe and was served just as the white customers. I had never seen a black man able to go into the front door of a white food establishment before in my life.

The 1958-59 school year was also an exciting one for those of us in the family who were left at home and still in school.

The year before, a television station had been built and started operating in the area between Laurel and Hattiesburg. The station was WDAM-TV, Channel 7, which was based in Laurel and Hattiesburg, but was physically located in the town of Moselle, Mississippi which was between the two larger towns. During that year, the station had started a program which was hosted by a black talent scout named Rick Darnell. Mr. Darnell had started a show called "The Rick Darnell Show" which was a local version of the famous "American Bandstand Show" hosted on national television by the renowned Dick Clark.

Rick Darnell was originally from New Orleans and his show was a talent show that featured black students from the all black high schools in the south Mississippi region, mainly from the southeast portion of the state. The schools from Jasper County were invited and participated on the show. The show would include dancing and students and other activity groups from the schools exhibiting their talents. The show lasted an hour and was on Saturday mornings during the school year.

During the 1957 school year was the first time that students from our school at Bay Springs participated on the show. On the show in 1957 the school choir had been the featured talent and sang several traditional songs directed by the school's choir director, Mrs. Claudia Singleton, who was also one of the English teachers in the high school. Mrs. Singleton was from Marshall, Texas and was an extremely talented, young and beautiful lady. She had taken a special interest in brother George and the three sisters because they could sing in perfect harmony without much coaching. All they needed was to either hear a song or to be taught the melody and the parts several times. During those years The Platters and The Drifters were among the most popular black rock and roll artists who were producing top hits. Mrs. Singleton was fond of both groups and taught George and the girls and also a quartet including George and three of his school buddies to sing The Drifters and The Platters songs.

We were fond of Mrs. Singleton and just loved her; I guess it was because she took so much time and gave so much attention to us children. When she went home to Texas for breaks or for the weekend she would always have one of the older brothers to go with her to help drive. Sometimes she would take one or all three of the girls with her. And when her three children, Harold, Percy and Orchid, would come to Bay Springs to visit her, they would usually stay at our house since they were about the same ages as the older children in our family. Mrs. Singleton was rooming with somebody in Bay Springs who had less room than we did, if that was possible. But her children loved staying with us and so they always did.

In the school year of 1958 George had graduated and gone which left the girls to sing as a threesome. Walterene, Brenda and Bobbie could sing as good or better than most of the popular women's groups of the time such as The Andrews Sisters, The McGuire Sisters and any others that were recording during the late 1950's. The girls had been singing since they were little girls in the church choir and the school choir. They also had been competing in talent contests in the 4-H Clubs, Future Homemakers of America (FHA), and in other school activities such as the annual Field Day talent contests. In the 4-H Club, they had been winning every talent contest they competed in for several years at the local, regional and state levels. They had become well known throughout the state for their singing abilities and success.

Ms. Willie Ruth King who was the black female County Extension Agent for the state's Cooperative Extension Service in Jasper County was their mentor. She thought the girls belonged to her because they were her pride contestants in the 4-H Club competitions. Brenda also was very successful in the public speaking contests and had won several regional competitions, but the talent contest was their mainstay. They knew and Ms. King knew that the girls could out-sing just about anybody they competed against in the state. And when it came to pure talent and singing they were hard to beat and were not to be denied.

Often times when they went to talent contests the other competitors would protest that the judging was rigged because the Lang Sisters always came out the winners. Over the years, competitors had tried all kinds of antics to attempt to tip the odds in their favor. For example, there had been requests that judges be brought from areas outside the region where the girls were widely known, which was done. Rules had been changed in other ways in attempts to make the competition more favorable for other contestants which was done also. None of these things worked against the girls because they were just so much more talented than their competition that they could not be denied.

The girls were daddy's pride and joy, and their singing talent had won them special places in his heart. They, like George, were in church somewhere every Sunday singing in a program or just singing in the choir. Many times they were with George and were singing with him. However, now that George was gone, they had a better opportunity for their talent to be recognized since they were not singing back-up to him but were on their own. When they went to church to sing it was just like them singing in the talent contests. Those who either had to sing before or after them knew they were in for stiff competition for attention and accolades.

The girls had been taught to sing perfect three-part harmony and it came as natural for them as breathing. When they sang together Walterene or Brenda usually sang the lead. Bobbie was a natural contralto and never really preferred to lead, she always would rather be in the background. But could lead if she needed to and sometimes would if one of the other girls was not quite up to par because of illness. The girls really had the talent and everybody around them was pushing them to reach to the heights.

It had never occurred to anybody that the Lang Sisters had the potential to be recording artists. During those times and being black in rural Mississippi such aspirations were not considered a real possibility even though they had some exposure to recording artists over the years. There had been one time that a popular gospel quartet, The Skylarks, had been touring in the area and for some reason had wound up at our house after their car had broken down and they had to stay over to wait for it to be repaired. As I remember, they had been performing in Laurel and had also done a program at one of the churches in Jasper County. On the particular night after they did the program in Bay Springs, which daddy and the brothers had attended, their car broke down and they needed places to stay. Since there were no public accommodations in the area where blacks could get lodging the only option was for them to stay with families in their homes. Of course daddy invited them to come home with him since they were one of the gospel groups that he and the older brothers had admired for years. Two of the group's members as I recall stayed at our house and several of them stayed with other people in the community for one or two nights until their car was repaired.

During those years black performers in all categories, especially those in small groups traveled mostly by cars rather than by bus, train or plane. And, when they traveled in the South they had to have lodging arranged with families before hand; this was especially the case when they were performing in rural towns where there were no black-owned hotels or boarding houses. Usually in places like Jackson, New Orleans, Memphis or Birmingham where there were black-owned hotels or motels they could find lodging.

Anyway, the girls got the chance to meet some live recording artists by chance when the members of The Skylarks happened to have the misfortune of their car breaking down in our town. I never really knew how daddy and the brothers got them to stay with us other than when their car broke down they had no other choice than to accept the hospitality of whomever offered it.

When the girls sang on The Rick Darnell Show on television he was struck by their raw talent and natural attractiveness. He immediately recognized what rare talent they had and wanted to do something to expose them to a broader audience. I remember after the first appearance on his show he came to our house one afternoon and wanted to meet their parents. He first wanted them to appear again on his show in a couple of weeks, which they agreed to do. The next thing he did was to arrange for them to appear on a television talent contest in New Orleans. Daddy agreed to allow them to go to New Orleans for that appearance if Ms. Willie Ruth King would agree to take them, which she did.

When the girls came back from the appearance in New Orleans sure enough they had won the talent contest against some of the best talent that New Orleans' schools had to put up against them. They were elated as were everybody in Bay Springs and Laurel who had heard about their success. The next thing they knew Mr. Darnell had arranged for them to audition with a recording company in New Orleans who had scouts at the talent contest and had been duly impressed with the girls' talent and brilliance. Mr. Darnell was absolutely sure that once they auditioned before the top executives of the company in New Orleans they would be offered a recording contract and the opportunity to begin recording and producing records. From there he felt the sky would be the limit for them.

There was just one problem in all of this that nobody up to that point had figured on. The minute that recording contract and cutting pop music or rock and roll records was mentioned, daddy wanted and would have no part of it. In fact, he had to be persuaded diligently to allow them to go to New Orleans to audition at the recording company. The thought and idea of his daughters singing rock and roll and performing in dance halls and nightclubs was totally against everything he believed in and stood for, whatever that was.

Daddy was certainly no saint, at that time he was not even a regular church attendant. He would go occasionally, but there were many times that the rest of the family would be going to church on Sunday and he would find some excuse to stay home. It was certainly not at the top priority for him although he made it the top priority for us in spite of him. We had to go whether he went or not. I guess he had been in enough juke joints and clubs in Laurel and Meridian to know what went on in them. But whatever it was, he felt like his daughters were too good to be in such places.

It took Ms. Willie Ruth King, Mrs. Thelma Peyton, Mrs. Singleton and even Mrs. Argell Falls who was a diligent churchgoer herself to convince him that the girls would lose nothing by at least going for the audition and interviewing with the company executives in New Orleans. I remember daddy sitting up most of the night one night lecturing the girls on the evils of rock and roll and the perils of singing and hanging out in nightclubs before they went to New Orleans for the audition. After all the persuading and cajoling Ms. Willie Ruth King took the girls to New Orleans with Mr. Darnell for the audition in the early Spring of 1959.

By the time the girls went to New Orleans for the audition they had written and arranged several original pop songs of their own to use for demos. They, of course, were super excited and were hoping that daddy would change his mind, but that was not to be. The audition in New Orleans as expected was a big success and Mr. Darnell was more excited than the girls were when they returned from the trip. They had gone to New Orleans on a weekend, leaving early on Saturday morning before day, staying all day and overnight, and returning late that Sunday evening. When they got home they were tired, but overjoyed and excited about the experience. Ms.

King was just as excited as they were and assured mama and daddy that they had been on their best behavior and that she had been with them every step of the way and every move they had made.

A week or so after the trip to New Orleans, Mr. Darnell accompanied by Ms. King came to the house to see daddy and mama to discuss with them to possibilities from the girls' audition. By then the girls' enthusiasm had waned because they had come to realize that there was no way their daddy was going to change his mind and allow them to pursue a singing and recording career under any circumstances. Mr. Darnell had indeed secured the promise of a contract from the recording company and assured that everything was all set and ready to go just as soon as a contract could be signed and approved. He explained all of the ins and outs, pointing out every detail, discussing all of the ramifications and what would be involved. Assuring that the girls would not have to leave home, they could do all of their recording in New Orleans. But, he made it plain and simple that yes the company would want them to perform during certain times across the country.

As dark-skinned as Mr. Darnell was, he talked until he almost turned another shade of black and blue, but there was no convincing daddy to change his mind, and mama was in full agreement with him. If daddy didn't want his daughters singing rock and roll and performing in nightclubs, mama was even more adamant because she was the real devout one of the faith at that time. It was proving to be a no-win situation, but Mr. Darnell went away that time with the promise that they would not make a final decision on the spot, but take a week or so to think about it and what it could mean for the girls and their futures, and he would be back to discuss it more. Nevertheless, from all indications right then and there it was a lost cause, and eventually that it was.

During the next few weeks though, everybody who could tried to persuade daddy that the girls were on the verge of a golden opportunity and that he should give them a chance. Mr. Darnell was in constant contact with Ms. King, Mrs. Singleton and all the high school teachers, and even Reverend Carter were all trying to convince him that it would be alright for the girls to take their talent to the next level. Still daddy would not be convinced; he stood steadfast on his conviction.

As we look back on that missed opportunity we all know now that the sisters could have very well been what The Supremes and The Marvelettes, The Sherells and other female pop groups became because they had equal if not superior talent as all of those groups. But daddy's decision was the rule of the house and being minors they could not go on their own. It was his way or no way. Not even the older brothers nor our uncles and aunts could convince him otherwise. So the girls had to pursue their life's dreams in other directions which they did. They never regretted the decision although they knew in their hearts that they could have been one of the best female vocal groups of all times if they had gotten the opportunity.

Somehow the demo records they produced got distributed anyway. Brother Charles recalls that some years later he was driving across the country in his big 18-wheel rig and early one morning in the upper Midwest a disc jockey on the radio played one of the songs they had produced and wondered who was The Lang Sisters and what ever happened to them. He had never heard of them but declared that they must have been some kind of talent whoever and wherever they were. Two years after 1958 the girls would be split up anyway after Walterene finished high school and left home. They would never be together again to sing like they did until many years later when they wound up together in the New Haven, Connecticut area for a few years in the late 1980's. The music world missed a golden and great opportunity because of one man's decision.

XII. OUT OF THAT CORN CRIB, ZOOK

The Summer of 1958 strikes a special note in my recollection for another reason. It was the summer that daddy had to take a leadership role on another issue that distinguished him from other men in the community. Early in that summer Mr. Rice Agee's house had caught fire and burned down. Mr. Rice, as he was called by all the teenagers and children of the community, lived right across the road in front of Blue Mountain Church. He was also known to all the grown men in the community as "Zook" a name they called him affectionately. Even his grown sons, R.J., Junie and Bill (Rice Jr.) called him Zook as did his sons-in-law and daughters-in-law.

Nobody ever knew how Mr. Rice's house caught on fire, but it was probably from the gas stove. Anyway, whenever a house caught on fire in the rural communities during those days, and even today in rural Mississippi, the odds are that it will burn completely down. The only fire stations are located in the small towns, and most of those are still volunteer today as they were in the late 1950's. I shall never forget when Mr. Rice's house caught on fire somebody called the sheriff's office, who in turn called the volunteer fire chief, who then called the volunteer firefighters in Bay Springs.

By the time the fire truck got from Bay Springs out to the Rock Hill Community, which is about five miles from town, Mr. Rice's house had almost burned to the ground. Many of the community people had gathered in front of his house, but the heat was too intense for them to do anything, and there was no running water in those days anyway. Everybody was still getting their water from wells situated usually in their back yards. When the fire truck did arrive, low and behold they had forgotten to check to see if there was water in the tank. Surely enough when they tried to pump water onto the fire there was none. So back to town the fire truck went to get water. By the time the fire truck returned over an hour later there was nothing but a pile of smoldering ashes. The house and everything else in it were totally gone up in smoke.

Mr. Rice had lost his wife, Mrs. Nola, in the early 1950's when she died an early death from long-term illness. So he lived in the house with his oldest daughter, Murtis Ruth, and her children. In recent years, Mr. Rice had been seeing a lady from the New Zion Community named Ms. Inez, who had also lost her husband some years earlier. Now Ms. Inez was a street-wise woman and was not an amen-corner church-going sister who would command the greatest respect of the ladies of the church. In fact, she was a whiskey drinking, shit-talking, street-walking woman who could out cuss most men, and could fight with the best of them. She carried a straight razor in her bosom and would "cut a son-of-a-bitch if they messed with her the wrong way" as she was known to say. About the only time Mr. Rice would come to church was on the Sunday they had the annual revival, and maybe one or two nights during that week that the revival was going on.

But Mr. Rice was a good man who meant well, and would do anything that he could to help anybody in the community who needed him. He and daddy got along really well because they would drink whiskey together on the weekends, and Mr. Rice was a cement finisher and bricklayer, so occasionally daddy would hire him to do those jobs for him on the houses he was building. As a result, Mr. Rice's sons had worked with him and daddy, and all of them had become excellent brick and stone masons; skills that had allowed them to stay in Mississippi and make decent livings.

When Mr. Rice took up with Ms. Inez it had been the scandal of the community because sometimes she would stay at his house and other times he would stay at her house. On weekends they could be seen riding together going drinking, both of them with their heads fairly ragged from the whiskey they would be drinking. Sometimes they would get into a slight skirmish which could cause some commotion. Although it was their business what they did, it was surely against the customs and mores of the community.

Their carrying on as they did had caused enough of a stir among the sisters of the church as it was. But when Mr. Rice's house burned down, for a while he had no place to live. His daughter and her children had moved in with her sisters and their families who all lived close by. Mr. Rice was too proud to put himself off on his children, so he and Ms. Inez were shacking in his corncrib which was not damaged by the fire and was located out back of where the house had stood.

Being situated right across the road from the church, this really caused the women of the church to start gossiping and complaining. As it was, whenever the women of Blue Mountain started complaining, the men had to take action and do something to address the problem, whatever it was. Mama and Cousin Rosie were the main ringleaders. Everyday mama would be complaining to daddy about how bad it looked for Rice and Inez to be shacking in a crib right in the church door. She would tell him the men of the church needed to do something. Somebody needed to go and talk to Rice and tell him that what he was doing was not a good picture for his children and was certainly not representative of the men of the community. Why don't the men do something.

Daddy didn't consider himself a devout man of the church since he only went occasionally and was not a deacon, although he was the church clerk, a position he held for years. He didn't see it as his duty or responsibility to be concerned about what Zook and Inez were doing since it wasn't bothering him. But mama was bothering him complaining about it and nagging him about it all the time. Every time she got a chance, every opportunity she had she would be talking about it and worrying daddy about it.

I guess daddy finally got enough of hearing about it and couldn't take any more of mama's moaning and complaining about Zook and Inez shacking in that crib. So one morning he stopped to talk to R.J. about it and tried to convince him that he needed to talk to his daddy and persuade him and Inez to move into the house with one of the children or go to her house and live until he could get his house rebuilt. R.J. told daddy he had offered his daddy to come and stay with him, but since he and Ms. Inez were not married she couldn't come with him; she would have to go home. Well, Mr. Rice had decided that if she couldn't come, then he wouldn't come; and the other children had offered him the same edict. So being independent and stubborn as he was, he had decided that he would just stay in the crib.

That is when daddy decided that Zook was just being fool hearted and that he would go and talk to him himself. So the next morning on his way to work daddy pulled his truck up in front of the crib, got out and walked up to the door. He knocked on the door and called out, "Zook! Uh Zook! Is you and Inez up in this crib? Come out of there, I want to talk to you." Here crawls Mr. Rice out of the corncrib with just his underwear on. "Yeah Otha, what is it?" Daddy said, "Zook, what you and Inez doing shacked up out here in this damn crib? Don't you know how bad this looks for you and for the community? All the folks of the church been talking about this, how you disrespecting yourself and your family shacking up right here in front of the church door in a crib with this woman. If you don't want to go and stay with one of your children, then come on over to my house and stay with me. But you need to do better than this right here in the church door."

Mr. Rice was so out done until all he could say was, "huh fellow, you know I hadn't thought about that, we just trying to git out of the weather. But you right Otha, we just need to do better than this. You know I appreciate you stopping by and bringing it to my attention." It was not long after that Mr. Rice and Ms. Inez got married and stayed at her house in the New Zion Community until he got his house rebuilt. Then they moved into the house with his daughter and her children and the both of them started coming to church and were faithful church members until they died some years later.

XIII. THE FIRST BRICK HOUSE

In the Summer of 1958 daddy traded the fancy 1956 Pontiac and bought a 1958 Pontiac Super Chief, red and white, four-door hardtop. All the trips back and forth to Wisconsin over the two years preceding had taken a toll on the transmission of the 1956 Pontiac. Back then American cars were not built for longevity and durability, they were built for style and quick obsolescence. The transmission was giving daddy some problems and he took it in for service at the dealership in Laurel where he had bought the car. Daddy had built the building that housed the Pontiac dealership in Bay Springs for Mr. Curtis Alexander, but for some reason he always bought his cars from the Central Pontiac Dealership in Laurel.

Anyway, when daddy took the car in and had it checked, he found out that it would need an expensive transmission overhaul. Two things daddy never liked; one was a repaired or overhauled car engine or transmission and the other was to have anything around him that didn't work properly, especially a car or tool. So instead of dealing to get the transmission fixed, he just traded cars on the spot. Red was not the color of choice, and four-door was not necessarily the style of choice, but that was what they had that day that was in his price range and would meet his needs. He had owned four-door cars before and it was much more convenient for all of us children getting in and out of the back seat; we loved it.

I shall never forget that day daddy bought that car on George's birthday, August 25, 1958. He would keep that car longer than any car he had ever owned. In fact, he kept it until all of us children had graduated from high school, me being the last one, from 1958 to the Fall of 1966, although he would buy several new pick-up trucks during that time.

In the Spring of 1959 work in the area had gotten slow again so daddy looked elsewhere for opportunities to build or work with builders. It just so happened that during the Winter and Spring of 1958-59 he and the older brothers had been working for a white contractor in the area of Simpson County near the town of Pinola building chicken houses and doing other work on project houses. When those jobs were completed the contractor had a group of chicken houses to build in the area of east Texas and west Louisiana between and around the towns of Shreveport, Louisiana and Marshall, Texas. He liked the Langs' work and invited them to go with him to Texas to work that summer.

So in early May 1959 daddy and the older brothers along with a crew of men from Bay Springs loaded up their vehicles with tools and suitcases and headed to Marshall, Texas. Mrs. Singleton was from Marshall, Texas and so was Mrs. Mignon Walls Crosby who was married to J.C. Crosby who has been a long time family friend. Mrs. Mignon had family living in Marshall and so she was instrumental in getting them connected with contacts there. As it turned out they were able to get rooms in the Wiley College dormitory since most of the students were gone home for the summer. Charles took his wife, Phyllis with him and his son who was almost a year old. Having been married less than two years she was not about to let Charles go off by himself.

In the meantime, while daddy was going off to Texas that summer, he had been working on arrangements to build a new house. Daddy had learned a lot about building over the years and was in the prime of his career. He knew the building business and he knew what was going on in housing financing during those times. He had learned from building houses for whites in the area that the federal government had programs to support housing finance such as the Farmers Home Administration (FHA) that were designed to assist people in rural areas in building decent housing.

Daddy had gotten to know the gentleman who was the director of the FHA office in Bay Springs who was a Mr. Walker. Having had to do the paperwork to meet the specifications for all the houses he had built for whites who were financing their houses through FHA daddy knew all the ins and outs of the application process. He also knew that the FHA was designed to serve all Americans, both blacks and whites. Hence, he wanted and needed to build a new house for his family, so he talked to Mr. Walker about the possibility of him applying for and getting financing through the FHA to build himself a house. Mr. Walker agreed for him to apply and offered to assist in helping him to go forth with the process. Yet, Mr. Walker was skeptical about the prospect of a black man in Jasper County, Mississippi building a brick house during that time.

Mr. Walker knew as well as daddy did that there would be many whites in the county who would not take well to a black man owning and living in a better house than most of them. He also knew that there would be whites of power and wealth in the county who would resent him for helping a black man to get financing for such a house. His initial impetus was to try and talk daddy into building an ordinary wood frame house perhaps with good siding on it; which would have been a decent house but just not brick veneer. Even mama tried to convince daddy that a brick house would cost too much and would be too fancy. She didn't want a house that would attract so much attention and would cause other people, both blacks and whites, to think that he had more than what his means were.

But daddy would hear none of it from either one of them. He wanted to build the best house that he could afford. His thinking was that if he could build good houses for white folks who were no better off than himself, then he should be able to build a decent house, and the kind of house he wanted for himself since he would be the one who would have to pay for it anyway. So Mr. Walker helped him to secure financing for $6000 from the FHA and he set out to build the first brick house that a black man would own in Jasper County, Mississippi and perhaps for several surrounding counties.

That Summer of 1959 was perhaps one of the hottest summers on record for the South. East Texas and northwest Louisiana can be one of the hottest areas of the country during the height of the summer. If daddy and the men had thought it got hot in Mississippi during the summers, they had not seen hot until they went to work in

Texas. It was so hot that it would be 120 degrees Fahrenheit in the open fields during the heat of the day. And where they were building the chicken houses was in open fields with maybe two or three trees in sight anywhere close by.

To avoid the dangers of sickness or injury from the heat what daddy and the men would do was to go to work around 4:00 o'clock in the mornings and work until around 10:00 o'clock midday. Then they would come back in and sleep and rest until late in the afternoon and go back to work until around 9:00 o'clock in the evenings. That way they would avoid the high heat period during the day and would still be able to get enough work time. Although the pay was good, the work was hard and treacherous. None of them had ever been in the situation where they had to endure such intense heat. Sometimes the temperature would be as high as 100 degree Fahrenheit in the shade.

While daddy and the men were in Texas he got the word from Mr. Walker that his financing had been approved by FHA, and that he could start building as soon as he returned from Texas. By the end of July or early August in that Summer of 1959 daddy and the men returned from Texas. Daddy immediately began the preparations to build his own house. The brothers agreed to stay and help get the house built, then they were heading back to Wisconsin. Work in southeast Mississippi was still slow although daddy did have one house that he had contracted to build while he was building his own. That would serve to provide him and the brothers income while they worked on our house.

Immediately after daddy returned from Texas he had the plot graded where the house would be located and was ready to begin the foundation. The plot where it was decided to build the new house was immediately next to the old house on the east side. It was an area that was between the old house and the field adjacent to the house which was about 150 yards away. A fruit orchard had been started on that plot and was just maturing to the point that it was beginning to bear fruits every year. There were apple trees and peach trees in addition to plum trees growing there, but it was the best plot of land for the new house that would allow for the most spacious lawn once the old house was torn down from in front of it.

Gone to Hell This Morning

Although everybody hated to see the orchard destroyed that all of us had worked so hard to develop, we were more excited to finally be having a house built that would provide separate rooms for those of us who were left at home.

It may be difficult to believe that the mere act of a man building a decent house for himself and his family would cause any concern, commotion, antagonism, or intrigue. But for a black man to build himself a brick house in rural southeast Mississippi in 1959, just four years after the Montgomery bus boycott was the cause of much concern, commotion, antagonism and intrigue for both other blacks and whites. Although daddy had not been able to borrow all the money he needed to completely build the house as he wanted, he was determined that he was not going to shortcut himself. He was determined to build the house to the same standards that he built houses for white men during those years.

All daddy could borrow from the FHA was $6000, so he put $2500 of his own money with that, yet he was still about $2500 short of what he needed to completely finish the house. So he went to old man Prentiss Alexander, the owner of the hardware store and lumberyard in Bay Springs and told him; "Mr. Prentiss, you know I have been buying materials from you for a long time to build other peoples' houses, and I buy a lot of materials here. I have never asked you to give me anything and I don't intend to do so now. But I do need your help to get my house built. I need you to extend me credit for about $2500 to get my house finished."

Mr. Prentiss was also the president of the only bank in Bay Springs and he was the largest depositor in the bank as well. He didn't change any word with daddy, he just told him to come go with him. They walked together across the street from the hardware store to the bank. Mr. Prentiss walked in and told the bank officer he wanted him to loan Otha $2500; Otha would be back in the bank tomorrow to sign the papers and pick up the money.

That was all it took. He still allowed daddy to buy materials on credit at the lumberyard and hardware store while he was building his house, just as he had done for him while he was building other houses.

There was certainly a lot of commotion and concern, and even some antagonism over our house being built. People would come from all over the county just to see the house being built; especially black folks who had never been inside or seen a brick house up close. On Sunday afternoons especially, people would come by just to look at the house even as it was being framed up and was in progress. Mama hated it that people made such a spectacle and were so intrigued by the house. Even in the Rock Hill Community some of the women stopped speaking to mama; others started to gossip about how we thought we were so much. Some of the children started to try and antagonize us and tried to provoke us into fights. It was so hard riding the school bus until sometimes we would drive a car to school. With the older brothers all having cars there was always an extra car at the house.

In Mississippi at that time and in some counties, especially in the Delta Region, there were already certain stipulations and laws about brick houses. For example, in the Delta there was a law in most counties that tractor drivers who lived on plantations had to live in brick houses if they were tenant farmers. Of course all of the tractor drivers were white men, thus this stipulation meant that black men would either not be tractor drivers, and thus they would not be living in brick houses as tenant farmers. This would tend to codify the segregation and discrimination against black tenant farmers de facto.

The word even got back to us that white folks were saying that this nigger must think that he is as good as a white man if he thinks he can live in a brick house. At the time the house did seem a bit extravagant with three bedrooms, a bathroom, built-in closets and appliances. We were excited but we certainly didn't feel like we were better than anybody else in the community. Mama was scared to death that somebody was going to come and set the house on fire and burn it down. If that had happened, as close as it was to the old house, it would certainly have burned down too. But daddy would not be deterred, he was determined to build and live in a decent house the rest of his life. I hate to think what would have happened to anybody whom he caught trying to burn his house down.

The house was started the first week in August 1959 and by the end of October it was finished. By Thanksgiving we were moving into our new house. As soon as it was finished the older brothers packed up their things and headed back to Wisconsin. Charles and Phyllis, George and Bubba all left for Beloit again. I remember the very day Charles and George left. Charles had just finished laying the bricks on the last windowsills and daddy was working on the fireplace. As soon as Charles had gotten through with that last window he came into the house and told Phyllis, well I guess we'll be heading back up the road. And no sooner than he had said the word, they packed their things into the car and away they went.

Daddy stayed on until after we got moved in, but right after Thanksgiving he too headed back to Wisconsin. He had completed his house and the only other house he had to build and didn't see anything else in the making in Mississippi. So with no new house to build and with both the black folks and the whites in the area in a rage of jealousy, he figured with a new house note to pay and the additional debt he had incurred to build it he had better go where he at least could be working every day. Daddy figured he could not afford to wait a month or even a few weeks to start making another paycheck. He had to move fast and in a positive direction, and that is exactly what he did.

XIV. THE WEDDING AND THE CALLING

Daddy stayed in Wisconsin over the Winter of 1959-60, but as soon as spring came he found his way back to Mississippi. Daddy came back that spring because now all the older sons were grown and gone and the two of us boys left, Otha and I, were only twelve and ten years old. Although we had been working in the fields ever since we could remember, daddy came back to make sure the crops were properly planted; he had to buy the seeds and fertilizer, and to make sure the grounds were properly prepared. By early March daddy was back home for good.

The oldest sister, Walterene, was graduating from high school in May 1960. By the time the school year was midway, she had decided after talking with daddy on one of his trips home that she would not be able to afford to go to college. At that time in our community not many of the high school graduates went to college; the parents still could not afford to send their children out of their household incomes and federal student financial-aid was not yet available. In 1960, out of a graduating class of 45 or 50 students, probably four or five went to college which was a pattern throughout Mississippi's segregated colored schools at the time.

Walterene had decided to get married upon completing high school and had become engaged during her senior year in school. Throughout that year she spent considerable time planning a wedding, which would turn out to be one of the biggest weddings ever held in Bay Springs even to this day. Where she ever got the idea to have a big wedding I never knew exactly, but I suspect she was influenced by sister-in-law Phyllis who had a small wedding when she and Charles were married in 1957. Phyllis loved weddings and talked much about the girls having big weddings when they got married. I'm sure Walterene was tremendously influenced by her.

In order to pay for her wedding Walterene had taken on a job doing house cleaning and ironing for one of the Alexander's households after school several days of the week. In those days there were no jobs for young African Americans after school except as domestic workers. There were no fast food places or other opportunities, and the few stores that were in town would certainly not hire young African Americans as clerks or cashiers; those jobs were taken by the owners, their wives and children.

Anyway, Walterene worked and saved her money, and with the help she got from her brothers and mama she planned and had one of the biggest weddings there ever could be. She finished school in early May and the wedding was held on the third Sunday in June 1960. It was so big until our little church, Blue Mountain, was not big enough to hold the wedding, although the new church building had been recently erected. In fact, the building, which was started in 1956, may not have been totally completed in 1960; anyway it was still too small to hold the crowd.

So Walterene requested and was granted permission to hold the wedding in the newest and largest black church in Bay Springs; the Bethlehem United Methodist Church which had been recently completed. When time for the wedding came, it must have been the biggest gathering of kindred ever held. On both sides of the family relatives came whom we had never seen before and some whom we have never seen since. Also, people from all over the county came; it was like a City-Wide Usher Board Homecoming. Invitations were sent out, but the word got out that this was to be the biggest spectacle ever to take place in the black community in Jasper County. People who had no business whatsoever being there came just to see what it was going to be.

The wedding was held at 3:00 o'clock in the afternoon on Sunday. Relatives started coming on Saturday and people were gathering at the church early that Sunday morning before the church could finish its Sunday School. We had so many relatives at our house until it was almost impossible to get dressed. All the brothers had come home for the wedding, and all the aunts and uncles from all over the state were there as was Grandpa Richard and Mama Lela along with her daughters and grandchildren. I can't begin to remember how we slept all of the people who were at our house on that Saturday night, or how they all got baths and got dressed for the wedding in time on that Sunday.

The whole thing was like one big festival. There were cars and people everywhere. It hadn't been too long before the wedding that daddy had torn down and sold the lumber from the old house and had the lot graded off to make a lawn for the new house. Thus, the yard didn't have grass on it yet, but was all bare red clay which was dry and dusty and was getting all over everybody's shoes and clothes. As many people were wearing white, the red clay dust gave them a reddish hue to their clothes. The only blessing was that it didn't rain either the day before or on the day of the wedding. Otherwise, it would have been a real red and muddy mess.

For some of the relatives, being at our house and at the new church where the wedding was held was their first time ever using an indoor toilet and bathroom. I can't imagine that they had never used and indoor toilet before but some, rather than using the filthy segregated toilets designated for blacks in town, simply refused to use them and would wait until they returned home. And, as they were not prone to travel great distances they had not chanced to use indoor toilets in other places. Thus, such was a novelty to them.

Another thing that was amazing about the wedding was that daddy agreed to participate and to give the bride away. At that time in his life it just didn't seem like something that daddy was prone to do; to put on a tuxedo and march down the aisle just didn't seem like something that he could be talked into easily. But the girls pulled it off; daddy was always a soft touch for the girls and they usually could talk him into doing just about anything they wanted him to do except to let them pursue a rock and roll singing career.

The man that Walterene married was Oliver Edwards whom everybody knew and affectionately called "O.L." He was the oldest son of a man whom daddy had known for a while who lived in Smith County in a community called "Warren Hill." Mr. Ollie, as O.L.'s daddy was known, had lived in Joliet, Illinois for a while and had built himself a house there some years before. However, he had left his wife and family in Joliet and moved back to Warren Hill where he lived and farmed most of the year. He would visit Joliet intermittently. Mr. Ollie owned several lots next to his house in Joliet and had offered O.L. one to build a house for himself and his new bride.

Before the wedding, O.L. had talked to daddy about coming to Joliet to build the house for him and Walterene in the Fall of 1960, to which daddy had agreed. So in the late Summer of 1960, daddy loaded his truck with tools and other equipment that he would need and headed to Illinois to build his son-in-law and daughter's house. He took with him two men who would forever be grateful to him for helping them to establish themselves in life. Those two men were Sammy Crosby and J.V. Tatum.

Sammie Crosby was a close friend of my brother George. He was the same age as George, but was a year behind him in high school. He and George had played on the basketball team together and Sammy saw George as a brother and mentor. Since they had finished high school, they had worked together off and on for daddy and practically did everything together while George was in Mississippi. Sammy had wanted to leave Mississippi because there was nothing productive for him to do there. He had relatives in Pennsylvania and in Chicago, but he had not been close to many of his relatives and did not feel comfortable going to join them.

J.V. Tatum likewise was a close friend of brother Claude, although he had finished high school in 1959. He just wanted to leave Mississippi and get a start in life. When daddy left in the Fall of 1960 both young men were with him. It would be a long time before they came back to Mississippi.

Daddy had served as mentor and guide for a number of young men over the years. Sometimes he did this in an official capacity and oftentimes in an unofficial capacity. For example, when cousin Chester had gotten in trouble in Laurel and had spent some time in jail, daddy had served as his guardian upon his release. Similarly, a son of a family that had relatives in Wisconsin who had gotten in trouble while he was in Wisconsin had been released to daddy's guardianship when he came back to Mississippi a year earlier. So providing guardianship to young men who needed a strong male presence in their lives was nothing new to daddy.

When daddy left Mississippi for Joliet, Illinois in the Fall of 1960 his intent was to build the house for O.L. and Walterene and to go on to Beloit, Wisconsin to join Charles, George and Claude who were already there. In fact, they were coming to Joliet to help build the house. However, when daddy got to Joliet and before he could complete the house and go on to Beloit his life took a strange turn that would cause him to come back to Mississippi never to leave for work or a long period again.

While daddy was building the house for O.L. and Walterene he received the gospel calling to the Christian Ministry. As he explained it he was on the roof putting on the shingles one day when he heard a voice calling his name, but none of the men who were on the roof with him nor anyone on the ground was calling him. He kept hearing this voice and then he decided to come down from the roof. When he got on the ground and sat in the garage of the house by himself, the Spirit of the Lord spoke to him and told him to go and preach the gospel of Christ. Daddy made up his mind there and then that he would heed the calling of God and not resist.

As soon as daddy finished building the house in Joliet, instead of going on to Beloit as he had planned, he decided to return home to Mississippi and pursue the preaching of the gospel. It must have been early Spring of 1961 when daddy returned home for good. He came back a changed man without doubt. You could tell by his demeanor, his attitude and his actions that something had happened to him. He talked differently, he looked differently, he thought differently, and he treated people differently than he had before. Those of us who were close to him and had been around him before knew that something beyond human design had occurred although we did not fully understand what it was.

Daddy's conversion and acceptance of the calling to the gospel ministry was the answer to many prayers both by mama and by others in the family. It had long been the fear of mama and others that whiskey would somehow destroy daddy. By the late 1950's he had become for all practical purposes a weekend alcoholic, for as soon as Friday evenings rolled around and his men were paid he would hit the jug. Each year his drinking had become worse to the point that it was amazing how he made it home sometimes. To now see daddy sober on the weekends was a miracle in itself, but to hear him talking about the calling of the Lord was beyond our wildest imagination.

Brother Otha has often talked about daddy's calling to the ministry being God's specific answer to his prayers. For he accounts that one time he remembers daddy came home so drunk that he couldn't believe he was even able to drive or even see the road. He says he went into the house and got under a bed and prayed to God to please make his daddy a preacher so he would not drink whiskey anymore. Preachers were the only men in the community we knew who did not drink whiskey, all the other men drank to some degree if for no other purpose than to show the other men that they were not henpecked and were macho enough to drink whiskey. When daddy came home and was not drinking, we knew something had happened that was a miracle.

Daddy's coming home when he did in the Spring of 1961 was of itself an act of great faith. Although it was time to plant the crops again and he needed to be there for that, he also would have to find work, and there was not much building going on at all at that time. Daddy's first priority though was to get started preaching.

It was and still is the custom in the African American Baptist Church that whenever someone declares their acceptance of the calling to the gospel ministry they must first come before the church and preach a trial sermon. The pastor and the church will then issue a license to preach. Whenever a licensed preacher is called to pastor a church, the home church will then ordain the person to pastor. Once this is done then the person is recognized by the state as being officially sanctioned to perform weddings, funerals, and all other official business of the church.

At the time daddy announced his calling, Reverend Frank Moore from Newton was the pastor at Blue Mountain. Reverend Moore had succeeded Reverend Carter who had left in 1958 or 1959 to accept the pastorate at a church in the town of Soso, Mississippi which was 25 or 30 miles from Bay Springs. Reverend Moore was a person whom daddy had known for a long time, and whom he had recommended for the pastorate of Blue Mountain because he was a supporter of the City-Wide Usher Board; and, he was one of the few pastors in the area who not only supported the organization but was also a local president of the organization in Newton County.

In late September 1961 daddy preached his first sermon at a special evening service at Blue Mountain. Supposedly, the preacher is supposed to be on trial and subject to the approval of fellow ministers and the church congregation. In reality it is a mere formality whereby the pastor will recommend at the end of the sermon that the congregation will accept the person into the calling and grant him or her license to preach by the local church which is recognized by other Baptist Churches.

Daddy's first sermon was based on the first chapter of Genesis and the first verse, "In the beginning God created the heavens and the earth." His text or subject was, "A New Beginning." I can't remember much about the content of the sermon as I was a mere 12 years old. I do remember the church was packed with people from all over the county and adjoining counties who knew daddy or knew of his work. Daddy was indeed well known throughout the county and surrounding counties. He had worked and built houses all around the county and surrounding area and had hired men from those areas as well. Many people had heard of him and knew of him and there seemed to be genuine excitement about his announcing a calling to the ministry. Others who may not have known him knew of him through mama's and her children's involvement in church work and his being her husband and our father.

The change that had occurred in daddy's life as the result of his accepting the calling to the ministry was tremendous; it was truly a miracle. Instead of getting drunk on the weekends as had been his custom for years, now every chance daddy got he was going to church. Every Sunday he was visiting a new church, and most Sundays different pastors around the area - in Jasper, Jones and Newton counties - were inviting him and giving him the opportunity to preach to their congregations. In the meantime, as he had done when he decided to become a builder, daddy began to search out and to buy books on preaching and on the Bible. Within a year or so he had bought volumes and several collections on interpretations of the Bible, and he began to read and to study to learn what he needed to know in order to become one of the best preachers he could become.

Learning the Bible and understanding its meaning became an obsession with daddy during the coming years. It seemed that every waking moment, and every opportunity he had was now spent reading and studying. Instead of coming home, eating dinner and retiring to his easy chair to watch television as had become his custom in recent years, now when daddy came home in the evenings he would eat dinner and immediately turn to his reading and studying. It has always been daddy's aspiration that whatever he pursued he wanted to be one of the best at it, and being one of the best preachers he could be now became his obsession. He would pursue his preparation for the ministry just as he had pursued his preparation to become one of the best builders of his time.

Photo Album

Members of the Lang Family at the home place in Tioch Community before their relocation after the Great Depression: L to R: Reedus, Otha, Elvira, and Richard Lang, Sr.

Reverend Otha Lang, Sr. during the 1970's.

Reverend Otha Lang, Sr. and Mrs. Hattie Lang in the 1970's.

The children of Otha and Hattie Lang at their Grandpa Richard's funeral in October 1978. L to R: Claude (Bubba), Charles, Brenda, Marvel, Bobbie, Otha Jr., Walterene, George.

The first 3 houses built by Otha Lang, Sr. on Mississippi Avenue in Laurel, MS, 1946-48.

The Lang Family home, the first brick house built and occupied by a Black family in Jasper County, MS, built in 1959. Now occupied by Claude and Berdia Lang.

Reverend Otha Lang, Sr. and grand daughter, Maya Susan, ca. 1985.

XV. NEW BEGINNINGS AND NEW DIRECTIONS

The changes in daddy as the result of his calling and preaching were enormous and truly amazing to not only his family but other people he dealt with. Whatever happened to him on that rooftop had surely given him a new outlook on life and had truly made a difference in the way he saw things and how he dealt with us, his children, mama and everybody else. His temperament was different, his personality was different, his whole person was different.

In the Fall of 1961, sister Brenda, the second oldest girl in the family was looking to enter college. She had finished high school in the Spring as the third Lang child to finish Bay Springs Vocational High School as the valedictorian of her class following the footsteps of Charles and George. Walterene had finished as the salutatorian of her class the year before. Brenda was truly the intellectual of the family. There was no doubt that she was intellectually gifted in every way she could be. She had been an outstanding public speaker and had won public speaking contests in the 4-H Club competitions statewide; she could sing and act, she had intellect and talent and she was destined to go to college.

Brenda had applied and had been accepted to attend Jackson State College and the whole family was determined that somehow she was going to be given the opportunity. All her teachers rallied behind her and were doing all they could to assist in getting her into college. By 1961 the Kennedy Administration was in the White

House in Washington, D.C., and the National Defense Student Loan Program and the National Work Study Program had been enacted. Mr. John Grantham, who was one of the teachers in the high school, and a noted alumnus of Jackson State, had helped to pave the way for Brenda to attend the college. He had been instrumental in helping to secure the necessary applications and seeing that all the papers had been filed on time for her to get into Jackson State. In fact, Mr. Grantham had taken Brenda to Jackson State on several occasions and introduced her to professors and administrators to let them know he had a favored student coming. By the mercy of God, Brenda was awarded a student loan and a work-study package to help with her expenses in college; so when the time came to enter Jackson State in the fall she was ready to go.

I shall never forget the day she left for college. Mr. Grantham was determined to see her securely in the dormitory, so he had agreed to take her over to Jackson State. On the particular evening she was leaving, he came to the house and picked her up along with mama and daddy and over to Jackson they went to get Brenda into college. Money was tight because daddy had not been working steady since he came home from Illinois in the spring. But he was in agreement that Brenda deserved and was going to college. Her high school accomplishments had truly been outstanding. In 1961, with the new federal programs to provide financial support for students from low-income families to attend college, quite a number of African American high school graduates from all over the South were going to college who would never have had the opportunity otherwise.

Brenda's going to college was in itself a new beginning for our family and the true renewal of a custom and tradition that had begun with Charles, but had been interrupted by the economic conditions of the time. As daddy made a new beginning for himself in the ministry, Brenda set the trend for the rest of us to follow in getting a higher education. With Brenda in college, the only children left at home in the Fall of 1961 were Bobbie, the youngest sister, brother Otha and myself, Marvel.

When daddy did go to work on a steady basis in October of 1961, it was the first time he had not worked as an independent contractor in Mississippi since he had begun contracting. He went to work for a white contractor from Mendenhall, Mississippi, a town in west central Mississippi approximately 50 or 60 miles from Bay Springs. Daddy didn't work for the contractor very long because for some reason the man's checks would bounce every time he would write one to daddy. Sometimes daddy would go two or three weeks without a paycheck, and then when he would get one it would come back from the bank because of insufficient funds.

This was a real test for daddy, and proved to show that he was indeed a changed man. He handled the situation calmly and with much patience. I remember one evening the man came to our house after daddy had left the job and came home from Mendenhall where he was working. I just knew daddy was going to forego his religion and give the man a good ass-kicking. But daddy was calm and really collected about the whole thing. In essence what he told the man was that he would give him a certain time to get him his money, or he was going to get a lawyer and file charges against him for writing bad checks. Daddy quit working for the man and did file charges against him, but he folded his business and filed bankruptcy. Evidently he owed everybody who had worked for him, both blacks and whites, as well as the companies where he had been buying supplies and materials. That was the last time daddy would work for another contractor; from then on if he didn't have a job of his own he waited until he found one.

In the Spring of 1962 things began to change for daddy as the whole country was changing its directions under the John F. Kennedy Administration. The New Frontier Programs of the Kennedy Administration were coming into being and monies were flowing from Washington in ways that had not been seen since the New Deal Programs of the 1940's. The Farmers Home Administration (FHA), which had provided the money for daddy to build his own house in 1959, had been amply funded to provide financing for rural housing development. With daddy having paved the way, other African Americans in Jasper County and throughout southeast Mississippi were now interested and seeking to build new homes for themselves, as well as low and moderate income whites. This would prove to be a tremendous blessing for daddy and his building business throughout the 1960's and 1970's.

As soon as the programs were announced and funded, blacks began to seek out funding to build new homes. In the Spring of 1962, daddy began a house for a single female household head, Clotee Jones, who was the daughter of Mrs. Gussie Darby and Mr. Hub Darby. Mrs. Gussie was the sister of Mr. Ezra Moffett. She and her daughter, Clotee, and Clotee's two sons, Calvin and Stanley, had moved to a rental house just outside the corporation limits of Bay Springs on Highway 18 west of town a few years earlier. Mrs. Gussie was a domestic worker and worked as the housekeeper for one of the Alexanders in Bay Springs and Clotee worked as a practical nurse in the office of one of the prominent doctors in town. Mr. Hub Darby, as he was known to most folks, was a civil rights activist and a known life member of the NAACP which was dangerous in Jasper, Jones and Smith Counties during those days; especially in Smith County where he lived. It was believed that Mrs. Gussie and Clotee moved out because they feared for his life and their safety as well as their jobs and livelihood. Their fears would later be realized as Mr. Darby was eventually murdered in his home mysteriously.

As soon as daddy finished Clotee's house, J.C. Crosby built one right beside her on Highway 18 west of Bay Springs. Both of their houses were built just across the road from where Clotee and her mother had been renting. J.C. Crosby's uncle in Chicago and his aunt in Bay Springs owned that land which had been inherited from their father and mother. A year after their houses were built, both of them were burned down mysteriously, but they both rebuilt in the exact same locations as before and their houses are still standing.

By 1963, the FHA program had become widely known and easy for blacks to apply to and receive loans to build new houses. Daddy had developed a firm and long-lasting relationship with Mr. Walker who was the county director of the FHA office, and had helped a young black man, Mr. Mitchell Howard to get the job as the assistant director. Mr. Howard had been a Cooperative Extension County Agent in Newton County for eight or nine years since he finished Alcorn College as an outstanding basketball player. He eventually had daddy to build him a new house just outside of Bay Springs which he and his family lived in for years before he became

Gone to Hell This Morning

the FHA County Director in Lauderdale County, sold his home, and moved to Meridian.

While the building business was beginning to boom in Mississippi and throughout the South under the new federal housing programs aimed at housing development in rural areas, things were slowing down in the industrial Northeast and Midwest. In fact, by the Fall of 1962, Charles and George were again out of work in Wisconsin. George had married in 1961 and so had Bubba. George married a young lady he had met in Beloit who was a cousin of sister-in-law Phyllis.

Bubba married a lady he had known for several years, Berdia Mae Luckett, who was a schoolteacher in Smith County. Bert, as we called her, had been around the family for a few years since she and Bubba had started seeing each other. By the time they married in June of 1961, she was already just like another sister in the family. When she and Bubba got married, they went to Wisconsin where he was living at the time and she stayed there during that summer until it was time for her to return to her teaching job in Smith County in the fall.

In the Fall of 1962, work had gotten so slow in Beloit that Charles and George decided to take their chances somewhere else. Bubba had already returned to Mississippi during the Summer of 1962 and was working in Jackson doing brick masonry work with a contractor there. Charles and George had packed up their truck and headed to Albuquerque, New Mexico to seek work there. Charles had a brother-in-law who lived there with his family, Leroy Johns, who had called and told him that the building business was booming in Albuquerque. Charles and George had packed all of their tools on their truck and headed to New Mexico to seek a new start. On their way, they decided to drive through Mississippi to visit with the rest of the family for a short while. They stayed with us for a few days and off to New Mexico they headed.

In October 1962 another tragedy hit the family. Daddy's youngest brother, Uncle Grover, was shot and killed in Laurel. It was on a Friday, the second Friday of the month that he was shot and killed in the street. Uncle Grover was a barber in Laurel as was Uncle Reedus, the oldest brother. At the time, Uncle Reedus had his barbering business in a shop on Front Street in the downtown section of the city, while Uncle Grover had his in the heart of the black residential section. Uncle Grover was the only uncle who had no children, thus, he was fond of his brothers' and sister's children. On occasions we youngest children (Bobbie, Otha and myself) would go and spend the weekend with him and his wife, Aunt Ruth, both of whom were extremely kind to us. Even after Uncle Grover was killed, we would still go and spend the weekends with Aunt Ruth on occasions until we finished high school.

Although we never knew the total story behind his death, bits and pieces were told by various sources. It was rumored that Uncle Grover was killed because he was fooling around with a woman who was the whore of another man. On several occasions the man had threatened Uncle Grover and on several occasions had even called his house and left threatening messages with Aunt Ruth as well. Uncle Grover, being a roughhouse character himself and not fearful of facing anybody, had resorted to carrying his pistol with him. He had long carried his gun because usually he left his barbershop late at night after all of his customers had gone and he had cleaned the shop. When he left late at night like that he would be carrying the cash receipts from the day's business with him.

On this particular Friday afternoon, he was leaving the shop to take a break and have some lunch before business got busy for the evening. Friday evenings were usually one of the busiest times for the shop besides Saturdays. Leaving for a short time and expecting to return, Uncle Grover neglected to carry his pistol with him. Although he had been receiving threatening calls from the man who shot him, he evidently didn't expect him to come after him since he had probably seen the man often hanging out on the corner close to his barbershop. Nevertheless, as soon as he walked out of the barbershop and locked the door behind him, the man stepped around the corner which must have been no more than fifty feet from the shop door and shot him with a twelve-gauge shotgun.

The impact of the shotgun blast was so great, according to witnesses, that it completely tore his abdominal section apart and as he fell dying his intestines fell to the street. By the time the police and ambulance got to the scene Uncle Grover was already dead.

Even if the blast had not killed him he would have bled to death by the time the ambulance arrived. In those days, there was no rush either on the part of the police or the medical services to save a dying black man in the ghetto streets of Laurel, Mississippi, or any other town in Mississippi and the South. Once again, daddy had lost a brother at the hands of a murderous rival.

Uncle Grover's funeral was an occasion for all the family to come together. Although Charles and George had gone to New Mexico just weeks before, they would come back for Uncle Grover's funeral. Bubba was living and working in Jackson at the time, his wife, Berdia, was teaching in Raleigh, MS and was pregnant with their daughter, Cassandra. They were at the funeral. Walterene and her husband, O.L., came from Joliet. Bobbie had just entered Jackson State College and Brenda was a sophomore there; they came for the funeral. All of our aunts and uncles and cousins also came for the funeral.

About six months after Uncle Grover had been killed, the man who was accused of his murder was put on trial. It seems the man worked for one of the big wigs of the Masonite Corporation in Laurel, and his boss wanted to keep him out of jail. Practically all of the witnesses to the murder either worked for the company or had husbands, sons or other relatives who worked for the company. Some years earlier, one of our uncles, either Uncle Reedus or Uncle Grover, had sued the company for injuries incurred while working in the plant. Thus, the Lang name was disdained by the company and the powers-that-be in Laurel, and no other Lang had ever worked for the company since that suit, which was only awarded a few thousand dollars.

Anyway, the word got around that the company didn't want any of their employees or their family members testifying at the trial. Thus, when the police and prosecutors eventually got around to questioning witnesses about what they had seen, nobody could remember anything and nobody had seen anything. Even people whom the family knew well and who had been Uncle Grover's so-called friends, they refused to testify or if they did they couldn't recall seeing anything that happened that day. Some were sitting on their porches across the street from his barbershop and would see him come and go every day, but were afraid or had been bought off from testifying. So Uncle Grover's death wound up being a tragedy for his family and a footnote in the pages of Mississippi justice for a black man.

A family rift developed as a result of Uncle Grover's death. Some time before he was killed he had told Grandpa Richard that he had taken out an insurance policy on himself for ten or twenty thousand dollars with Grandpa as the beneficiary. So if anything happened to Uncle Grover, Grandpa would have a little nest egg of money for himself. When Uncle Grover was buried, Grandpa had asked Aunt Ruth about the policy and if he could have it and a copy of the death certificate in order to collect the benefits. Evidently Aunt Sis (Caroline Macmillan) also knew about the policy as Uncle Grover had informed her. We never knew whether such a policy did not exist or whether Aunt Ruth didn't want Grandpa to receive the benefits, but she would not produce the policy if there were one. That's when Aunt Sis cut ties with her and assured her that neither she nor Grandpa would ever set foot in her house again. In fact, in all the years that she lived after that, neither Aunt Sis, Grandpa, Uncle Reedus nor daddy ever visited her again. I can remember her coming to our house on one or two occasions after that.

Shortly after Uncle Grover was buried in the Fall of 1962, daddy was called to pastor his first church which was Phalti Baptist Church a few miles northwest of Bay Springs. Phalti, like many of the other black Baptist churches in the county, was dominated by two or three families. In its case the families were the McLaurins, the Paytons, and the Pages. It was a small church situated in a small wood frame building. It was one of the two or three churches that had not been rebuilt during the heyday of the City-Wide Usher Board although it was an original member of the organization. Its membership was just not large enough to support any kind of building program. Another reason was the church was located on property that belonged to a white landowner who had donated the church for his tenant farmers to have a place to worship some years prior. Thus, the church was actually owned by the white landowner rather than the church members.

Gone to Hell This Morning

Daddy found out about the church's ownership situation after he had accepted the call and began pastoring. Thus, his first initiative was to try and help the members of the church to gain ownership of the land and building that the church was situated on. He met resistance both from the members themselves who were beholding to the white landowner, and the white landowner who had no intentions of either selling the land and church to the black members or giving them a clear deed and title.

Some of the members, in fact one of the head deacons, still lived as a share cropper on the white landowner's land and did until he died in the late 1970's. When the man died his wife had gotten too old to work for the white landowner any longer, so she was required to move out of the house where they had lived and it was torn down. Evidently, the church must have been allowed to buy the land and the church because in the Spring of 1999 when I visited there a new church building had recently been built.

Daddy pastored at Phalti until 1968 when he was called to pastor at Pleasant Grove Baptist Church in Moss; a small town community about 20 miles south of Bay Springs. Part of the reason he left Phalti was because there was no headway being made in the progress to either buy the land and build a new church or to relocate from that location and buy land somewhere else and build a new church. Daddy under no circumstances was in agreement with doing anything to the church building as long as the white landowner held the deed and title to the building and land. He strongly believed and advocated that in lieu of doing anything to that building under those circumstances they should buy land somewhere else and start over.

By the late 1960's daddy had settled into a routine for the remainder of his working and preaching years; he was building houses and preaching. After he left Phalti as pastor and was called to Pleasant Grove, he was also called to a church in Laurel, Union Baptist, which he accepted for two Sundays a month. So he was at one church for two Sundays a month and at the other for two Sundays. He would continue this routine for many years before he would be forced to resign both by health and circumstances. A few years after he accepted the call at Union Baptist, he was also called to pastor for one Sunday a month at Ebenezer Baptist in Heidelberg, which he did for a few years.

Daddy didn't last long at Ebenezer as the pastor. He was a staunch traditionalist in his views and beliefs, and pretty much a fundamentalist in his perspectives on church traditions. He believed in the old way of thinking and social ethics. At Ebenezer the congregation was made-up mostly of extended families who knew each other and looked out for each other. The young lady who was the pianist for the choir got pregnant and had a child out of wedlock. Traditionally when this happened in the Southern Baptist Black Church, the young woman would be required to come before the congregation after the child was born and to make a public apology and ask for forgiveness of the congregation. By the early 1970's when daddy became pastor at Ebenezer this tradition was no longer being widely enforced.

Nevertheless, daddy believed that as pastor it was his prerogative to require the young lady to do so, especially since she was director of the choir. Thus, he directed the deacons to inform the young lady that this should be done by the next church business meeting. Well, the young lady was one of the main deacon's daughter, another's grand-daughter, and the niece of several of the others. None of them were willing to have her come before the church and make a public apology.

When that next business meeting came around daddy inquired of the deacons when the young lady was coming before the church. They had no response; so daddy adjourned the meeting, went into the pastor's office collected his things and went home. Before he left he told the deacons that until they were willing to accept his leadership he was through and they could look for another pastor. As always, whenever daddy left a job of any kind, whether it was finished or not, he was through. He never returned to Ebenezer again after that business meeting. Shortly thereafter Union Baptist went back to two Sundays a month with their services. Daddy continued to pastor both there and at Pleasant Grove until he retired.

XVI. TRIED AND TESTED

In 1962 daddy began to build the house that in my opinion would be the masterpiece and crowning jewel of his work and his career as a builder. It was the house he built for a Mr. Mitchell Asmar in the outskirts of north Laurel. Mr. Asmar was the son-in-law of an older Arab gentleman named Mr. Mony Rhamm. Both men were of Arab descent, and were prominent business owners in Laurel. Mr. Rhamm owned one or several restaurants and perhaps an icehouse in Laurel. He might have even owned a beer and soft drink distributing business in the city also.

Over the years, off and on, daddy had done work for Mr. Rhamm. He had remodeled his house, built several of the buildings for his businesses, and had done work for some of his family and friends as well. Being considered a minority themselves and of Arab descent, Mr. Rhamm and his family sought out and trusted daddy to do all of their building work. It was only natural that when his son-in-law got ready to build his own house he came to daddy to do the work. Mr. Asmar's house was by far the largest single house daddy would ever work on. It was the largest house I had ever seen or ever been in. It would take at least two years to build the house as it was built not all at one time, but the work was done in stages because the house was being paid for as it was being built.

Mr. Asmar's house was a large tri-level house that must have been at least 80 feet long. It was definitely an exceptional house for the times and for the area. There was not another house in all of Laurel owned by anybody that could match the design or the materials that would be used in this house. If the owners had not been Arab, there was no way that a black man would have had the opportunity to build such a house in Laurel, Mississippi at the time. Some of the materials used to build the house were shipped from overseas, so some of the delays in building were because of delays in the shipment of those materials.

By 1963 and 1964 the Civil Rights Movement was at its peak in Mississippi. Tensions were very high, especially in Laurel and Hattiesburg, two of the most racist towns in the South and definitely strongholds of the Ku Klux Klan. In 1962, James Meredith had enrolled at Ole Miss, and everybody, both blacks and whites, had been drawn into the emotions of the Civil Rights Movement whether they wanted to or not. I can remember vividly sitting and watching the evening news after coming home from school during those days of early October 1962 when the federal troops were escorting James Meredith to be admitted to Ole Miss. All of Mississippi held its collective breath as Governor Ross Barnett barred the way of his entry into the building to register at the Oxford campus. It was as if the Civil War was on the verge of beginning all over again.

Some months or even a year or so later, Cleve McDowell, who had also been a student at Jackson State University would enroll at Ole Miss also. Both McDowell and Meredith were contemporaries of my sisters, Brenda and Bobbie, who were attending Jackson State at the time. Brenda, in fact, dated McDowell while he was there. The Christmas after he had entered Ole Miss he even came to Bay Springs to visit her and spent several days with our family. We didn't think much about it, but the folks in Bay Springs thought it was a big deal. I remember him going to town with my sisters, my brother Otha and I, and people were stopping on the sidewalks and staring and pointing at us as we walked down the streets with him. There was no doubting who he was because his face had been plastered on all the television news shows and newspapers for months.

It didn't phase daddy at all that he came to visit or about all of the other ruckus that had gone on about the Civil Rights Movement. For some reason daddy just didn't get excited about what was going on in the movement. He just went about his business everyday as usual until somebody rubbed him wrong.

Otherwise, one would have thought that he was totally removed from the rest of society and its goings on. Anyway, intermittent to working on the Asmar house daddy would work on other projects here and there. But Mr. Asmar was determined that nobody else was going to build his house, so whenever the materials would come in and the money was there he would contact daddy to come back to work on it. Meanwhile, as the work progressed on the building, the tensions between blacks and whites in the state, across the South, and across the nation continued. You could tell and feel the hostilities as you attempted to do business with white merchants and retailers. Still, daddy continued to build and he would continue to buy from those who wanted and showed appreciation for his business.

By 1964, daddy had shifted much of his material buying to the Laurel Builders Supply Company in Laurel which was owned by a Mr. Tatum who also owned the concrete plant next to the builders supply and the concrete plant in Newton as well. This Mr. Tatum was the same one who was one of the sons of the Tatums who had lived on the Old Missionary Place in Rose Hill in the 1930's, and who had let the family use their milk cow to provide milk for brother George when he was born. This was after the land had been lost on the Souin Lovey Creek and the family had become share croppers. Mr. Tatum was around the same age as daddy and they had done business for years ever since daddy had gone into the building business.

In the early 1960's the Alexanders in Bay Springs became somewhat fastidious in dealing with their black contractors, especially after the Old Man Prentiss Alexander died, who was the founder of the company. The sons who took over the business, in compliance with all the other white merchants in town became hesitant to allow the black builders to have extended credit, so daddy took his business elsewhere. Mr. Tatum, who had known daddy all those years continued to do business with daddy the same as he had all the time. Daddy, in fact, during the early years and later in the 1960's was one of his best customers. When daddy shifted his dealings away from the Alexanders in Bay Springs and began buying most of his materials and concrete from Mr. Tatum, daddy was in fact one of his biggest customers if not the biggest in sales volume.

The allegiance of Mr. Tatum to a loyal customer was put to the test in the early summer of 1964. By then Mr. Asmar's house was finally coming to a finish, and daddy was trying to get it finished because he had other jobs on hold and pending as the building business was definitely picking up under the Lyndon Johnson Administration and his newly declared "War on Poverty." The FHA was lending money going and coming, and Negroes and whites across the South and even in southeast Mississippi were beginning to build houses en masse. One can see the results of this era even now if you were to ride through Jasper, Jones, Newton and Smith Counties in Mississippi. You can hardly see a family living in a dilapidated house in the rural areas of either of these counties. Almost anybody and everybody who wanted a decent house during that era were able to borrow the money and to afford to build a decent house if they had any kind of job and an acre of land.

Anyway, as daddy was finishing Mr. Asmar's house we were pouring the concrete for the driveway one sunny day in June. Any builder and concrete finisher knows that the secret to making the job of pouring and finishing concrete easy is to make sure that the driver of the concrete truck who delivers the concrete spots the truck right so that the laborers don't have to work too hard in spreading the concrete. The truck drivers know this and are usually willing to cooperate with the spotter to make sure he stops the truck in the right places. When pouring foundations and driveways this involves moving the truck every few minutes to get it at the right spots to pour the concrete.

Usually when he was on the job and concrete was being poured, daddy was always the spotter. He would stand near the back of the truck, but far enough away from its side so that the drivers could see him and hear him when he would yell at them to stop the truck, move it up, or back it up before unloading concrete through the long chute coming out of the back of the truck. Drivers expected this and knew this procedure very well. Good drivers made it their prerogative to cooperate and work with the spotter without impunity.

On this particular day the driver was a young white man in his early thirties. He obviously was a fairly new employee with Mr. Tatum's company because we had never seen him before and he had never delivered concrete on any of the jobs we had worked over the past few months or the last year. It was just after noon that day when he finally got out to the job at the Asmar house with the load of concrete. In the middle to late June in Mississippi it is already reaching into the mid to high 90 degrees by early afternoon. So it was on this particular day. We had already finished eating lunch and all of the men were just sitting around and laying around in the shade waiting for the concrete truck to arrive.

When the truck did arrive and came into the single-lane road which spanned the quarter mile of so from the main street coming into the Asmar house, it seemed to be going rather fast for a loaded concrete truck. You could tell that the driver was rushing and was somewhat in a hurry. As he approached the house all the men got up and grabbed their shovels and other tools and got ready to spread concrete. Daddy took his position out front so the driver could recognize him as the spotter and the person in charge. The driver recognizing the driveway as the area where the concrete would be poured turned the truck around and backed it into position to begin pouring near the garage entry where the driveway began.

When the driver stopped the truck he got out and walked to the back to get the chute set-up and ready to pour the concrete. When he got out of the truck daddy spoke to him as he would usually greet anybody, but the driver didn't respond. In fact, he didn't even look at daddy or acknowledge him in any way. He acted as if neither daddy or any of the rest of us were even there; to him we were totally invisible. He positioned the chute on the truck and started to pour the concrete. He poured the first batch and got back into the truck to move it forward to get ready to pour the next batch.

It was also the usual procedure in pouring concrete to wait until the men get a batch spread and leveled out before pouring the next batch; that way the concrete does not begin to set-up before it is spread. The driver got back in the truck, however, moved it forward and was about to begin to pour another batch of concrete before daddy gave him the order to do so. I knew we were in for trouble. Before he could pour another batch daddy yelled out to him: "Hey! Wait a minute until we get this spread!" The driver just sat in the truck and waited. When we got that batch spread, the truck needed to be moved forward before he poured the next batch. Daddy yelled at the driver to move the truck forward, which he did, but he moved it too far.

Daddy hollered out to him again; "Hey, back-up you went too far." The driver backed-up, but he backed-up too far. Daddy yelled out to him again; "Hey! You backed-up too damn far, move that truck up." This time the driver stopped the truck and jumped out in a flash and came back to where daddy was and hollered at him; "Nigger why don't you make up your goddamn mind where you want this goddamn concrete, I ain't got all day." Before he could turn around, daddy didn't say a word, he just came up with the shovel with which he had been leveling concrete with a swing. Before the driver knew what was happening, daddy hit him upside the head as hard as he could with that shovel full of concrete and knocked him to the ground.

Blood shot out of the side of that driver's head as if he had been stabbed or shot. He just lay there on the ground, he was stunned and couldn't moved; he must have been knocked semi-unconscious. That didn't make any difference. Daddy was standing straddle him with one foot pressed in his chest and the blade of his square-point shovel pressed against his neck within a few seconds. In a minute the driver was crying and daddy had tears in his eyes. He began to lecture the driver:

"Peckerwood who in the hell do you think you talkin' to? I'll take your goddamn head off and throw it to the dogs if you so much as grunt. Fart goddam' it!! And I'll cut you goddam' head off with this goddam' shovel right now. If you want to we can both go to hell this morning!! Don't you know I'm the one paying for this goddam' concrete. Don't you say a word or I'll take you motherfuckin' head off right now.

If I let you up from here you git your goddamned ass back in that truck and take that damn concrete back where you got it from and pour it up your ass or somewhere. I don't need no damn concrete from a sorry-assed cracker like you today or no other day. Now you git your goddam' ass up and you haul ass, 'cause I'm gonna be right behind you."

One of the men threw the driver a sweat towel to wipe blood and concrete from his face, neck, and off his clothes. He looked like a hog that had been stabbed to drain the blood from his body at a hog-killing. He was a bloody mess. But he got up in a hurry and grabbed the towel and got in the truck and took off. He stopped at the end of the single-lane road before entering the main street and positioned the chute at the back of the truck where the concrete was pouring out to keep it from swinging wildly across the road. Then he headed back to town.

Daddy got in his truck and took off behind him just as he had said. Nobody said a word to daddy because we all knew he was not to be messed with right then. He would have lit into whomever tried to talk to him right then and there. We didn't know where daddy was going, but he took off down the road right behind the concrete truck. We finished leveling the concrete that had been poured and we had to finish it out before it got dry and hard. That's what we did, then we went on to clean up the trash around the job and prepare for the next tasks.

Daddy returned to the job around three-thirty that afternoon. When he got back he sat all of the men down and told us what had happened and how sorry he was that he had almost taken the young driver's ear off when he hit him with that shovel. Daddy had followed the driver back to the building supply place where he found Mr. Tatum and went in to talk to him about what had happened. He met with Mr. Tatum and asked him why he would hire such racist white drivers to supply his black customers. Then he related to him what had happened with the driver that afternoon.

When Mr. Tatum heard the story, he had his secretary to page the driver and have him come to the office. When the driver arrived Mr. Tatum had another office assistant to write a check for the driver for the time he had put in already since the last pay period, and gave him an extra hundred dollars to go see a doctor for his injury. He informed the driver that he would no longer need his services and that he could take the rest of that day off to go to the doctor if he needed to. He told him that he had known Otha Lang for most of his life, and not only did he consider daddy a friend, but also a loyal customer who had bought more materials from him over the years than any single customer he ever had, black or white. He was not about to let some stupid racist like this young man drive away a good customer like that; he could find more drivers but good customers were hard to come by.

Mr. Tatum apologized to daddy and assured him that he would hire some black drivers and laborers, and that he could be assured that such problems would never happen again with his drivers. Mr. Tatum had a black driver at his Newton concrete plant, Quiller Morris, who had grown up with daddy and had delivered concrete to his jobs out of the Newton plant for years. True to his word, within a few weeks Mr. Tatum had hired some black drivers and they were delivering concrete and building supplies not only to daddy's jobs, but to other customers as well.

The incident with the concrete driver was indeed a source of great concern and fear for us and the other men working with daddy at the time. Jones County and the town of Laurel, and Forrest County where the town of Hattiesburg was located just south of Jones County were hotbeds of Ku Klux Klan activity. A few years later (in 1966) Vernon Dahmer's home and business would be bombed and burned by the Klan just outside of Hattiesburg. One or two of the men working for daddy quit shortly after that incident because they were afraid the Klan would come after daddy and them because of what happened to the driver. Yet, it didn't phase daddy one bit. He kept on working like nothing had happened. The Klan never came.

XVII. THE MOVEMENT COMES HOME

Throughout the mid-1960's and into the 1970's the building business was booming in southeast Mississippi. The Johnson Administration's anti-poverty programs were certainly making a difference in the rural South and the small towns as well. By the late 1960's most of the houses daddy was building were for African Americans, both low-income and middle-income families. As the Civil Rights Movement was making a tremendous difference, blacks were getting better jobs and access to the opportunity to make a better living than they had ever had before in the South. New jobs were being created as small and medium-sized industries were moving to the rural South and to small towns where labor was both abundant and cheap, and taxes were low and land was cheap and easily available.

Also, by the mid-1960's cotton was no longer king in the South. Most of the family farms had stopped planting and growing cotton as the staple of their family's economy. Prices had gotten ridiculously low, and it had become more profitable to work off the farm than to try and make a living strictly from farming. Plus, the labor pool was dwindling as most of the older children in African American families were finishing high school and migrating north rather than settling at home as their parents had done before. This trend would begin to change toward the end of the 1960's as the national economy would begin to expand and that expansion would make its entry in the South.

The Johnson Administration's anti-poverty programs and the consequent economic expansion had definite positive effects in the rural South in several ways. Instead of having to move to the North and other regions to find decent employment, blacks were now able to find work and stay home. They were taking advantage of these opportunities since most of the new industry coming to the South was being developed by people from the North and other regions who did not hold to the southern traditions of hiring only white males. These companies were hiring blacks not only as laborers but also as supervisors and mid-level managers. The stream of migration of young blacks from the South to the industrial northern cities almost dried up completely during the late 1960's and 1970's. Where it had been the custom in the 1950's that as soon as young blacks would finish high school they would migrate north, now they were staying home in significant numbers. The new employment opportunities were making this possible.

In 1966, I finished high school at Bay Springs Vocational High as the last of my generation of Lang children to do so. My graduation from high school and the events of the preceding year would put our family in the middle of the Civil Rights Movement and struggle for equal rights. This was certainly unintentional and purely by accident of circumstances. Sometime during my junior year of high school I had to write a term paper for my English class. Since I was looking for opportunities for scholarships and financial aid to pay for college after my senior year, I decided to do research and write the paper on "Ways to get a Free College Education."

In doing the research for that term paper I happened across information on the Armed Services Academies: West Point, The Air Force Academy, The Naval Academy, and The Coast Guard Academy. Although I had heard about West Point before, the information about the other academies was totally new. I knew nothing about how to apply or how to get admitted to these academies, and I certainly did not know that a person could receive a free college education by attending one of the academies and committing to serve in the armed forces for a few years. Although I was not particularly interested in serving in the armed forces, the possibility of attending and getting my college education paid for was certainly exciting.

The major obstacle I saw to availing myself of this opportunity was to get a U.S. Senator or Representative to sponsor and nominate me. This was no minor obstacle in those days for it was unheard of for a black person from the South to be nominated and admitted to one of the Armed Service Academies. In fact, in 1965 there were less than five blacks in each of the academies except the Air Force Academy which had six blacks. Once I learned what the admissions criteria were, I figured I had an excellent chance and with the Civil Rights Movement in full swing the timing was right. I decided to pursue the opportunity.

I still remember how excited I was that one day in the Spring of 1965 when I ran into the high school principal, Mr. Edmund King, Sr., in the hallway during the lunch hour and told him about what I had learned doing my term paper and what my plans were. Mr. King was a good friend of our family and daddy was building a house for him during that same time. It disappointed me to no end when I shared my plans with Mr. King and his reply to me was that I was wasting my time because it was impossible for an African American to get nominated to one of the academies by the state's senators and representatives. His final edict was that I could not get nominated or admitted. That was all the motivation I needed to go forth. I had to show and prove to him that he was wrong.

During those times two of the most racist bigots to ever serve in the U.S. Senate were the senators from Mississippi: John Stennis and James O. "Big Jim" Eastland. Also, the first Republican from Mississippi to serve in the U.S. House of Representatives since Reconstruction was from our district in Mississippi: Prentiss Walker. I wrote to all three along with the governor and asked each to nominate me for an academy. The only positive response I got was from Mr. Walker who sent me information on the process he was using to select his nominees for the various academies and invited my to apply using the procedures outlined, which I did.

Mr. Walker's process for selecting his nominees involved a series of qualifying tests that candidates would take over the course of several months. These tests were to be taken at Keesler Air Force

Base in Biloxi, a three-hour drive from Bay Springs. I signed-up to take the tests, and sometime during the Summer of 1965 I went to Biloxi and went through the better part of a week of written and physical testing. It would be late in the Fall of 1965 that I would learn the results of the tests.

When I did receive the results, I had done exceptionally well. A few weeks later I would hear from Mr. Walker that I had come out at the top of his candidates and that he was nominating me for the Air force Academy. I couldn't wait to show the letter to Mr. King. He was just as excited and surprised as I was; he couldn't believe that I had actually gotten nominated.

A few weeks later in early 1966 all hell broke loose in Mississippi politics over that nomination. Somehow the media in the state got wind of the news that Mr. Walker had nominated an African American for an armed services academy. By this time Mr. Walker was in the thick of a campaign for the U.S. Senate. He was seeking to become the first Republican to be elected to the U.S. Senate from Mississippi since Reconstruction. And he would have stood a good chance except for the fact that he had nominated an African American for an armed forces academy. The media and the opposing forces had a heyday.

The first thing I knew reporters from The Clarion Ledger, which was the largest newspaper in the state located in Jackson, were at the school in Bay Springs one day looking for me for pictures and an interview. Next thing we knew my pictures were on the front pages of newspapers and on the news broadcasts across the state and the South. Our family was caught up not only in the senate campaign but also in the Civil Rights Movement as my seeking the nomination to the academy was seen as another civil rights ploy by the media and the powers that be, and became a major issue of the senatorial campaign.

Daddy didn't take too well to all the publicity and mama was totally against it. She wished it had never happened, as she was never one to want to be in the spotlight, and especially during those times. Locals saw it as a connection between our family and Cleve McDowell and James Meredith, since they knew that McDowell had visited us earlier. Local blacks began to spread the rumor that daddy was connected with the Civil Rights establishment and the NAACP. Little did they know that the furthest thing from daddy's mind was to be involved in the Civil Rights Movement in any direct way.

It turned out that Mr. Walker withdrew his support of my nomination in an attempt to regain momentum in the senatorial campaign. It was too late for him, and I had decided I did not seriously want to be a military man anyway, especially with the Vietnam War in full swing. I had proven my point, and scholarship offers were coming in from all over as the result of the publicity I had received and Mr. Walker's withdrawal of his support of my nomination. I decided to follow my siblings to Jackson State University where I would eventually earn my undergraduate degree.

By the mid-1960's daddy was no longer dependent solely on whites for work as most of his building was for blacks. Thus, there was no real slowdown in work as a result of the publicity gained from the Air Force Academy nomination. Yet, in the Summer of 1966 he was working on a job in Bay Springs that did cause some ire.

Sometime in the early to mid-1960's mama had decided she wanted to go to work outside the home. Of course, daddy almost had a fit because this was totally against his beliefs. But mama decided that since all but the last two children, my brother Otha and I, had finished high school and left home she wanted to do something else beside be a homebound housewife. So she decided to find a job outside the house. In those days the only work for black women in southeast Mississippi was either at the poultry processing plants as chicken pluckers or as domestic maids. Mama found a job as the cook and housekeeper for the James B. McBay, Jr. family whose property joined ours on the east, and whose daddy had bought the 60 acres from daddy some years prior.

Mr. McBay, Jr. was the principal at the white high school in Bay Springs and his wife, Paula Jean, was the new director of the county welfare office in Bay Springs. They had two young daughters, one was in elementary school and the other was a pre-schooler whom they needed someone to care for during the day.

Mama thought this was an excellent opportunity for her to do something different and make a little money to help her children in college. Daddy thought it was a lousy idea, but eventually he went along with it.

Mama worked for the McBays a few years until both their children were in school and then their grandmother who lived just behind them agreed that she and her husband could look after them for the hour or so until their parents came home from work everyday. Mama decided that she enjoyed being out of the house every day and found another job. This time it was as a housekeeper at the only motel in Bay Springs at the time, the Hinton Motel. The motel was located on an elevated lot in the heart of Bay Springs at the junction of Highways 18 and 528 where the Hardee's restaurant now stands.

The owners of the Hinton Motel were a Mr. Haskell Hinton and his wife. Mr. Hinton was known throughout town as an alcoholic; but he was a respectable drunk because he was one of the important business owners in town and he had money. He was mainly a drunk because he didn't have much else to do everyday but drink. He didn't really have much to do in terms of work because his wife took care of all the business in running the motel. Mama went to work for him at the motel partly because I had gone to work for him on Saturdays during the school year cleaning up the yards around the motel buildings. I would work one or two Saturdays a month during my junior year of high school. I wanted to have a work experience different than just working for daddy.

As the result of both mama and me working for him, Mr. Hinton had contacted daddy to do some remodeling work around the motel buildings for him during the summer of 1966. When I returned home from a six-week College Readiness Program at Jackson State University in early July, I went to work with daddy along with my good friend Llewellyn Peyton, who was like another brother to my brother Otha and me, and was the son of Mrs. Thelma Peyton.

Usually Mr. Hinton just stayed in his house and drank whiskey all day for the most part. But when Llewellyn and I came to work with dad he got in the habit of coming out everyday to where we were working and joking around with the two of us. We didn't take too kindly to his joking because we had learned over the years not to joke with white men, especially drunk white men. Tradition and our parents had taught us that their joking with blacks almost always turned into racist degradation. So we were respectful, but not very talkative or responsive to Mr. Hinton. In fact, we tried to ignore him and go about doing our work because we knew that his antics toward us annoyed daddy, so we tried to get him back in the house as quickly as possible by responding to him as little as possible.

One day right after we had finished eating our lunch and were just getting back to our work routine, Mr. Hinton came out of his house just as drunk as he could be and still walk. We were all working in two adjoining rooms in the motel building. There was daddy, Mr. Lawrence Moore, Uncle Bud, Llewellyn and me. We were putting up paneling on the walls and refinishing the window casings. Mr. Hinton came staggering into the room where Llewellyn and I were nailing up paneling. We were into a good work routine and really didn't want to be bothered by him at all that day. Obviously he had begun to get on our nerves. You could smell the whiskey clearly across the room. He started his joking and talking as usual, but we didn't say much; we just kept on nailing paneling to the walls.

Evidently he must have become annoyed at our ignoring him and decided he would do something boldly to get our undivided attention. He screamed at us as loudly as he could: "Don't you young nigger sons-of-bitches hear me talking to you!" He was standing all the way across the room from us but next to the door going into the next room where daddy and the two men were working. Before we could say anything and before he realized what had happened to him, daddy had reached in the room and grabbed Mr. Hinton in the collar of his shirt and thrown him to the floor and was down on him with one knee in his chest. He went to draw back his hammer to hit him in the head with it when Mr. Lawrence Moore caught the hammer before daddy could swing it down. The hammer came out of daddy's hand so he just hit him with his fist. "Who in hell are you calling nigger sons-of-bitches? Don't you know these are my boys, and that it is my wife and their mothers you're talking about? Do you think I'm gonna stand here and let you talk about my wife and my child's mother like that, peckerwood." Daddy hit him a few more times while he was talking to him.

Mr. Hinton lay there on the floor and was crying like a baby when daddy got up off him. For a few minutes I thought daddy would beat the man unconscious, which would not have taken much as drunk as he was. Mr. Hinton started begging and pleading with daddy. "Otha I didn't mean no harm, I was just joking with your boys like I always do," he said. Daddy lit right back into him verbally: "That's the problem with you white folks, you don't know how to joke with Negroes. Your joking is gonna always end up calling somebody a nigger if they're black. You go on back in your house and you stay in there if you want us to finish this job. If not, you let me know and we can leave here right now and never come back. It don't make me no difference one way or another. But don't you ever let me hear you call one of my children a nigger or a son-of-a-bitch ever again in my life or even after I'm dead and gone. I'll come out of the grave and kick your ass if I so much as hear tell of you doing it."

Needless to say, the next week mama quit working at the motel as soon as Mrs. Hinton could find somebody to take her place. Mrs. Hinton wanted her to stay on, but daddy wouldn't hear of it and mama knew she couldn't work there any longer after that incident. We did finish up the work remodeling the motel building in a few weeks. Mr. Hinton never did come back out there to the building while we were still there. After that incident Mrs. Hinton would talk to daddy and take care of all of the business. Mr. Hinton just seemed to try and drink himself into oblivion, but he never came back out there joking again.

XVIII. HELP FOR TIMES TO COME

As a family we had always been taught and we believed that our lives and destinies were divinely arranged and that God always had us in his care. We were taught to believe that God would make the best divine arrangements for us in spite of our trials and troubles if we trusted in him and did what was right by ourselves and others. We didn't realize how true this would be until years later. In the mid-1960's we never thought much about this reality because things were going so well for our family. In the years to come it would prove to be a truth we would embrace wholeheartedly and come to understand why our parents had taught it to us.

As fate would have it, in the Fall of 1966, just after I had entered my freshman year of college at Jackson State University, mama wrote and informed us that brother George was coming back home to live and work with daddy. At the time, three of us - sister Bobbie, brother Otha, and myself - were at Jackson State. Bobbie was in her senior year, Otha was in his junior year, and I was a freshman.

Brother George had just gotten out of the Army a little over a year prior. He had spent most of his three years of Army duty in Germany playing basketball on a traveling Army team. When he returned home to Albuquerque, his wife had squandered all of their money partying and having a good time, and was three or four months pregnant by another man. He was in a devastating situation. Nevertheless, he had managed to go to work and to help her to get situated and have the baby, and to begin to get his financial situation back into some kind of order. He had also filed for and gotten a divorce by the Fall of 1966.

As the building industry had slowed down in Albuquerque when George had returned from the Army, he had inquired of daddy as to how building was in Mississippi. Of course, daddy confirmed that it was booming, which it was, and welcomed George to come back home and work with him and to stay as long as he wanted until he got back on his feet again. George made it to Mississippi in early October 1966 and immediately went to work with daddy. With George as another lead man, daddy could now double his building schedule since George could take one crew and work on one project while he could take a crew and be working on another. They started building houses like there was no tomorrow.

The three of us who were in college were absolutely thrilled to have our big brother back in Mississippi. It meant somebody to come over and visit us occasionally, and to pick us up at times to go home for the weekend. And, as George was always the most generous brother we had, he would always share clothes and money with us when we had needs. He was also a confidante that we could talk to and share things that we would never share with our parents. George had always been a surrogate parent for us, even when he was in high school. He was like the strong pillar of the family; he was caring and didn't mind sharing whatever he had. He had come to daddy's rescue several times over the years when money was tight and he was working; he would help daddy out with bills and other needs the family had even when he was away. He was the one that everybody in the family had come to rely on when things got tight.

With George back home to help him, daddy began to build more houses and to make more profit than he had ever made in his entire career. For the first time in his life daddy was able to begin to put away a few dollars for hard times. It was profitable for George as well because he was able to pay off the bills that had been left from his wife's squandering, and he began to create a substantial savings for himself. Daddy shared the profits from the houses with George in addition to his regular wages, so it was a profitable situation for the both of them. When George returned to Mississippi he had become a master builder and had learned a lot of shortcuts to making the work go faster. He and daddy were building houses and finishing them faster than any other builders in the area.

In the Fall of 1968, George was offered the job to become the vocational education teacher for the colored high school in Bay Springs, which he took. The public schools in Mississippi did not become integrated until the Fall of 1970. Sometime during the late Spring of 1968 work had slowed down a bit, and he had decided to move to Joliet, Illinois where sister Walterene and brother Otha were living. Brother Otha had just finished college that May and was getting married in August. He had secured a teaching job in the school system there, and he and his wife, Shirley Jeanette, would be settling into an apartment after the wedding before the school year would begin.

When the vocational education teacher's position came open during that summer, Mr. Edmund King, Sr., who was still the principal of the colored high school, thought about George's talents in carpentry and woodworking and decided to help George secure the position. George had spent some time taking college courses in Wisconsin in the 1950's, so he would be able to receive a special teaching certification because of his experiences and could attend college in the summers to take the necessary courses needed for regular certification in vocational education. George decided to take the job offer and to return home again. This time he would be there for good.

Sometime during that Summer of 1968 George had gone on a blind date and met the woman whom he would marry that December. A mutual friend had told him about Agnes Robinson who lived in Indianola, and he had called her on the telephone and arranged to fly from Joliet to Indianola to meet her. It was love at first sight for the both of them, if there is such a thing, for they made immediate plans to be married in December. Agnes was a teacher in the Indianola public schools where she planned to finish the 1968-69 school year and then take a teaching job with the schools in Bay Springs which she did.

With George back home for good, and with him getting married and building himself a nice home, which he did in 1971, daddy and mama became very comfortable and settled into a regular routine.

They would go to church every Sunday, and maybe visit George and Agnes on Sunday evenings and one evening during the week.

In the Summer of 1970, George began contracting on his own and hired some of the students whom he had taught during the year to work with him. By the Fall of 1970 the school officials had decided to change the vocational education program from what it had been to more of a sheet-metal and industrial technology oriented program. Thus, they closed down George's shop at the previously all-colored high school. That school became the elementary school for the entire school district. The white vocational education instructor was kept on to teach all of the classes and George's job was phased out. He became a full-time contractor and began contracting and building on his own. He and daddy still worked together to help each other out whenever one or the other needed extra help on their jobs. Daddy even hired some of George's best students who had finished high school that year to come to work for him. Both he and George now had some of those students working for them and they would go on to become excellent carpenters themselves. Daddy's tradition of training men to be self-sufficient was being carried on through George's teaching.

During the last two years of my high school years when I was the only child at home, my daddy and I became closer than we had ever been before. I might have become closer to him than any of the other children beside George. He and I spent a lot of time over those two years getting to know each other as I had never known him before. Those were good years for me and for the two of us. Daddy told me things during those years that he had never told any of the other family members. And although I was far from being a perfect child, he showed a lot more tolerance for my shortcomings than he had shown for any of the other children. I think daddy felt some guilt for being away over those crucial years of my childhood and could sense that I had missed something very vital during those years. His tolerance of my mischief was his way of making up for those lost years and opportunities.

I know I tested his and mama's nerves and patience during those two years perhaps like they had never been tested before. There were several occasions I remember that I should have been busted, and if it had been at any other time in his life there is no telling what daddy would have done to me. Once I was hanging out late one Sunday night with some of my buddies. I must have been no more than sixteen years old at the time. Anyway, we had gone out with some older girls who had finished high school and who already had babies and their own cars. We went to Laurel with them and somehow were admitted into a bar. We sat in that bar until very late drinking good whiskey until we were all fairly well drunk. When we got back to Bay Springs, it was around midnight, and it was raining like all hell was flooding.

I had left the car at one of my buddy's house. Instead of my just staying the night at his house, I decided to drive home which was at least five miles. To avoid getting stopped by the police, I decided to take the back roads which were all dirt roads at the time. The way I chose to go was a dark and dreary road that usually became impassable when it rained; thus, it was slick as wet glass on this particular night. With my vision impaired from the drinking, of course, I wound up in the ditch. It was impossible to get the car out of the slick ditch without a wrecker or having somebody pull me out with a truck. Thus, I ended up having to stay all night in the car stuck in the ditch and drunk.

I woke up occasionally during the night and let the car idle for a while in order to keep warm. It was in mid-January and it was cold even in Mississippi; the temperature was at least in the lower 30's because frost had formed on the windshield and windows over the night. In the morning when I awoke around 6:30 o'clock, I just got out of the car and walked home which must have been at least two miles from where I had gotten stuck in the ditch. By the time I got home, daddy and mama were coming out the door on their ways to work. Neither one said very much to me, but I could tell by their demeanor that they were fuming mad, especially daddy. I knew he wanted to take a belt and tan my hide, but realizing that I was almost grown, he showed restraint. But I knew I was in serious trouble.

Mama asked what happened and I told her that I had gotten stuck in the ditch and could not get out. Since it was raining, obviously I had chosen not to walk home in the rain and just slept in the car. I stayed far enough away from the both of them to try to avoid them smelling the whiskey on my breath, but I knew I was not really fooling anybody, especially daddy. He could tell by the look in my eyes that I had been drinking, he had seen that same look in his own eyes too many times to be fooled by me. He didn't say anything about it then, but I knew that I had it coming when he came home that evening from work.

I knew I had better not miss a day out of school. So even though the school bus had already gone, I had to get to school and I had to get that car out of the ditch as well. I went up the road and got Cousin John's son, Tamp, to take his pulpwood truck and go with me to pull the car out of the ditch, which he did. Then I came home and got a bath and got ready and went to school. Somehow I got to school by the end of the first class period.

When daddy came home that evening from work, after he had dinner he sat me down and had a long talk with me about responsibility and manhood. He was angry, but to my surprise he was reasonable and rational. He talked to me as if I was another adult rather than a child, but it was still painful. I think I would have rather he gave me an old fashioned whipping like he had done when I was a child.

Another time daddy showed such passionate compassion was during my senior year of high school in the Spring of 1966. The high school band of which I was a member had gone to Jackson for the annual band festival day at Jackson State. Mr. Elijah Cross, the high school band director, was also my girlfriend's father and one of the teachers whom I admired very much. He was responsible for my getting a marching band scholarship to play in the band at Jackson State during my college years. On this particular band trip about half of the boys in the band had gotten drunk after our performance. On the way home they started vomiting on the bus, and the bus driver had to stop along the road to let them get off the bus to relieve themselves.

The next day Mr. Cross called certain ones into his office and began to issue punishments. In doing so, some of the fellows told him that I had been drinking also, but I had not gotten sick on the bus on the way home. I had indeed drank some wine, and had took some of the other boys and showed them where to buy the wine and beer they had drank. I knew where to go because I frequented

Jackson often to visit and pick-up my brother and sisters to bring them home on their visits home. Mr. Cross reasoned that in order to not show prejudice and favoritism toward me since I was dating his daughter, the thing to do was to punish me also. I at first refused the punishment and protested since I had not gotten caught doing anything wrong and I had not pointed the finger or turned in anybody else who got caught.

Mr. Cross did not agree and insisted that I would either take the punishment or be expelled from school for a few days. Daddy was building a house for Mr. Dessie B. Young at the time just a few blocks from where our school was located. Mr. Cross put me in the car and took me down to where daddy was working for us to discuss the situation with him before he made up his mind. This was just three months after the previous incident where I had slept in the car all night. Daddy was not too happy to see us coming on his job under these circumstances. Anyway, I went in to see him with Mr. Cross; we both explained our positions to daddy.

Daddy's first response to Mr. Cross was to ask him did he need him to help do his job at the school. "If I've got to do your job and mine, then maybe you need to come out here and start building houses and let me go to the schoolhouse and teach the children and direct the band. Tell that boy what you want him to do and tell him when you want him to get started. Then, if he don't do what you tell him that's when you come see me, after you done put a limb on his ass first." That was the end of that, I went back to school and had to pick-up paper on the grounds after school for a week and help the janitor clean the halls and rooms after school along with the other boys. Daddy never said another word about the whole matter after that. I was totally shocked, and I knew for sure he was a changed man just as I was.

XIX. SAVING GRACE

The 1970's and 1980's were certainly golden years for daddy and mama and for the family generally in many ways. But the 1970's had both an adverse and not so adverse beginning. In the Spring of 1970 I was graduating from college at Jackson State and had planned to attend graduate school at the University of Pittsburgh in Pennsylvania. One weekend in early April I came home for the weekend on Friday evening to bring some of my belongings and to visit and found daddy and George preparing the pickup truck and themselves to head up to Joliet in all due haste that evening.

Over the years Walterene and her husband, O.L., to whom she had been married for almost 10 years, and with whom she had four children by then, had been having marital problems. It seemed that during this particular week their situation had come to the breaking point. As I recall the night before I arrived home on that Friday evening, she had followed him to another woman's apartment somewhere in Joliet. She had waited until he had gone inside and made himself comfortable, to the extent of getting undressed and getting into the woman's bed and whatever else. She shot the lock off the apartment door, kicked the door open and went inside. By the time she had made her entry, he had already jumped out the window of the second floor and was making a hasty exit on the ground below, leaving his shoes behind. She fired a few more shots out the window just to make sure he kept running.

Upon returning to her house Walterene called daddy to let him know what had happened. Daddy had been in the middle of their marital problems for far more years than he had wanted to or even hoped he would be. In fact, he would have preferred if they had left him out of it altogether. But it seemed that every time she and O.L. would have a spat, he would get on the phone and call daddy for him to talk to her and try to convince her to see things his way. Daddy had been exceptionally patient with this situation over the years, but his patience had grown thin, and his tolerance of the entire matter had long waned. This episode was the last straw.

When Walterene had called daddy and told him what she had done, that was the end of the matter. He told her to stay put until he got there. In fact, he told her that she could just as well make up her mind that their marriage was over, because it was. She could make up her mind that she was moving to somewhere else in Joliet, or she was coming home, but she was leaving the house the two of them were sharing when he got there; and he would be there just as soon as he could get there. She could start packing and be ready to move when he got there. Daddy meant business because in his opinion the situation had gone on too long already, and with this shooting incident it had reached the danger point. Somebody would wind up getting killed.

As fate would have it, by the time Walterene had arrived back home that evening she had a call that our first cousin, Harold Bell, Aunt Euralea's son from California, had arrived in town. Harold was a truck driver and an ex-convict who weighed at least 350 pounds, and was as mean as a bull. She went to the truck stop to pick up Harold and called daddy back for Harold to talk to him. Daddy told him to stay there until he and George got there. They left Bay Springs about midnight that Friday evening with pistols loaded and under the truck seat. They were in Joliet by noon that Saturday. Harold stayed at the house with her that night to make sure no trouble went down. Anyway, O.L. didn't show back up at the house that night, or for a few days.

When daddy and George arrived in Joliet, daddy arranged for Walterene and O.L. to meet. He wanted them to get together one last time to discuss whatever they needed to talk about with each other. He let them know that the next time they were going to meet was going to be in divorce court. He let them know that he had enough of their marriage even if they hadn't, and since they had seen fit to keep him involved in it, he was calling it off.

So they needed to get together and decide how they were going to end it, because it was over. He made it clear that he didn't make that hasty trip there just to sit down and talk with them. It was time for somebody to make a move and he was there to move them. He was moving her and the kids somewhere before he left.

After two days, she decided on what few items she wanted to take from the house, and that she and the children would return to Mississippi with daddy and George. So they loaded those things on the truck for daddy to drive back and she, George and the children would drive her car back to Mississippi. By that Wednesday, they arrived back in Bay Springs and the marriage was over. It really hurt mama because she did not believe in divorce or separation; she had always encouraged them to try and work out their differences. Daddy, on the other hand, believed that if they could not get along they should get apart.

A few weeks after they arrived in Mississippi, Walterene decided she would go to California and try to make a new start there. Two of her friends came down from Illinois and helped her drive her car to California. She left the children with mama and daddy across the summer and came and picked them up in late summer before it was time for them to enroll in school. She spent a year in California then returned to Illinois where she married again a year or so later.

In the Fall of 1970 I went off to the University of Pittsburgh to study for my master's degree. I had graduated from Jackson State in May 1970 and had worked in Jackson for part of the summer and with George and daddy building houses for the remainder of the summer. I was part of the class of 1970 at Jackson State that never graduated because of the riot on campus and the killing of the two students in early May. The two students at Jackson State were killed just days after the Kent State University massacre, but most have forgotten the Jackson State incident except those who were students, faculty and staff there at the time. I suppose that people who were living in Jackson during that time also remember.

Anyway, my first year at Pittsburgh was a total success. I was the top student in the master's program in geography, although I came from the most unlikely background to be a success at such a distinguished university. By the beginning of my second year, I had grown tired of the social isolation, and was generally burned out and wanted to leave. I had completed most of the credits I needed to get the master's except the thesis. In the middle of the term I decided I had enough. I didn't want to return to Mississippi, but I had little choice. Plus, I had co-signed a year's lease on the apartment I was sharing with three white students in the program. I had lost my spirit for school and just didn't want to do it anymore. I didn't know how I was going to get out of Pittsburgh in a dignified manner and not be seen as a quitter.

I called daddy and talked to him and shared with him the dilemma I was in. He couldn't understand what was going on with me or why I wanted to drop out of school since I seemed to be making such good progress. Yet, he assured me that if that was what I wanted to do and needed to do it would be okay, if I left with the option that I could return to complete my degree the next year or next semester. With his assurances, I made up my mind to return to Mississippi to regroup. Daddy arranged to send me the money to pay off the remainder of my portion of the apartment lease, and I made arrangements to withdraw from the university in the middle of the semester.

As fate would have it, the apartment manager allowed me to leave without paying off my portion of the lease. So when I returned to Mississippi I brought all of daddy's money with me, which was approximately $800. That was a considerable amount of money even for 1971. Daddy was usually always generous in terms of helping his children out of situations as long as he believed they were doing the right things and trying to advance themselves in the right direction. He had done it for others and had no hesitancy about doing it for me.

I returned to Mississippi in late October 1971, in the midst of the autumn season. When I got there, daddy was working on two houses and George must have been working on two or three. I went to work with daddy the very next day after I arrived. I was somewhat ambivalent about being there, because although I knew the circumstances under which I had returned, I subconsciously felt that I had failed myself and let my parents down. I felt comfortable though knowing that I had done what I felt was best for me at the time. Daddy and mama welcomed me home with open arms, and I immediately started planning how I would go on to become what I hoped to become in life with their encouragement.

Shortly after I returned to Mississippi in 1971 I met the young woman whom I would first marry, Sharon Payton. She was a person I had known all of her life since she was a child. Sharon was four or five years younger than me and she was in her senior year of high school in 1971-72. She would graduate from high school in May 1972. Although she was only seventeen when I met her that fall, she seemed very mature for her age and was undoubtedly a very sharp and intelligent young woman. She was as pretty as she could be as well; very attractive and well spoken. The public schools in Mississippi had recently integrated in 1970 and in Bay Springs, Sharon was one of the brightest young black students in the local high school.

Sharon and I started talking when I ran into her one Sunday evening at Mrs. Thelma Peyton's house. Mrs. Peyton was like a mother to me as her son, Llewellyn, and I were classmates and the best of friends in high school. We became very close after his brother, L.C., had died from being critically burned in a tractor accident in 1964, and his father, Mr. L.C. Peyton, Sr., had died suddenly of a heart attack during the summer of 1965. His brother and my brother, Otha, were the best of friends in high school as well. When Mr. Peyton died, daddy was just beginning to build a new house for him and his family.

When Sharon and I started dating and spending time with each other she was already engaged to another young man who was away in the Army. I talked her into breaking the engagement in January when he came home on a visit, and she and I were engaged in March to be married in June. Of course when we decided to marry we agreed that she would continue her education by going to college in the fall. Thus, we began to do applications for her to get admitted to Jackson State for the Fall of 1972, and we began to make plans to be married after she graduated in May 1972.

When we decided to get married I wanted my daddy to perform the ceremony. When I asked him if he would do this for me, he hesitated and decided that he needed to think about it before he gave me an answer. I remember well the Saturday afternoon when we talked about it and the hesitation he showed. I had presumed that his answer would be automatically yes; but I was mistaken. When we talked about it that first time daddy seemed somewhat confused and distraught. To me it was like he felt that it might not have been proper for a father to perform the marriage vows for his son, but I could tell that it was something deeper than that. Anyway, he said he would think about it and let me know soon.

A week later daddy and I sat down again on Saturday afternoon and talked about my getting married to Sharon. He assured me that he was supportive of my getting married, if that was what we wanted to do. However, he was not in favor of my marrying Sharon; there was something he felt that was wrong about it, but he couldn't quite articulate what it was. It was just his intuition. He didn't want to discourage me, but he felt deeply within his heart that she was too young and that she was not as serious about marrying me as she was about getting away from her home situation and becoming independent. Anyway, he explained that since he felt that way, it would be best if we got somebody else to perform the marriage ceremony, which I agreed to do. I could never hold a grudge against my daddy for not performing the marriage ceremony because I had too much respect for him and his decisions.

Sharon and I were married on Saturday afternoon, June 17, 1972 on the front steps of Mrs. Peyton's house beside Highway 18 west of Bay Springs with 25 to 30 people in attendance. Daddy's good friend, Rev. J.W. Crosby did the ceremony. Our plans were for her to go to college at Jackson State in the fall, and I had originally planned to go back to Pittsburgh to finish my master's degree that fall. My plans changed after we realized that Sharon would need my support to help pay for her college expenses. I decided I would delay going back to Pittsburgh until she had gotten settled in school and had at least a semester behind her. We would live with my parents until she went to Jackson State in the Fall of 1972.

When the time came for Sharon to go off to school, she really hated to go. She resented the idea of leaving her family; although she was married she was still strongly connected to her mother and sisters more than she was connected to me. It was really them that she dreaded having to leave. I never shall forget the day I drove her over to Jackson, she cried all the way there. Although she would be only 65 miles away from home and would have the privilege of coming home any weekends she chose, it seemed to her that she would never see them again.

It didn't take Sharon long to find comfort for her loneliness at Jackson State, for not long after school had begun she met and fell for another young man for whom she would have a child a year or so later. She joined the cheerleader corps and became involved in college to the extent that she decided that no matter how liberal her marriage situation was, she wanted total freedom. I knew what was going on because I had friends and fraternity brothers on campus who kept me informed of her comings and goings and other activities. Even when I would go to Jackson on weekends to be with her, she was so busy she hardly had time to spend with me. Of course I became disillusioned and knew that something would happen sooner or later to our relationship that would not be good.

Things came to a head when she came home for Thanksgiving. Jackson State and Alcorn State played their annual arch rival game on Thanksgiving Day during those years. So I went over to see the game and to pick her up to come home after the game. This was the first time she came home since being away in school.

Our communications had already almost totally broken down, so I didn't force it. Instead of bringing her home to my parents' house, I brought her and left her at her parents to stay with them over the weekend. She didn't seem to want to be bothered with me so I didn't persist, because I knew our relationship was virtually over anyway; at least as far as I was concerned. Since I had taken a couple of my friends with me to the game, I didn't try to confront her during the ride home. She was tired and wanted to sleep, so we didn't disturb her.

I had decided to take a position as an instructor at Jackson State starting the second term to begin a week after Thanksgiving. In fact,

I had already been interviewed and had accepted the position; I had even rented an apartment and bought the furniture and had it set up before Thanksgiving. I didn't tell Sharon because I wanted it to be a surprise for her. I would tell her during the weekend or when I took her back to Jackson.

I thought that in spite of whatever was going on, if I moved to Jackson and we lived together we could make the marriage work, at least that was my hope. My dad and mother had encouraged me to take the position and finish my master's thesis during my first semester working at Jackson State rather than going back to Pittsburgh. I had decided that I would not continue for the doctorate at Pittsburgh anyway. So taking the job at Jackson State seemed to me a good plan to save our marriage and support her in college.

Over the Thanksgiving weekend I came to realize that Sharon's interest was somewhere else. During the time she was at her parents she didn't call or say anything to me the whole time. It was as if I no longer existed to her, except as a provider of money to support her. I picked her up at her parents late that Sunday afternoon to take her back to Jackson. On the way there I told her about my accepting the job at Jackson State and that I would be moving there the next weekend. In fact, I was going to New Orleans that next weekend for a conference and wanted her to come with me since football season was over and there were no more games for her to be cheerleading on weekends. I also told her what I knew about her seeing another man, and assured her that if she would end the relationship before I moved to Jackson I was willing to forgive and forget about that if she were willing.

Early that Tuesday morning, as daddy and I were sitting at the kitchen table drinking a cup of coffee before going to work, the telephone rang and it was Sharon. She called to tell me she had decided she no longer wanted to be married to me and that she would not be moving out of the dormitory into the apartment with me on the weekend when I moved to Jackson. I was devastated! It was like the world was coming to an end for me and I didn't know what to do. Daddy was sitting there listening to my end of the conversation and I could tell that he was getting upset as well. I told Sharon that she could have some time to think about her decision and let me know later, but she was determined that it had to be this way; She was through with the marriage.

I told Sharon that I wanted her to go with me to New Orleans for the weekend trip I was taking and we could talk about it then, but she would not entertain that thought either. So my final words to her that morning was that I would give her thirty day to decide if she wanted to change her mind. After that I would be seeing a lawyer to start divorce proceedings. I let her know what my address would be in Jackson and the telephone numbers both at my office and at the apartment, if she wanted to talk to me or if she changed her mind she could give me a call. But I would not try to contact her since that was the way she wanted it to be. I hung up the phone and started to cry as I walked out of the kitchen and toward the front door.

Daddy got up from the table and walked out behind me. He wanted me to tell him the details of what Sharon had said to me, which I did. Also, for the first time I told him about what had been going on between us, which he already sensed as we did not stay together during the Thanksgiving weekend when she was home. He became livid and I assured him that there was no need for him to be upset or involved in this, but he wanted to take drastic measures. I told my dad I would not have any part of what he was talking about doing to Sharon, because it wouldn't change anything, and I certainly did not want to be married to anybody who did not want to be with me. We both agreed that she was probably too young to be married in the first place, so I had to move on with my life.

I never shall forget the words daddy said to me that morning that made all the difference in the world. He reached in his pocket and pulled out five crisp one-hundred dollar bills and handed them to me and said to me, "Son the best thing to mend a broken heart is to find a new one as soon as you can. There are plenty women in New Orleans where you are going this weekend and in Jackson where you will be next week. As soon as you can find you one of them and let her make you happy. You'll be all right after you do." I took him at his word and that was exactly what I did.

It was in 1984 that I finally had another conversation with Sharon. I was home for Christmas and stopped by her mother's house just to say hello, and lo and behold Sharon was sitting in the living room when I walked in. If I had known she was there I probably would not have stopped, but I had heard that her mother was ailing so I wanted to pay my respect. The Christmas after we broke up I had stopped by to give her mother and father a Christmas gift and she was there. That time her mother asked if Sharon and I could talk, or if we needed to talk. I asked Sharon if she had anything she wanted to say to me, and she said no; so I said that I didn't have anything to say to her either. So we didn't have a conversation; there appeared to be nothing for us to talk about.

But in 1984, when I was leaving out the door to get in my car and drive away she followed me out the door and asked if she could talk to me before I left. I said surely if you have something you want to say. She walked out to the car with me and grabbed my hand as I was opening the car door. Standing there facing me she looked me in the eyes and said she was sorry for leaving me and she had realized over the years that she had made a mistake. I told her that I had realized that she was young and I was too, but I had long forgiven her for whatever pain she had caused me and there was no need to apologize after all those years. She started to cry and put her arms around me. We kissed as if we were young lovers all over again, but that was surely the end. I was glad in my heart that she had said those words to me. I asked her if it had been something that I had done that caused her to leave and she assured me that it was nothing I had done. We just kissed again and said goodbye. I still don't know why we kissed each other so fervently that night. I guess in my heart there was still some love that we shared.

XX. GOOD AND BAD TIMES

I went to work at Jackson State University for the second term of the 1972-73 academic year in late November 1972; the week following the Thanksgiving holiday. I moved into my apartment and only saw Sharon occasionally as we passed each other on the sidewalk on campus between classes. I would be going to teach my classes and she would be changing classes. I would cordially speak to her, and she would respond in kind, but we never stopped to have a conversation. Finally, in late January 1973 I went to see a lawyer, Hermel Johnson, a friend of mine who had been in school at Jackson State with me and who had recently finished his law degree at Ole Miss. When I went to see him and told him what I wanted to do, he agreed to handle the divorce for me and informed me that I needed to find out from Sharon if she was going to contest the divorce.

As I was sitting in Hermel's office that day, he handed me the phone and said I needed to call Sharon and find out if she was going to agree to the divorce, or if she was going to contest. I took the phone and dialed the number to the dormitory hallway where she was staying on campus. When she came to the phone, I handed it back to him and told him he needed to ask her those questions because he was the one who needed to know and that was what I was paying him to do, which was to handle the matters relating to the divorce. He talked to her and she indicated she had no plans to contest the divorce.

During the time I worked at Jackson State that year I continued to go back and forth to Bay Springs every chance I had to work with daddy and George building houses. They were both building a lot of houses during those times and I was drawing blueprints for them on the weekends and during all the spare time that I could afford. I also busied myself doing all that I could to advance my efforts at Jackson State. Daddy, George and my mother were all very supportive and probably my close connections with them kept me sane. Going through the divorce, even though Sharon and I had only been married for a short time, was the hardest and most emotionally draining experience I had ever had.

In the Summer of 1973 I took the opportunity to attend a Graduate Institute in Liberal Studies at St. Johns College in Santa Fe, New Mexico. I wanted to go there for several reasons. I wanted to get away from Mississippi for a while, and it was an opportunity to begin work on another master's degree program. I was somewhat ambivalent about ever returning to Pittsburgh to finish up my degree from there. Yet, I knew that if I were to remain in academia I would need to complete a master's in order to work on the doctorate. I saw going to Santa Fe as a potential option since the program there was strictly a summer program that could be completed in three summers.

I went on to Santa Fe that summer and worked hard. Another colleague from Jackson State and I drove out together in his car. The program was based on the classics and great books. It didn't take me long to decide that I was going to complete my master's from Pittsburgh some way and go on for the doctoral degree in geography rather than pursue any further the program at St. Johns. For some reason, I just couldn't get into reading the classics and becoming serious about studying them. Aristotle and Plato and the rest of the classic philosophers just didn't excite my intellectual juices.

I did meet the next woman I would soon marry during the summer at Santa Fe. It must have been the second week there that I saw Mozell sitting with another friend of hers on a bench in the plaza. When I looked her over I liked what I saw and decided to go over and introduce myself to the two of them. They invited me to sit down and join them for conversation, and so I did. Mozell told me some time later that she and her girlfriend, Norma Cotton, had been sizing me up and trying to decide which of the two of them would go after me, but I beat them to the point by making my move first.

Mozell and I spent a lot of time together that summer. Every weekend we would go somewhere together away from the campus. Often we would spend the weekend at my brother's and sister-in-law's home in Albuquerque - Charles and Phyllis. Their son, Chucky, was a young teenager and their daughter, Cheryl, was a pre-teen. Charles was busy driving his van across the country and some weekends Phyllis would fly out to meet him in Denver or L.A. Mozell and I would go spend the weekend in Albuquerque with the children or just the son if the daughter happened to go with her mother.

We became very close to each other during those six to eight weeks we spent together. When the program ended for the summer we had to decide what we would do. We were sitting and talking one evening during the next to last week of the program, and I asked Mozell what she was going to do when she returned to New York City after the program was over. She said that since she had finished her master's degree that summer she was moving to Atlanta and would look for a job after she got there. She had some money saved and was going to relocate and make a new start. I suggested to her that if she was going to relocate to the South why not move to Jackson and come with me. She said she could do that but only if we were going to get married. That is when I proposed to her and we announced our engagement.

After I left Santa Fe in early August I returned to Jackson and began making preparations for our getting married. I had to find a larger apartment since the one I was living in was not in the best of neighborhoods and was only a one-bedroom. I also had to trade cars and get a nicer one since the one I was driving needed some major repair work. Within the first week of returning to Jackson I had those things done and was off to Bay Springs to work with George and Daddy for a few weeks.

On the Labor Day weekend I flew off to New York to help Mozell pack her things and prepare to make the move. By the end of that week we had things picked up by a moving company and we were off on our way back to Mississippi driving her vintage Volkswagen beetle. We left New York on Friday evening and by Sunday evening we were at the airport in Jackson picking up my car which I had left in the airport parking lot.

The next weekend, on September 15, 1973, Mozell and I were married by a Reverend McLaurin, who was the father of the wife of one of my fraternity line brothers, at his church on the corner of Lynch and Rose Streets a few blocks from the campus of Jackson State University. Only the minister, his wife, my cousin Clayborn Lang, my good friend James Watkins and his wife JoAnn attended the marriage. Clayborn's wife, JoAnn stayed home and fixed dinner for us. After the marriage we went to their house for dinner and spent the afternoon eating, talking and listening to music together with them. It was a simple marriage, but since both of us had been married before and had each recently gone through divorces that was the way we wanted it.

That evening after we had left the group at Clayborn's and JoAnn's house, Mozell and I drove out to Bay Springs so she could meet my mother and father, Brother George and sister-in-law Agnes. Their first child, Angela Delphia, had just turned a year old on August 27, and just beginning to walk. My folks could hardly believe Mozell and I had gotten married that fast. I had told my mother and my brother that I was going to New York to pick up Mozell and that we were going to be married when we returned to Mississippi, but they did not realize it would happen that fast.

My mother had told me before I left not to bring her to Mississippi unless I intended to marry her. My mother and father would not have stood for us living together for any length of time without being married. Such arrangements were not acceptable to my family and had never been indulged by any members of the family. So I knew that we needed to be married as soon as possible upon arriving in Mississippi, and that is what we did. Not so much to please my parents and other members of the family, but because those values were so deeply rooted in my own spirit that I could not be satisfied with myself unless we were married.

During that year while still working at Jackson State, Mozell and I decided that I would go on to work on my Ph.D. the next year. Neither one of us particularly wanted to stay in Mississippi at that time. So I went to work collecting the data to do my master's thesis. I had made contact with the Geography Department at the University of Pittsburgh and gotten my thesis proposal approved. The previous year I had gone back in April to complete my comprehensive exams and had passed those. All I had to do was to complete my thesis and I could defend it and receive the degree. I had proposed to do my research on the relocation of retail businesses from the central business district of Jackson to outlying retail shopping centers over a five-year period. Therefore, during that year I worked hard to get as much of the data collection and surveying done as I possibly could.

I also applied to the doctoral program at Michigan State University and had been accepted provisionally. This meant that I would have to complete the master's during the first year there. During the Summer of 1974 I worked at Jackson State one summer term and spent the remainder of the summer working on my thesis to get as much done as I possible could. I was determined to have most of it completed by the time I arrived at Michigan State in the Fall. Mozell and I visited my parents in Bay Springs as often as we could during that summer before we left Jackson. We didn't know if we would be returning or when.

During those years living was good for daddy and mom. George and his family lived close by and my mother kept their children while they worked which was her joy. She had always wanted to have grandchildren live close by so she could pamper them. The late 1970's and 1980's were definitely good years for all of them. The building business was going good; both daddy and George were making as much money as they possibly could and living was easy. Those were undoubtedly the best years of their lives. No one could have possibly predicted how or when things would change, but they certainly would and they did within a few years.

During the time we were living in Lansing and I was attending Michigan State, Mozell and I would return to Mississippi as often as we could on holidays and during the summers. Brother George and Sister Agnes would come and visit us occasionally, and even brought mom and dad to visit us once or twice. During those years the other members of the family were having their children, especially Brother Otha, Sisters Brenda and Bobbie, and mom would go and stay with them during the first two or three weeks after their children were born.

For some reason we had never thought about all getting together as a family at one time. Probably because we had not been apart from each other for that long, and one brother or sister was always visiting the other brother or sister. Or, two or three of us would be in Mississippi for the Christmas or Thanksgiving holidays, or one or two would be there together for a week in the summers. It was like we were always visiting each other or we were often together somewhere for a brief period. Plus, we have always kept in touch with each other on a regular basis. Every since the oldest brothers left home there has hardly been a month gone by that we have not talked to or heard from each other. It seems that we visit each other all the time because we have kept in such close touch.

Somehow, the girls decided that we needed to have a family reunion in the Summer of 1976. One of the reasons was that some of them had children that the others had never seen by then, and Grandpa Richard was getting far along in his years as was Mama Lela and the girls wanted him to see all of the great grandchildren before he passed away or became deathly ill. They planned for us to all gather in Mississippi for a family reunion in July 1976, which we did. All of the brothers and sisters made it except Brother Charles, who sent his oldest son, Chucky, in his stead. Being a trucker, summer has always been Charles' busiest time of the year; that is when truckers try to make all of their money for the year just in case the weather is bad enough during the winter to not be on the road as much.

In the Summer of 1977, Mozell and I returned to Mississippi in early June to spend the summer. As a result of us having the family reunion the summer before, I had gotten interested in learning more about our family history and the history of black settlement in Jasper County. In the course of having the family reunion and attempting to explore our family's history, it occurred to me and the rest of the family how little any of us knew about our grandparents, and even our parents' history for that matter. That's how I decided during that academic year that I would do my doctoral dissertation on the history of settlement and racial residential segregation in the county.

This would also allow me the opportunity to explore as much as I could about our family's history in the county at the same time.

So in the Summer of 1977 we came home to spend the summer with mom and dad. I worked with dad and George building houses several days during the week and I would do my research, conduct the surveys, and collect the other necessary data during the other parts of the week. During that summer I traveled every main road and back road in Jasper County. I found roads and houses in the county I never knew existed and talked to people whom I never knew even lived in Jasper County. I also learned a lot about our family, but I also learned that there was much more that I nor anybody else would ever get a chance to know because all those who knew were either dead and gone or had forgotten.

When we arrived in Mississippi, mama was in Connecticut visiting and assisting Brenda who had just had her second child, a son whom she named Asim. Mama must have been gone for two weeks before she returned. Shortly after we arrived and just a few days after mama returned from Connecticut, Mama Lela died suddenly of a heart attack. There were no apparent warning signs, and she had not suffered any recent illness; it was just the toll and toils of the years that finally caused her to succumb. Since it was such a sudden thing, none of the family who were at a great distance away came. Just mom and dad, George and Agnes, and Mozell and me were the only members of our family who attended the funeral. Of course, Aunt Caroline was there because of Grandpa Richard having to be there; she never had much to do with "Ms Lela" as she always referred to Mama Lela.

By the end of the Summer of 1978 I had completed most of the work on my doctoral dissertation and had completed the draft of my dissertation. Mozell and I had decided to return to Jackson where I had agreed to a position back at Jackson State University. Actually, I came back to Jackson State because they offered me the best salary of any of the offers for positions that I received. Being in graduate school for four years I had accumulated some debts, so I needed to make as much money as I possibly could. So we bought a nice house in Jackson and came back.

In October 1978, just two months after we had settled back in Jackson, Grandpa Richard died. After Mama Lela died in 1977 Aunt Sis had brought him to live with her and her husband, Uncle Sandy. She had married him after Uncle Cap had died in 1974 while we were living in Jackson before. One reason Aunt Sis had married Mr. Sandy Davis was because after Uncle Cap died, the white man on whose place she and Uncle Cap had lived all those years decided she could no longer live on the place. Just about the time she was about to be evicted, Uncle Sandy came along. He had recently lost his wife and was looking for a "biscuit cooker" as he would call it. His and Aunt Sis' marriage was one of mutual benefit and consent; he found a "biscuit cooker" and she found a place to live. Both of them were into their elderly years; well over 60 years old and probably in their early seventies.

Of course all of the family came home for Grandpa Richard's funeral. It was like a family reunion and family homecoming all over again. In fact, his funeral was a bigger family reunion than the one we had in 1976 because all of our uncles and aunts and cousins who were living made it to the funeral. And although Aunt Sis and Uncle Sandy had a small and simple house way out in the middle of the woods, we all gathered at their house after the funeral for a great potluck dinner. At Grandpa Richard's funeral we started a family tradition that continues and shall continue for as long as a Lang lives and dies. Brother George lead the song "God Has Smiled On Me" which was written and recorded by the late Reverend James Cleveland, one of the greatest gospel singers of all times. We decided after Grandpa Richard's funeral to make that our family anthem and vowed that it would forever be sung at any Lang's funeral that any of us attended, and we would pass it on as a legacy to our posterity forever.

After Mama Lela died, Aunt Sis brought Grandpa Richard to live with her. Although Mama Lela's children and grandchildren had always looked up to him as their surrogate father, and he was the only grandfather that their children had ever known, the place they lived on belonged to her. When she died her daughter who lived next door and her daughters who lived close by vowed they would continue to see after grandpa. Aunt Sis said then that would not be the case, but they wanted it to be that way. A couple months later grandpa got sick and there was nobody there to look after him every day. That was when Aunt Sis went and got him and brought him to live with her and Uncle Sandy.

Grandpa Richard was content and did not object to the move. Although he was old he was still in his sound mind and could still get around relatively well. There was nothing wrong with his mind, it was his physical body that was worn out. One evening in that October he was sitting in a rocking chair watching television and nodding. He just nodded right on away and never even made a sound. Aunt Sis was in an adjoining room sewing on her sewing machine. She missed his snoring and came in to see about him and he had just slept away without any pain or stress.

We didn't really know how old Grandpa Richard was when he died. Some speculated that he was over 100 years old, but nobody knew for sure. It was a few years later when checking his social security records that it was learned that, according to their records, he was 97 years old when he died in 1978. Therefore, he had been born in 1881, but there was no record of where he had been born since there was no birth certificate on record of his birth. We still believe he was older than that. Although his mental faculties were good until the end, by his later years he had forgotten when and where he was born.

Of course daddy and Uncle Reedus had to pay for Grandpa Richard's funeral and burial. He never had any means and certainly didn't have any when he died. Daddy and Uncle Reedus didn't hesitate and didn't ask anybody else to help. They simply got together and talked among themselves, came to an agreement and went to the funeral home and paid for the funeral and burial. Nobody else ever knew what it cost, how they split the costs and who decided on what. They included Aunt Sis in the discussion, but they didn't expect her to contribute anything because they knew she had nothing to contribute. She had contributed what she could when she had taken him to live with her and never asked them to contribute anything to that effort. Their agreement and commitment on matters of family was unspoken, unwritten and unquestioned.

Daddy and Uncle Reedus had to do the same thing when Aunt Sis died in 1989. When Aunt Sis had married Sandy Davis after Uncle Cap died, she admitted that it was a marriage of mutual convenience. He needed a wife and she needed somewhere to stay. She knew that she was about to be put off the white man's place where she and Uncle Cap had lived and worked for nearly 50 years. If Mr. Davis had not come along she would probably have wound up moving to Memphis to live with Cousin Purvis and his wife, or she would have wound up coming to live with daddy and mama. The latter would have most likely been the case because by that time Purvis' wife Neller Mae was bed-ridden from chronic deteriorating illness. His hands were full just seeing after her as he had retired to do so.

Aunt Sis and Uncle Cap had lived their entire lives and never owned so much as an acre of land, and certainly had not even earned a pension since neither of them had ever worked publicly. Uncle Cap never held a job at anything, and Aunt Sis had mainly supported them through her sewing which she did for both whites and blacks. She had continued to support herself with her sewing after she married Mr. Davis as he was just a dirt farmer still trying to make a living by raising and selling a few cows and hogs on his farm of 40 acres more or less.

A month or so before Aunt Sis died she had become severely ill. I still don't know what was the cause of her illness other than old age and years of neglect of her health looking after others, both Grandpa Richard and Uncle Cap. Nevertheless, when she became ill she stayed home until one day mama called just to check on her, not knowing that she was severely ill. After mama talked to her on the phone and found she was so severely ill she informed daddy and they went to see about her. By this time mama's health had started to fail as well and she was not fully able to see after herself let alone somebody else who was deathly ill.

Anyway, when daddy and mama got to Aunt Sis' and Uncle Sandy's house they found her in bed where she had been for several days. To complicate matters, the house and especially the kitchen were unsanitary and she had eaten something that Uncle Sandy had fixed the week before that was evidently spoiled. Thus, on top of her main illness she undoubtedly had food poisoning as well. Daddy helped her get dressed and immediately took her to Bay Springs to the hospital. They were living a few miles west of Rose Hill and a good 25 miles from Bay Springs. She was immediately hospitalized and stayed there for several weeks. Every day daddy and mama would go to the hospital twice a day to see about her. During the whole time she was there Mr. Davis came to see her only once in three weeks.

When Aunt Sis was released from the hospital daddy insisted that she come home with him and mama until she was back on her feet, which was never to be. She agreed and came home with them, but after a few days she insisted on going home. Still, Mr. Davis had not seen fit to come and visit her, or even to inquire as to where she was. To comply with her wishes, daddy called Mr. Davis and explained to him what the situation was and that he was bringing her home which he did. Mr. Davis' fear evidently was about the expenses of her hospitalization and whether he would be liable for the bills. However, the hospital had made arrangements for her hospital bill to be taken care of by Medicare or Medicaid.

Daddy knew that her condition was such that her chances of overcoming her illness and being able to function on her own again were slim. But he wanted her to be as content as she could be in her last days, so every day he and mama would go and spend the day with her and make sure that she was taken care of and had decent meals to eat. Mama was weakening herself as her health was failing her, but she stuck with daddy every step of the way. Eventually Aunt Sis passed away after a week or so and daddy was there at her side as she was back in the hospital when she expired. Mr. Davis was nowhere to be seen.

Daddy, Uncle Reedus and Cousin Purvis put the money together to give Aunt Sis a decent burial. When they caught up with Mr.

Davis a day or two before the funeral he was home dead drunk. They sought to discuss the funeral arrangements with him, but he was both defensive and adamant. Daddy didn't expect him to pay for her funeral after the way he had avoided coming around while she was in the hospital. When they asked him if he wanted to contribute anything toward her burial, his reply was, "that's y'all's sister and mother, y'all can bury her if you want to." Cousin Purvis was ready to beat him to death, but daddy and Uncle Reedus restrained him and wouldn't let him touch the man.

Cousin Purvis didn't want to allow the man to come to Aunt Sis' funeral, but daddy and Uncle Reedus insisted that he would be allowed to come to the funeral and would be respected if he showed up. I remember at the funeral it took Brother George, Uncle Reedus, Brother Otha and me to restrain Cousin Purvis from beating Mr. Davis to death. As soon as the funeral program was over, Mr. Davis high-tailed himself away from the church and we never saw or heard from him again as long as he lived.

XXI. GOLDEN ANNIVERSARY

In 1984, the sisters decided it was time to have another family reunion since we had not all gotten together in one place since Grandpa Richard's funeral in 1978. In addition, January 1985 would be the 50th Anniversary of daddy's and mama's marriage and the sisters decided it would be an appropriate gesture to have a big celebration for them which would include a rededication of vows in a wedding ceremony since they never had one when they were originally married. All the family members agreed we would share the expense of sponsoring the banquet that was planned for the evening following the ceremony. The major concern was how would we get daddy to agree to participate. We left that task to the sisters since they had always been able to get him to do most anything they asked. Over the years he had flown or taken the train to Connecticut to participate in Brenda's and Bobbie's weddings, which he felt he had to do since he had done the same for Walterene when she was originally married.

So with the plans all set and everything in order, the family gathered in Bay Springs at Christmas time in December of 1984. Just about all of the family members, including grandchildren and great grandchildren, cousins, aunts and uncles living on both sides, cousins on both side, and numerous family friends and well wishers were all there. It was to be a joyous time and another celebration to be remembered as well as a first of a kind event for Bay Springs. The sisters, especially Brenda and Bobbie along with Brother Otha, spared no expense in planning the event to the finest details. The ceremony itself would be held at Blue Mountain Church with an open reception to follow in the church's fellowship hall immediately after the ceremony.

I don't remember on what day Christmas fell in 1984, but I do remember the ceremony and banquet were held on the Saturday afternoon and evening. At the time, both daddy and mama were in good health except for a bit of arthritis. While their steps had gotten shorter and they had both slowed down a bit, they were still able to participate fully in most activities they decided to. At the time Mozell and I were living in the suburb of Oxon Hill, Maryland just outside Washington, DC where we had moved in the June of 1984. Our children, Martin and Maya, were the youngest of the grandchildren and were 4 and 1 years old respectively.

Reverend J.W. Crosby who is now deceased, and who had been over the years one of daddy's closest friends in the ministry was invited to perform the rededication of vows ceremony. The ceremony was beautiful and gracious with all the brothers and daddy dressed in tuxedos and the sisters in formal dresses serving as ushers, attendants and hosts. The sisters had bought mama a lovely golden formal dress for the occasion which was simply elegant. I had never in my life seen my mother look so good and be so proud of herself and her family. Charles who is the oldest brother was the best man and Walterene the oldest sister was the maid of honor. The banquet was planned for just the immediate family, uncles and aunts, cousins and closest friends of mama and daddy. It was held in the ballroom of the Ramada Inn hotel in Laurel.

On that Christmas day we had a buffet dinner at the house where all of the family could come and share the meal at different times during the afternoon. We were staying at the Ramada Inn in Laurel since there was not enough room for all of us to stay either at daddy's and mama's house or at Brother George's and Sister Agnes' house. During the mealtime, several of us were shocked while sitting at the table enjoying conversation after eating. Daddy all of a sudden got up from the table and took his plate with him over to the sink in the kitchen. He raked the scraps from his plate into the garbage can sitting nearby and went to the sink and began fixing dishwater and washed his plate. Upon noticing what he was doing, all of a sudden the room grew quiet and everybody focused on daddy. I was sitting there, as I was sure the others were, wondering what was wrong with daddy. I thought he had gotten mad about something or with somebody sitting at the table and would start into an angry rage just as soon as he finished washing his dishes.

After daddy finished, Brenda walked over to him and asked if anything was wrong. He said no there was nothing wrong, why did she think anything was wrong. We all breathed a collective sigh of relief. In all our years none of us had ever seen daddy get up from the dinner table and so much as take his dishes to the sink. It was unthinkable that he would wash a dirty dish. Hence, we thought he had gotten mad with somebody or something that had been said at the table and was fixing to go into a rage.

Once again we realized how much daddy had changed over the years, and how times had changed. When we further inquired of him he indicated that as he and mama were getting older and she was no longer able to do all the chores around the house so he had begun to wash the dishes and even to fix some of the meals in recent years to help out around the house. The joy we felt was unimaginable.

After that fiftieth anniversary celebration, it became our custom to have a family reunion in Bay Springs every two years around Christmas time. We continued this tradition until mama died in 1996. After that nobody has really been in the spirit of having a reunion since we have been called together on some sad occasion at least once every two years since then.

XXII. EXPERIENCING THE SUPERNATURAL

When we celebrated daddy's and mama's golden anniversary we all came to realize just how blessed we had been over our lives and just how fortunate we had been to have our parents live so long and in fairly good health. Throughout our years we had never really had any chronic illness or sickness in our family. Everyone's children had been born healthy, and none of our siblings had ever had a miscarriage or an infant die in childbirth or at an early age. We had never lost a sibling and had only had a few untimely deaths among aunts and uncles and close relatives. That would begin to change much faster than any of us had ever expected.

In the meantime, we enjoyed getting together to have a reunion every two years and visiting with each other on occasion in between if we happened to be traveling somewhere nearby. By the late 1980's and certainly by the early 1990's we realized that our parents were getting to the point where they would no longer be able to carry on as they had in the past. They were getting toward their late seventies in age and certainly mama's health was beginning to decline. We came to realize this more and more as we would visit them during the years. Mama has always kept an immaculate house and although she could be somewhat junky, she loved cleanliness. But we began to notice that each time one of us would visit, the house would be less tidy than before and dust would have accumulated more each time.

It had gotten to the point that each time one would visit, the first thing that would have to be done would be to give the house a good cleaning inside and out. Mama had gotten to the point where the chores of cleaning, mopping and dusting, along with washing and ironing, folding and putting away clothes, and even cooking big meals as she had always done had become too much. Occasionally she would mop the kitchen and bathroom floors and would get daddy to do one or the other on occasions, but consistently the house was becoming too much for them to manage by themselves.

It was around the late 1980's or early 1990's that we started trying to persuade daddy and mama to let us have somebody come in at least once or twice a month to clean the house thoroughly for them. We wanted to relieve them of that duty and try to make it easier for them to live in comfort, but they would hear nothing of it. They swore they could manage on their own and were managing on their own; they could not realize what we were realizing and would not admit that they needed help. That is the way of most elderly parents I guess; to admit that they need help is to admit that they are getting older and less able to manage their affairs. Our parents were no different than others in this regard, and the more we would talk about it the more upset and obstinate they would become at the thought that they needed help.

It was around the Spring of 1992 that we came realize that we would have to make a decision to get someone to come in and provide help for dad and mom regardless of their thoughts on the matter. Brother Otha was visiting them during the Easter holiday or during his spring break as often he would during that time of the year. Fortunately he was home at that time. During the past year or so mama had gotten to where she would have a black-out occasionally every two or three months. Her heart was weakening and when she would have episodes of weakness she would become semi-conscious or unconscious. Luckily, she had never injured herself as daddy, Brother George or Agnes would be with her at most times.

But during this time while Brother Otha was there visiting mama had a black-out and fell in the bathroom and broke her wrist. He and daddy rushed her to the hospital and her arm was incapacitated in a cast, and would remain that way for four to six weeks. Brother Otha knew then that some arrangements would have to be made for somebody to come several days a week at least to look after mama and daddy and to cook and clean for them. He called several of us brothers and sisters that very day and got our input on what he saw that needed to be done and how he should go about doing it. We decided collectively that we would each pitch in enough money to help cover the costs of hiring somebody to come in. That part was easy; the hard part was finding somebody reliable in the area that they would trust to come into their home and provide such help.

Brother Otha had two or three days that he could spend there to try and get the arrangements made for their assistance. He called around to people he knew and got suggestions of names of people who might be available and willing to come in and do what needed to be done for mama and daddy. There were not many and even fewer whom they felt comfortable with. Finally mama thought of Mrs. Winnie Cook who was one of daddy's church members at Pleasant Grove Church where he had been pastoring for over 20 years. Her husband whom everybody knew as "Fat Sam" was the head deacon at the church as well. Mrs. Cook had done domestic work most of her life, but always for white folks as had most of the black domestic workers in the county. Hardly ever had black folks hired domestic help, and rarely had other blacks worked for black folks as domestic workers in the county. We knew it would be hard to find a black person who would agree to work as a domestic worker for another black family. That had not been the way of the South throughout history. Again, the Lang family was about to break new ground in Jasper County and start a trend that would prove to be a benefit for many other families to follow.

Brother Otha immediately got on the telephone and contacted Mrs. Cook and her husband and had them to come to the house that very evening to discuss the matter with them and to seek an agreement. He knew Mrs. Cook from the times he had visited the church over the years on visits home, and he had known her earlier in life as they had been in school together during their high school years. They came to the house that evening and before Brother Otha left to return to his home in Illinois he had an agreement with Mrs.

Cook. She would begin coming three days a week the very next week. The timing was perfect as she was between jobs and was looking for another. She was delighted to come and look after mama and daddy as she was like a surrogate daughter to them anyway. Her mother had been deceased for a number of years and she had admired mama and had great respect for daddy. She was the one person mama and daddy could unequivocally agree to allow to come into their home and look after them without hesitation.

It was a great relief for the whole family to have somebody coming in to see after mama and daddy. It was a great relief for Brother George and Sister Agnes because it took some of the strain off them of having to check on them almost daily. It gave us all comfort knowing that there was somebody making sure they had decent meals cooked every day, and that the house was clean and sanitary and that their clothes were being washed and taken care of so that when they went out they were decent. We were so thankful that Mrs. Cook had agreed to take the job. We could all sleep a little easier every night knowing that our parents were being looked after on a regular basis.

It was also during this time after mama had fallen and broken her wrist that we all made an unconscious effort to visit her and dad as often as we could. Every chance either of us got we would go and spend a few days, if no more than two or three days at the time. I had the most flexibility as I could take off whenever it pleased me, so I made it my business to go to Mississippi every two or three months for three to four days just to check on mom and dad and to make sure they were all right. I did that for four years, and mostly I drove by myself from Michigan. It was something I felt compelled to do.

As fate would have it and as God would divinely arrange it, in the spring of 1993 a good friend of mine had a 1989 Mercedes Benz 300SE, the large body Mercedes vehicle, that he had leased for four years and was about to turn in. He offered me the chance to take over the lease of the vehicle with the option to buy it. I could lease it for the remaining three months on his lease and then I could buy it outright; which I did. The car only had 45,000 miles on it and it was virtually like new. I bought the car and for three years I drove it back and forth to and from Mississippi to see my parents every two or three months.

Sometimes, if he were off or if he could get away, I would go through Illinois and Brother Otha would go to Mississippi with me. Or Sister Walterene would ride down with me if she could get away. In the meantime, Sisters Brenda and Bobbie would go down from Connecticut, and Brother Claude and his wife Berdia would go down from Connecticut as often as they could. Brother Charles would stop in while passing through the area, or if he were off and had the time he would drive from New Mexico to see about them.

It was in April 1994 that Sister Walterene and I went down to Mississippi together for a visit. I had to attend a conference in New Orleans and she had a week off at the same time, so we decided to drive down together. It just happened to be our luck that mama was going into the hospital for a few days during the time we were going to be there. Since Sister Walterene had been working as a surgical nurse for a few years by then, it was a blessing that she was going to be able to go so she could ask the doctors all the right questions about mama's condition while she was in the hospital.

While mama was in the hospital during that week the doctors ordered a series of tests to determine just what was the condition of her heart and other organ functions. Her doctor had thought that she had some blockages in her arteries that were causing her to have the black-outs. These tests would allow for some certainty as to her condition. What they found was that mama had an abdominal tumor and she had a small brain tumor at the front of her brain, and of course her heart was failing gradually just from old age.

The doctors offered several options; they could operate and remove the abdominal tumor, but there was a fifty-fifty chance that her heart was not strong enough for her to fully recover from the surgery. That was a chance she would have to decide to take. The possibility of operating to remove the brain tumor was even riskier, as the doctors felt confident that her heart was not strong enough to even make it through that surgery. Mama decided that she would have neither. That was the end of that discussion.

When we learned the extent of her condition, and when she had made her decision to not have surgery which we knew was the best decision, we fully realized that mama was on the decline and that her time would not be long. We didn't know exactly how long and the doctors could only make a prognosis based on the rapidity of the growth of the tumors. It became our goal to help make her as comfortable as possible for the remainder of her time and to see that she didn't want for anything that we could possibly provide. Daddy had long stopped building houses and had worked with George during the last years that he had done carpentry work. George had stopped contracting around 1989 as the business had slowed so much and the competition had become so stiff that it was no longer profitable to contract to build houses in that area. He had taken a job as the vocational building trades instructor with the Smith County Public Schools in Raleigh, and daddy had come home to be with mama every day to look after her when her health had first started to fail.

During the years of mama's failing health Brother George and Sister Agnes had become the anchors of mama's and daddy's well-being. They had assumed the roles of caretakers and advisors. Hardly a day went by that one of them or both didn't go by to check on them or call if other obligations kept them from visiting. Mrs. Cook really took charge on a day-to-day basis seeing that mama and daddy had decent food to eat everyday. Even on those days that she didn't come to the house she would leave enough cooked from the previous day. Often she would even leave the plates already fixed so that all daddy had to do was to put the plates in the microwave and heat the food for the lunch and dinner meals. He could fix whatever needed to be fixed for breakfast with mama giving him instructions.

By the fall of 1994 we began to notice that daddy's memory was beginning to fail him and his capacities were declining rapidly. We noticed that in his conversations he had begun to repeat questions and sometimes would go over the same parts of the conversation he had stated before. He was still pastoring the two churches, but his effectiveness both in preaching and in leadership had seriously eroded. Our concern became heightened when upon a few occasions Brother George had reported that daddy had shown up at the wrong church on the wrong Sunday. When he needed to be at the church in Moss he had gone to the one in Laurel. He was beginning to show signs of confusion and forgetfulness. We knew it was time for him to give up trying to pastor the churches, but neither we nor the church officials knew how we would get him to resign. This became our newest struggle.

All along mama had continued to go to church with him each Sunday when she felt any way good enough to do so. By the summer of 1994, however, her condition had become so fragile that it was necessary to have somebody stay with her on Sundays while daddy went to church. Sometimes either George or Agnes would go and stay with her after they left church service at Blue Mountain until daddy came home in the afternoon. Although mama's physical health was failing her mental condition remained strong and she thus became the mind for both she and daddy and he provided the physical strength for both of them.

I still don't know how he did it, but sometime during late 1994 and early 1995 George talked daddy into resigning from the churches. He had tried to get the officers of the church to ask daddy to step aside, but out of respect and loyalty they had declined because he had been with both churches so long, they just couldn't bring themselves to asking him to quit. They felt it would be an act of betrayal and insult. But Brother George always had a way of getting daddy to concede when nobody else could. I guess it was because George had been there with them so long and they had always relied on him as a pillar of support as everybody else in the family had for so many years. When George talked, usually everybody in the family listened, even daddy.

When daddy did resign from the churches there was no fanfare and no big celebration or program, he simply told the churches he felt it was time and because of mama's condition it had become necessary for him to devote his undivided time and energy to her. He thanked the churches for all their years of support in a final worship service at each one and quietly retired to mama's side to provide her daily assistance along with Mrs. Cook. It was a few months before the family knew he had given up the churches. We were all glad because we knew it had become dangerous for daddy to try to drive back and forth during weeknights as his eyesight and his memory had both gotten very bad. We rejoiced that nothing had happened to him during the months before he resigned. On several occasions he had lost his way just trying to get from town back home during the day when he had become confused, or had a memory lapse. Several people had reported to George that daddy had stopped them on the road to ask them for directions or to tell him where he was. We could only hope and pray, and God had answered our prayers so far.

Throughout the years of mama's illness daddy had become a totally different person than what we had known over the years. He had become her complete servant and handmaid. He showed sensitivity, compassion and concern that we never expected or would have believed. The devotion daddy displayed toward mama and her care was remarkable and was an inspiration to all of us and to those outside the family who knew them. He was constantly and daily by mama's side and was genuinely concerned that she had anything and everything that she thought she wanted or needed. He became to her what she had been to him for over 60 years.

By the late fall of 1995, mama's condition had reached the serious stages and she had become almost totally bed-ridden. The week after Christmas Sister Walterene and I had gone down to spend that week to give Brother George and Sister Agnes some relief. Her state of mind and health was such that we decided it was time to make some arrangements for mama to either be placed in a nursing home or at least be provided with 24-hour assistance at home. We knew that daddy was no longer going to be able to manage at nights by himself, and Walterene and I thought that it was going to be impossible for George and Agnes to provide them the assistance that would be needed. But George was insistent that he didn't want mama to go to a nursing home and that he would be able to spend the nights there with her and daddy so she could stay at home.

We even sought to have somebody to come in just to be there with mama and daddy at nights, but the cost of providing support to pay for that person and for Mrs. Cook during the days was more than anybody could afford out of pocket. Although George had made the arrangements for mama to go to a nursing home, he was not readily in agreement that she should go. He insisted on trying to manage it his way. So Walterene and I returned home after our week's visit not knowing what the outcome would be, but feeling assured that mama's situation had become grave. Hardly a week had passed after our return when we received the call from George informing us that he was looking seriously at putting mama in the nursing home as soon as they had a space available for her. He had tried staying at the house with her and daddy, but the strain of being up with her most of the nights and trying to go to work the next day was just too much; other arrangements had to be made. He had come to realize sooner than we thought he would that he would not be able to do what he desperately wanted to do; that was keep mama out of the nursing home.

By early February 1996, mama was placed in the Rolling Acres Retirement Center which is located just a few miles south of Raleigh in Smith County; just a mile or so from where George was working at the Vocational Education Center as the building trades instructor. George had wanted mama placed there so he could go by and visit her on his way to work in the mornings and on his way home in the afternoons. Some days he would go during his lunch hour and have lunch with her. From the first day mama went to the nursing home daddy began coming to visit her in the mornings and afternoons every day. He would keep up this routine for as long as mama remained there. It was amazing how he couldn't remember how to go anywhere else by himself with any certainty, but he would drive the twenty-five miles one-way to the nursing home and back twice a day without fail and without getting lost. Some days Mrs. Cook would go with him in the mornings on those days she was at the house, but with or without her daddy went every single day.

It was around the end of May 1996 before I was able to go back to Mississippi after mama was placed in the nursing home. When I arrived at the nursing home to visit her for the first time on my trip mama was somewhat responsive but only for a few minutes. In fact, she did something that I had never seen her do before. After we had been in the room with her for about fifteen minutes, she asked if we would leave her alone so she could get some rest. That was when it really dawned on me that my mother was deathly ill. For all of her years she had always been the most gracious host and accommodator. To see her ask guests to leave, even in her condition, to me was the surest signal of the real state of her health. She had become physically so weak that all she could do was to just lie there and whisper a few words; not really in conversation. When I left the nursing home that day I cried over her condition for the first time because I could sense in my heart and in my soul that her time was not long on this earth. I could feel her spirit drifting and I grieved in my spirit.

I really didn't want to go back to see mama before I left to return to Michigan. I just didn't want to see her in a sad condition again. I wanted to remember my mother as herself, always smiling and always wanting to see everybody around her in a pleasant mood. But I had to go back anyway, and so I did. But I didn't stay long; I went and prayed with her and then I left after a few minutes and headed back home. Off and on during the next month I was constantly on the phone with Brother George and with the other brothers and sisters keeping abreast of how mama was doing and of any changes in her condition. All of us were in our own way preparing ourselves for what we knew was sure to come, and by talking to each other constantly we were able to help each other to grieve and to comfort each other as much as possible as we prepared ourselves.

It was on the evening of the 30th of June that I received a call from Sister Agnes. Mozell had gone to Grand Rapids that evening for a work assignment that would keep her there for a few days. I had gone out to get something to eat and to visit with a friend for a while. When I returned home around 9:00 p.m. just as I sat down to read the newspaper, the telephone rang. Sister Agnes was calling to tell me that she had just left the hospital and that mama had taken a turn for the worse. In her groaning mama had been calling for me and asking why I was not there particularly and why weren't her children there to see about her. Sister Agnes said they had her moved from the nursing home to the hospital and if I could come. I didn't ask for details I just told her I would be leaving the next morning as soon as I could get packed, take care of a few business matters, and go to the bank and get some money I would be on my way.

I had to go to my office and take care of a few matters that evening; and I had to make some phone calls to make arrangements for others to cover some of my assignments that night as well. By the time I got to bed it was around 2:00 a.m. and I knew I had to be up early to finish packing and doing the other things I knew I had to do in order to be ready to get on the road as soon as the bank opened at 9:00 a.m. I went to bed but it was a while before I fell off to sleep; too many thoughts were racing through my mind. As badly as I hated to think about it, I couldn't help but think about the possibility of mama passing away before I could get there. I prayed and asked God to not let her go before I got there to see her alive one last time no matter what condition she was in.

 I awoke around 5:30 o'clock in the morning which was unusually early for me, especially during the summer months since I am officially off from work during the summers and don't have to keep regular hours. That summer, however, I was doing a bit of consulting training as well as some research and was going to the office regularly. When I arose that morning I laid in bed a few minutes contemplating what I had in front of me that day and the coming days before getting up to get started. As I was lying there I heard a voice speak to me as clearly as any voice I had ever heard, and it came from the hallway just outside my bedroom door. The voice said, "Lo I am with you always." When I heard that voice I was astounded and sat up straight in my bed. I knew there was nobody in the house beside me because both the children were away in summer programs and Mozell had spent the night in Grand Rapids.

 As I sat there on the side of my bed listening and trying to figure out where the voice had come from, it seemed that I heard somebody moving around in the kitchen downstairs. I thought maybe Mozell had decided to come back early that morning to see me off since I had called her the night before and told her about the call from Agnes and that I would be leaving in the morning heading to Mississippi. So I went downstairs to see if the movement was her coming into the house. But when I got downstairs there was nobody there. Again I was puzzled. I went back upstairs to the bedroom and went into the bathroom to relieve myself. As I sat on the toilet contemplating, I heard the same voice again speaking in the bedroom. This time I knew it was the Spirit of God speaking to me. Fear and trembling came over me as I sat there thinking how was I going to make that sixteen-hour trip to Mississippi that day all by myself on three hours of sleep. I knew what I had to do so I just sat there praying to God and saying Lord you must be with me for I can't make this journey without your help. I got up and took a shower, got dressed and began to do the things I needed to do to be packed and ready to go by the time the bank opened at 9:00.

It seemed I was moving in a daze, I was in awe of what I had experienced that morning, but somehow it didn't seem out of the ordinary even though it was the first time I had such an explicit spiritual experience. By the time the bank opened I was packed, had eaten some breakfast and was ready to go. I went by the bank and withdrew some money and hit the road heading to Mississippi.

It seemed I made it just fine that first hour of driving until I crossed the Michigan-Indiana state line which is eighty-one miles from Lansing. By the time I got just into Indiana I got so sleepy I could hardly keep my eyes open. I started to nod and to go into those phases where my eyes would be wide open but my mind would be tuned out. I knew I was in trouble and began to panic thinking about how late in the morning I was leaving, how far I had to go, and how late in the night I would be getting into Mississippi. Usually when I would leave for the drive to Mississippi I would always try to be on the road at least by 6:00 a.m. at the latest. That way I can usually be in Mississippi by 8 or 9:00 p.m. I really began to get scared and didn't know what I would do. At the first rest stop I came to, I pulled over and stopped. As I sat there with the engine of the car still idling all I could do was begin to pray. I asked God as fervently as I knew how to help me; I remembered the voice I had heard earlier that morning assuring me that He would be with me. I began to cry as I laid my head against the steering wheel.

As I was crying and praying I must have fallen asleep with my head against the steering wheel. I woke up about fifteen minutes later and felt fully refreshed. I felt as if I had just finished a good night's sleep of eight hours or more. It felt like something supernatural had suddenly come over me. I backed the car up and pulled out into the expressway with a new determination and a feeling of assurance that I could make the journey safely. I headed down the road with that Mercedes wide open. My determination was to be in Mississippi by midnight.

Gone to Hell This Morning

It was as bright and as sunny a day as I had ever seen. Of course it was the first day of July and as I headed south the temperature was soon in the mid-90's. All I could think about was my mother lying in a hospital bed moaning and groaning and the possibility that she would not be alive when I got there. I was driving eighty-five and ninety miles an hour with my eyes peeled to the road ever looking at the next oncoming car to see if it was the state trooper. I was lucky not to see one until I got into the hills of Kentucky. As I was about fifty miles out of Louisville around 2:00 o'clock in the afternoon I came around a curve doing about ninety or ninety-five and my radar detector immediately picked up the signal of a patrolman's radar.

I could see the trooper coming toward me on the other side of the expressway about a quarter-mile out; I knew he had me on his radar. I began to cut my speed down to the seventy miles an hour speed limit. I could see the trooper in my rearview mirror as he crossed the median and came up on my side of the highway about a quarter-mile behind me. I just knew he was going to stop me but I just kept driving at the speed limit; I never touched my brakes. He never put his patrol lights on but he kept following me at a distance for a few miles, then suddenly he speeded up and came after me in a hurry. My heart started beating fast and I began to sweat as he rushed up behind me; then all of a sudden he passed right by me. He never so much as even looked at me and just kept driving right on by me. He hurried down the road in front of me and took the next upcoming exit. As he did I breathed a sigh of relief and said a silent prayer. I just knew he was going to stop me and give me a ticket. I don't know why he passed me by and didn't so much as look my way, but I was thankful anyhow.

Practically the same thing happened to me when I got into Tennessee and was heading south out of Nashville a few hours later. I had stopped just south of Nashville at my favorite place along the way to have something to eat around mid to late afternoon. As I headed on toward Alabama through the hills section of southern Tennessee I came over a hill and there was a state trooper coming up on me seemingly driving as fast as I was around eighty-five or ninety miles an hour. He immediately picked me up on his radar and put his patrol lights on before he could even find a place to cross the median and get behind me. Again my heart started racing and I just knew I had a ticket coming. I let off the accelerator and let my speed come down to the seventy miles per hour speed limit and kept driving. Again the patrolman turned off his lights and followed me for a few miles until he reached the next exit. Then he too took the exit and I kept going.

By the time I reached the Tennessee-Alabama state line it was getting on toward eight or nine o'clock in the evening and I knew I had at least five or six more hours of driving ahead of me if I kept the pace I had been traveling all day. But I knew that when it got dark I would be getting sleepy and I would not be able to keep moving at that pace because I couldn't see far enough ahead or behind myself to keep driving at the speed I had been driving all day. Although I had been alert all day since I had stopped and prayed and took the brief nap in northern Indiana, I felt that as it got dark I would begin to get sleepy. I had about two hours to go before I reached Birmingham so I decided to call my sister Bobbie in Connecticut and get brother-in-law Randy's mother's phone number in the city and call her and maybe stop by her house and sleep for a few hours.

I called Bobbie and she assured me that it would be okay for me to stop by Mrs. Ellis' house in Birmingham to rest for the night. She even called her mother-in-law for me and called me back on my cell phone to let me know she would be expecting me around 10:00 p.m. which I figured would be my arrival time. That was the plan I would follow. As the sun was setting that evening I was still rolling along at my break-neck speed as long as I could see a distance in front of myself by natural light.

As I was heading south of Huntsville there was a long open stretch of highway where you can see for a few miles as you cross over the Tennessee River. When I got into that stretch I thought I was seeing clearly ahead of me, but out of nowhere came a state trooper all of a sudden coming toward me. My radar detector started beeping profusely as we passed each other on opposite sides of the expressway. I just knew for sure that this time my luck had run out and I was surely getting that speeding ticket I had been missing all day. I was just trying to make it to Birmingham and to Mrs. Ellis= house before it got too late and I got too tired.

Sure enough the trooper's car made a quick turn across the median and was heading back down the highway behind me with all haste. By then I had gotten my speed back down to the seventy miles an hour speed limit but I knew it was too late. All of a sudden as I was expecting the trooper to put on his flashing patrol lights to signal for me to pull over, the patrol car pulled out of the lane behind me and rushed to pass me by. The car was up beside me in no time and sped up as it went by with all haste. As it passed me by I looked over at the car but I could see nobody in it. I did a second take as it went on by; again I didn't see anybody behind the wheel. I couldn't believe my eyes or my senses. This was the strangest thing I had ever seen in my life. There was another car in front of me about three or four car lengths ahead. As the patrol car passed by that driver he also looked over at the patrol car and the next thing I knew that driver almost lost control of his car when he took a look into the patrol car. Evidently he must have seen the same thing that I did. By then my palms were sweaty; I was trembling and my mouth had gone dry. I was almost a nervous wreck. That patrol car just seemed to disappear into nowhere ahead of us in a few seconds and all of a sudden it seemed the darkness set in.

Until this day I still cannot believe what I saw or did not see. I still have not come to grips with whether I was over exhausted; whether my vision was overwhelmed by the transition from dusk to dark; or whether I truly experienced something supernatural. The only assurance I have of my sanity at that moment was the fact that the driver in front of me must have seen something very unusual in that patrol car as I did. I just wanted to hurry and get to Birmingham and get off the road so I could rest. I knew for sure I had no business trying to make it to Mississippi that evening.

When I arrived at Mrs. Ellis' house on Third Street in Birmingham she was expecting me and had some good food prepared for me and the guest bed ready. I arrived there at almost exactly 10:00 o'clock as I had anticipated. I ate and took a shower and prepared to lie down for the night after talking with Mrs. Ellis for a while. Before I went to bed I called my sister Bobbie in Connecticut to let her know I had arrived at her mother-in-law's house for the evening. I had to share my experiences of the day with her. I thought she would be shocked and amazed at what I was telling her, but to my surprise her reply was simply, "huh, that was just the Lord sending his angels to protect you and make you slow down and be careful." She also informed me that she and Sister Brenda had decided they would come to Mississippi also to be with mama, and to share in her witness with me while I was there. When I thought about what she had said about my events and experience of that day I had to agree with her for I realized that must have been what it was. What else could explain what happened to me that day?

XXIII. SORROW AND REJOICING

I awoke around 5:00 a.m. the next morning and immediately decided I would get up and get on the road again so I could be in Mississippi and get to the hospital as soon as I could that day. I got up and went to the restroom and washed up, then I got dressed and without waking Mrs. Ellis I eased out of the house and got on the road. I arrived in Bay Springs around 8:30 that morning after stopping in Meridian and having breakfast on the way. When I got home, daddy and Mrs. Cook were finishing breakfast and he was getting ready to go to the hospital in Raleigh where mama had been admitted. I got there just in time to drive him over there.

When we got to the hospital that morning, mama was in a semi-conscious state in which she would remain during the time I was there. We got to her room just as the nurses were getting her bed changed and getting her cleaned-up for the day. When they finished daddy and I walked into the room and over to her bedside. I took her hand in mine and began talking to her. She never opened her eyes, so I had to figure out a way to get her to let me know if she was hearing what I was saying or not. I asked her if she could hear me as I spoke to her to move her head or squeeze my hand. I could feel the slightest pressure coming from her hand on mine to let me know she could hear me.

Later that morning her doctor came to check on her and to instruct the nurses as to what he wanted them to do. I had the opportunity to question him about her condition, and so I did. He informed me that from the tests he had run the day before it seemed that the tumor in her head was putting pressure on her brain, causing the semi-consciousness and the deterioration of her functioning. But more seriously was the weakening of her heart. The overall summation was that her organs were shutting down gradually as her brain was getting less and less oxygen as her heart was deteriorating. At some point she could be put on oxygen, but even with that the prognosis was not good. I knew it was mama's wish that she would never be maintained for a long time in a vegetative state so I communicated that to the doctor as we talked.

After the doctor finished talking with us and had left from the reception area where we had been sitting with him, daddy turned to me and asked me what did I think. Did I think mama would recover and ever come home again? At that moment something came over me that I had never felt or realized before. It seemed that something spiritual had just occurred and had given me a revelation. All of a sudden it dawned on me that surely enough daddy was expecting mama to come home from the hospital well one day. I suddenly realized that he had not comprehended fully what the doctor had been saying for the last half hour. It was at that moment I came to realize that old age and senility were truly having a severe effect on my daddy. I just took him by the hand and said to him as gently as I could, "daddy, I don't think mama will be coming home soon, she is really sick this time."

I think it was the next day that Brenda and Bobbie made it home to Mississippi from Connecticut. When we had a chance to talk away from daddy I shared with them what the doctor had told me, and of course Brother George and Sister Agnes already knew what I had learned since being there. So we all got a chance to discuss the situation and we called the other brothers and sister to update them as well. Brother Claude and Sister Berdia were already making plans and would be in Mississippi in just a few days to spend some extended time since they were already retired.

We realized there was not much we could do at this point except seek to assure that our mother was kept as comfortable and as free of pain as she could be. On that day when the two sisters arrived until I left five or six days later, each day we would go to the hospital at least twice a day and spend several hours each time. We would

Gone to Hell This Morning

take turns holding mama's hand and talking to her; we would read some of her favorite scriptures from the Bible to her; we would sing some of her favorite songs and hymns to her softly; and we would say prayers constantly so she could hear them if she was hearing us at all. We could see the change in demeanor in her countenance and we could feel the comfort in our own spirits. We could tell she was in no pain and that she was content and at ease during the entire time. We also realized her time would not be long; but just how long we had no way of knowing.

I must have stayed in Mississippi about a week and the sisters stayed a few days longer than I did. Before I left, Brother Claude and Berdia arrived prepared to stay a few weeks until after the first Sunday in August when her annual family reunion was usually held. I returned to Michigan feeling and knowing in my heart that it would not be long before I would be going back to Mississippi. The feeling I had as did all of my brothers and sisters was not a good feeling, but it was a sorrow we had to bear. The only comfort we had was each other and that of knowing that at least we had time to prepare ourselves for the worst. Our greater concern now was about daddy and his condition and how all of this would affect him. In spite of it all he continued to drive back and forth to the hospital twice a day when there was nobody there to drive him. Luckily now there was somebody there practically everyday which was a relief because there was no way to keep him from going and we all knew that. Daddy, just like the rest of us, did what he felt and knew he had to do; and as dangerous as we thought it was for him to be driving at all, there was no way to stop him.

When I returned home to Michigan I kept a daily vigil of calling to Mississippi every day to check on mama's condition. She stayed in the hospital at Raleigh for two or three weeks and then was transferred to another regional hospital in the town of Magee which is located about 45 miles southwest of Raleigh in Simpson County. Since Brother Claude and Sister Berdia were there and staying in the house with daddy, they would take him back and forth every day to Magee, or Brother George would take him in the evenings when he got off work. They also kept everyone in the family informed of mama's condition which didn't change much from day to day.

On the evening of August 7, 1996, Mozell, Martin, Maya and I were up until late that night because we were having one of the worst thunderstorms in Lansing, Michigan that we could ever remember. It must have been raining about two or three inches an hour for several hours. The lightening was flashing so bright that you could see down the street for a block each time, and the thunder was so furious that it was impossible to sleep. So we were sitting together in the family room waiting for the storm to cease so we could go to bed. After the storm ceased and the children had gone to bed, I was busy mopping and cleaning up water in the lower level of our house where the sewer had backed up in the shower and washroom drains and was covering the floors on that level of the house. It must have been around 1:30 a.m. when the telephone rang. I knew in my heart that with it being that time of the night that the phone was ringing, it was not going to be good news no matter who was calling, whether it was local or long distance. Reluctantly I picked up the receiver.

It was my Sister Brenda calling to tell me that mama had died about a half hour earlier. Brother Claude had called her to let her know and asked her to call me. I was not surprised but rather stunned, for this was a call I had been expecting since I had left Mississippi a few weeks earlier. I guess I just felt numb; I really didn't know how to feel or what I was feeling. In a way I was relieved, but knowing my mother was dead was a strange feeling. My brothers Claude and George had been with her at the hospital when she expired as the hospital staff had called them earlier and requested that they come. They hadn't taken daddy with them because he was already asleep for the evening, and in his state of mind there was no need to disturb him.

I assured Brenda that we would begin immediately to make plans to head toward Mississippi the very next day, just as soon as I could get my family packed and ready to go. I made a few calls to other brothers and sisters, and then I went to bed to try and get some sleep, but sleep did not come right away. Mozell and I just lay in bed and talked for a while until we both must have just talked ourselves to sleep. It was already into the early morning hours when we finally got to bed, and we knew we had much to do the next day before we could get on the road to Mississippi. It wouldn't have taken much time if I were going by myself, or if just the two of us were going, but with all four of us having to get prepared to go together, I knew it would be a chore for us to be ready to leave even by noon.

It was important for me to get to Mississippi as soon as I could because the family was depending on me to play a major role in the funeral plans, especially since I had the obituary written and with me, and Brother George and I along with Brother Otha and Sister Brenda were coordinating the funeral program arrangements. It was a tremendous blessing that we had all of these already done, as it would have been difficult to handle these under the circumstances and the emotional state that all of us were in.

We managed to leave Lansing around 4:00 p.m. on that Thursday afternoon after getting the telephone call in the early hours of that morning of August 8th. I knew we wouldn't be able to drive very far, but I hoped we would be able to make it at least to Nashville, Tennessee where I had a good friend who had moved there with his family a year earlier. Perhaps if we could make it that far by around midnight we would spend the night with them. I called them to let them know we were on our way and to alert them in case we made it to Nashville. We drove to Indianapolis by 8:30 p.m. and stopped to have dinner. After we ate we all began to get sleepy and I knew I wouldn't be able to drive through the mountains of Kentucky and into Nashville as tired as I was feeling. When we got into Louisville, Kentucky around 10:30 p.m. I called my friends to let them know we were stopping for the night in Louisville.

We got a good night's sleep at the motel in Louisville and were able to be back on the road by 6:00 a.m. the next morning. By 2:30 p.m. that Friday afternoon we were in Bay Springs. When we arrived at daddy's house that afternoon Brothers George and Claude along with Sisters Agnes and Berdia were there with daddy. They had cooked dinner in anticipation of our arrival. We unpacked the car, ate dinner, and immediately headed to the funeral home to make the arrangements. We set the funeral for that Tuesday, August 13, 1996 at 11:00 a.m. George had checked with the other brothers and sisters to make sure that would give them enough time to arrive over the weekend and have Monday to rest.

On that Monday morning we had to decide where mama's final resting place would be in the community cemetery. Brother George had consulted with mama sometime before she became deathly ill about where she wanted to be buried in the cemetery. She had shown him the plot where she wanted to be laid. But daddy was unaware of this arrangement. And in his emotional state of stress and with his confusion associated with the early stages of Alzheimer's which was beginning to set in, he was in total disagreement. He somehow decided that the whole cemetery was unfit for mama to be buried in and that she should be buried in the front yard of the home place which to the rest of us was totally out of the question. We had to convince him that it was illegal to bury someone there without the plot being designated a cemetery by both the county and the state. It took Brothers George and Charles along with the funeral director, Jesse Crosby, who was a long time friend of the family and one of George's closest personal friends to definitively declare that what daddy was talking about would definitely not happen. Daddy almost went off, but somehow the girls were able to calm him down and convince him that what the brothers were telling him was the best thing. He finally consented to go along with the plans.

On that Monday evening at 7:00 p.m. we held a family hour and visitation at the funeral home. From around 6:30 o'clock until after 9:00 p.m. people never stopped coming into and through the funeral home. There a line four people wide that stretched out into the parking lot continuously. And there were more flowers in the funeral home than anybody could ever remember seeing at any funeral in that area. We knew that mama was well respected in that area, but the outpouring of people at the visitation that evening and for the funeral the next day really showed just how many lives she had touched with her kindness and generosity.

We had mama's funeral that Tuesday morning at 11:00 a.m. at Blue Mountain Church there in the Rock Hill Community where she had labored diligently and faithfully for many years and in numerous capacities. When we arrived at the church in the family procession the small church and the adjoining fellowship hall were fully packed as was the yard of the church. Cars were lined up on both sides of the roads leading to the church for at least a half-mile in every direction. Although people knew they would not be able to get inside the church they just wanted to be there to show their respect and support. The funeral was a rejoicing celebration of mama's life and service to the community rather than a sorrowful occasion. Brother Otha gave a resounding tribute on behalf of the family which highlighted mama's life and her faithfulness. Brother George sang a stirring rendition of her favorite song, and the family together sang a medley of some of her favorite songs with Bobbie's oldest son, Randy, playing an accompaniment on his saxophone. It sounded like an angelic choir was singing indeed. Mama would have been proud and would have rejoiced, which I'm sure she did in spirit.

After mama's funeral we all left Mississippi and returned to our separate homes knowing that soon different arrangements would have to be made for daddy. We knew he was no longer capable of staying by himself, but trying to convince him of that was a chore for which none of us were up to right away. Brother George assured us that he would be looking after him and Mrs. Cook would be there with him during the days. Just weeks after mama's funeral the evidence of daddy's declining mental health became evident. It was obvious that he was depressed and confused, and that his memory loss was becoming worse. For one thing, daddy had a severe loss of appetite and for the next several months he loss a significant amount of weight. Then he started getting his sleep times mixed up. Brother George reported to us that some mornings daddy would be at his house around 3:00 or 4:00 a.m. thinking it was time to be up and about. Often he would even show up at George's house in the middle of the night thinking it was either early evening or early morning.

Brother George knew then that the best thing was to try to get daddy to stay with him and Agnes. They started picking him up in the evenings and bringing him home with them to have dinner and spend the nights. But in the mornings when they left for work they had to take him back home. He refused to stay at their house during the days, even though Mrs. Cook would be there with him. For a while we were afraid we were going to lose daddy, he had lost so much weight and was so frail and depressed; but he hung on. He finally got into a routine of staying with George and Agnes at night and going back home and spending the days with Mrs. Cook. After six or eight months that routine seemed to work well and daddy had gotten fairly content with that arrangement as long as he could be at home and in the Rock Hill Community.

XIV. WAITING AT THE END

We had no way of knowing just how tentative the situation would be with daddy being in the state of mind that he was. Brother George kept us informed of his condition as he and Sister Agnes noticed just how rapidly daddy's memory was failing, even though his health was improving. Still it was becoming increasingly difficult to reason with him and to keep him under control. He still wanted to be totally in charge of his life and to determine daily his own destiny. George and Agnes seemed to be managing the situation very well, but nobody can ever fully understand a situation unless you are there on a daily basis. Between them and Mrs. Cook they managed somehow to keep daddy off the road in his car as much as possible. Mrs. Cook would drive him to town or wherever he wanted to go during the day when she was with him. Some days she would even suggest they go for a ride just to keep the desire of driving and going out of his mind.

Still those of us who were not there on a daily basis could not fully appreciate just how stressful it must have been dealing with the constant monitoring of daddy's daily actions. I had an opportunity to observe the situation firsthand in August 1997 when I went to visit for a few days. It had been almost a year since mama had died and I had not been back to Mississippi since then. Never in my life had I ever been away from the home place more than a year without visiting my mother and daddy. So I decided that before a year was up I would go and visit, which I did that first week of August just before the anniversary date of mama's death. Being there for those four or five days I could see the difficulty George and Agnes were facing trying to keep daddy in check and trying to keep him from doing something detrimental. I could tell they needed a break, but I didn't know how and could not convince them that they did. During early June after Sister Agnes had gotten out of school for the summer, they had gotten somebody to stay with daddy and they had taken a few days and gone to visit Brother Otha and Sister Walterene in Illinois.

As I was leaving from my visit in Mississippi, George promised he was coming to visit me in Michigan over the Labor Day weekend as he had never visited me since we had returned to Michigan in 1986. I welcomed his visit and assured him that we would be expecting him to come. I assumed that he would be bringing Agnes with him and maybe even daddy, but he came by himself. We were glad to host George over that weekend and we invited Otha and Jeanette to come and spend the weekend also. They all went to church with us that Sunday morning and we had a big cookout and invited a number of friends to come and spend the afternoon having dinner and fellowship with us.

Brother George enjoyed himself and seemed at ease. That Sunday evening Otha and I sat a long time with him on the patio talking about the situation with daddy and trying to help him sort through the things he needed to be planning for in terms of daddy's long-term care. From the conversation we had it seemed that eventually other arrangements would need to be made such as admitting daddy to the nursing home. Yet again George was committed to keeping him out of the nursing home as long as possible.

When George left for Mississippi early that Monday, Labor Day morning, we had no way of knowing it would be the last time we would see him alive and in good health. We had questioned him about his and Sister Agnes' health as we talked with him that evening on the patio. We had admonished him to be sure to look after himself, and that he and Agnes needed to take some time for themselves by getting somebody to look after daddy for some weekends while they got away from the situation for a break together occasionally. Or let one of us know and we would come and give them a break whenever we had some time off from work. He assured us that he was looking after his own health and taking care of himself. We were worried because we knew he had problems with his blood pressure in the past and we wanted to feel assured that he was doing what he needed to do to keep it under control.

I remember talking to George the weekend after Thanksgiving when he was telling me about the severe pain he was having in his leg. I told him he should see the doctor about it and he assured me that he would see his doctor soon the next week. I talked to him a week or so later and the leg was still bothering him, but he had not seen the doctor. Again I urged him to see the doctor as soon as possible, and again he assured me that he would.

When Christmas came, Mozell and I along with our children packed our things and headed to South Carolina to visit her mother for a few days. We must have gotten to South Carolina on that Monday and Christmas Day was on that Thursday. That Wednesday evening, which was Christmas Eve, I decided to call my brothers and sisters to wish them a Merry Christmas as I usually did in recent years. I called Brother Otha in Illinois first that evening probably just because he and I are closer than the others. When he answered the telephone and determined it was me calling he breathed a sigh of relief. He was so glad I had called because he was wondering how he was going to get in touch with me. I could tell something was wrong.

Sister Agnes had called him earlier to let him know that George was in the hospital. In fact, she had called him from the hospital. George had a stroke that afternoon while visiting with his good friend, J.C. Crosby. What had happened was that while George was with J.C. he had experienced some numbness in the leg that had been bothering him. J.C. had brought him home and luckily Agnes was there cooking for Christmas dinner. She had dropped everything and put George in the car and taken him to the emergency room at the hospital in Laurel, over twenty miles away. It was the closest hospital with an emergency room since the one in Bay Springs had been closed several years before. Why J.C. didn't rush him to the hospital and call Agnes to meet them there we still don't know.

After talking to Otha I called the hospital and finally got Agnes on the phone and talked to her. She told me what had happened and indicated that it had been a severe stroke. They had managed to get George stabilized, but he had some paralysis on the right side and his speech was slurred. She didn't yet know just how bad the stroke was totally, but she was worried that it was worse than she could really tell. Her concern was also about daddy as she had left him with their son Adrian who was home from college where he was attending Mississippi State University. Luckily Adrian was at home for Christmas and had not gone away to visit with his girlfriend for the holidays. I assured Agnes that I would stay in close touch with her the next few days and would be making some arrangements to come there directly from South Carolina, or take Mozell and the children back to Michigan and come there immediately depending on what George's condition would be the next day or two.

On the next day, that Thursday afternoon I called Sister Agnes again. By that time she was at home preparing to go to Jackson. The doctors in Laurel had transferred George to the University of Mississippi Medical Center in Jackson, the largest and best hospital in Mississippi. He had been transported by ambulance that Thursday morning and Agnes had come home to pack some clothing and prepare to go on to Jackson. Their daughter, Angela, was in her second or third year of medical school at the same center and she and her husband, Derrick, had bought a house in the suburbs of Jackson. Agnes spoke with much more distress when I talked with her that time. She had found out from the doctors that morning that George's condition was very grave; that was why they had transferred him to Jackson because there was a special stroke treatment unit at the University Medical Center.

That Thursday was Christmas Day, but she expressed the desire for me to come as soon as I could. She didn't know what the prognosis would be once she got to the hospital in Jackson, but she knew that somebody needed to be there with her as soon as possible, both to help her and to make sure that daddy was seen after. I assured her that I would be on my way by that next day, Friday morning, and other family members would be coming as soon as possible as well. I called Sister Brenda in Connecticut and she made arrangements to fly into Jackson that Friday morning. Brother Otha was also coming by Saturday morning, and brother Charles was on his way as soon as he could make arrangements.

We spent Christmas Day with Mozell's mother and those of her family who came to have dinner with us that day. We hurried through dinner that evening and got to bed early to get a good night's rest so we could leave for Mississippi early that Friday morning. By six o'clock that morning we were on our way. We stopped in Atlanta by Cousin Clemertine's house for lunch and by early evening around 7:00 p.m. we were in Meridian, Mississippi.

We made it to Bay Springs around 8:00 p.m. just as Brenda, daddy and Adrian were getting home from the hospital in Jackson. Brenda had arrived in Jackson around ten o'clock that morning and Adrian and daddy had met her at the airport and they had gone to the hospital and spent the day.

As we unpacked our things and got into the house we began to talk with Brenda and Adrian about how George was doing and what was the prognosis. They reported that they had talked with George several times during the day and he seemed stable and resting comfortably. The doctors had discussed with them the situation and indicated that the first 72 hours would be critical considering the intensity of the stroke he had. If he made it through that critical period without the process repeating itself he would have an even chance of recovering in time. They had warned, however, that often times the stroke process would repeat itself during that time and it could be severe and mean disaster. Even the doctors had suggested that all we could do was to hope and pray. Even as we talked daddy was unsure who or what we were talking about although he had just left the hospital with them after spending all day. I realized then just how badly his dementia had progressed since I had been there that past August. I knew we were in serious trouble.

Just as we were finishing our conversation around 8:30 p.m. and were about to prepare something to eat, since we were all hungry, the telephone rang. It was Sister Agnes calling to let us know that George had taken a turn for the worse, and that we needed to get to the hospital as soon as we could. The stroke process had begun again and they were putting George on life support. His condition had gone from serious to extremely critical. We dropped everything right away and got ready to go to Jackson immediately. Brenda, Adrian and I would go and Mozell, Martin and Maya, our children would stay there at home with daddy. The three of us left for Jackson within 10 or 15 minutes. We didn't wait to eat.

We made it to Jackson within the hour driving at break-neck speed all the way with our emergency flashers on. We used the car phone on the way to call the other brothers and sisters, and the pastor of Blue Mountain Church, Reverend Booth, to inform them of the situation and to ask them to be in prayer. By the time we reached the hospital Agnes and Angela were already there along with George's two twin daughters by an outside relationship along with their pastor and his wife who had brought them as they were only sixteen years old. When we got there Agnes and Angela were just coming out of conference with the doctors and informed us that the prognosis was poor. The situation was not good and the chances did not seem good. Brenda was dismayed because when she had left the hospital just a few hours earlier, she and George had been talking and except for the partial paralysis on his left side he seemed to be doing just fine.

The hospital staff made the hospital chapel available to us and we all went in together and said prayers at the altar and read scriptures. It was all we could do. When I got a chance I went into the room where George was to see him. I opened his eyelids to get a look at his eyes; it was obvious to me that he had gone into a coma for there was no response in his eyes at all either to the light or to the movement of my hand in front of his eyes. That's when I knew we were facing a desperate situation. I returned to the chapel where the others were and we held an all-night prayer vigil off and on in between getting whatever sleep we could.

As morning came we called the other family members to let them know what the situation was we were facing. Brother Otha was preparing to catch a flight to Mississippi that morning, as was Brother Charles with his daughter and son-in-law who were returning to North Carolina after spending their Christmas with their parents in New Mexico. Sister Walterene was making arrangements to get off from work and would be flying in just as soon as she could. Later in the morning the doctors came back in to make their rounds and to review the results of tests they had ordered on George the evening before. They essentially reconfirmed what they had pronounced the evening before. The stroke process had begun again and blood clots had moved into the cranial area causing the brain to swell and major portions of the brain to shut down also causing some bodily functions to shut down. They were honest in telling us that George's chances were not good for recovery, and even if he did regain consciousness and survive he would likely be in a vegetative state for the rest of his life. At some point within an unspecified time they informed us that the decision would need to be made to take him off the life support to see if he could make it on his own. From all indications they could surmise the life support was what was keeping him breathing and keeping his heart functioning at whatever level it was. By then we all knew that it was a seriously grave situation.

By that Saturday Brother Charles had flown into Jackson with his son-in-law and daughter from Albuquerque and Sister Walterene arrived that Sunday along with Brother Otha from Illinois. A critical mass of us brothers and sisters were there and the other two, Claude and Bobbie, would be on their way as soon as we gave them the word to come. Poor daddy hardly knew what was going on, and every day we would have to repeat to him who it was that was sick and what had happened to him. The Alzheimer's disease was taking a toll on him and, although he was fighting as hard as he could to maintain control of his faculties and everything else around him, the severity of the disease was too much for him to handle.

As we brothers and sisters talked among ourselves we decided that we would yield the decision about when to remove the life support to Sister Agnes and her children. We all knew that George would not want to be left in a vegetative state and be totally dependent on anybody; we had heard him say that so many times in later years. We decided that we would give Sister Agnes and the children our support and assure them that we would be behind them in whatever decision they would make when the time came. The doctors provided us with ample information and kept us informed every day, and with Angela, George's daughter, being there in medical school at the University Medical Center she was close enough to the doctors in the neurology unit to get access to all the information available. They decided there was no use performing any brain surgery because the pressure and swelling on his brain was so great that it would probably explode if the cranial area was opened. And with the loss of so much brain function what good would it do anyway. All anybody could do was to wait, hope and pray. That is exactly what we did.

By New Year's Day, January 1, 1998, the decision was made to remove George from the life support. If he was going to make it he would have to make it on his own. As long as he was on the life support systems we would never know whether he had enough life functions operating to sustain him alone or not. Sister Agnes and the children invited our input and the decision was made to remove the life support that evening. We all gathered at the hospital around 6:00 p.m. that New Year's evening and a room was prepared to which George would be moved away from the Intensive Care Unit. At around 7:00 p.m. he was moved to that room and shortly after with all of us gathered around him, his pulse ceased, his faint breathing if there were any stopped, and he quietly and peacefully expired. In a moment of silence he was gone.

We stood around him and had prayer, a few tears were shed, we comforted each other and in our own ways we said goodbye to our dearest and beloved brother and contemplated what we would need to do next. The funeral home in Bay Springs was owned and operated by one of George's best friends and a long-time friend of the family, Jesse Crosby, was called to come and pick up his body as soon as they could and bring him back to Bay Springs. The other family members and cousins were called to be informed of his death. We spent maybe another hour at the hospital taking care of whatever needed to be taken care of there, then those of us who were not staying in Jackson for the night returned to Bay Springs.

Our most immediate concern then was what would we do about daddy's situation. The sisters thought that he could be taken to Connecticut and either brought to live with one of them or put in a nursing home there in the New Haven area since three of the siblings lived there. We all knew that even with the onset of Alzheimer's disease daddy would have to be sedated to get him away from Rock Hill Community and out of Mississippi. That part would be easy, but how would anybody keep him away and in Connecticut or anywhere else for that matter. In addition to getting George buried we had a much more serious problem on our hands now.

Brother Otha has been the one in the family with the most wisdom for a long time. He can always think through difficult situations and come up with solutions that can change impossible circumstances into manageable ones. Everybody may not always agree with his solutions, but they will be practical and reasonable in the end. In his wisdom he came up with the idea that maybe, just maybe, we could persuade Brother Claude and Berdia to come to Mississippi and live with daddy to keep him there and in the house. They were both retired now and we had an inclination that Sister Berdia wanted to return to Mississippi in her retirement anyway; especially since they had long ago bought land back at her old home place where she had grown up.

We put our heads together and decided that if we could make them an offer they could not or would not be inclined to refuse our problem could be solved easily. We would each give them our inheritance in daddy's property, the house and all sixty acres of land, if they would come back and see after him and be responsible for him for the remainder of his life. We agreed to call them and propose the offer to them before they left Connecticut headed to Mississippi for George's funeral. If they accepted they could bring whatever belongings they needed with them to the funeral and be prepared to take over the caretaking of daddy when we all left to return to our separate homes. It was a long shot but it was our only hope. We had to make some arrangements for daddy and we had to do it quickly. It was a no-brainer, he could not and would not be left there by himself; he was in no condition to even consider that thought. Brother Claude and Berdia realized that fact as well and that is probably what caused them to make the decision to accept our offer on short order. What choice did any of us have?

Claude and Berdia thought about it overnight and called us the next day to let us know they would accept the offer and were leaving Connecticut on their way to Mississippi with the intentions of staying after the funeral to look after daddy. There was some hesitancy on the part of some to give up their rights to inheritance just like that, but when all was said and done we had no choice.

Claude and Berdia made it clear after they arrived and we sat down and discussed the matter that they were not out to take anybody's inheritance. So if anybody else wanted to take on the responsibility they were about to assume they were welcomed to do so. But once the deal was made there would be no reversal and there would never be any discussion about it ever again. We all agreed and the deal was sealed with a handshake and a hug.

Our mother and father had trained us from children until we became adults that as family we were never to argue or fight one another. Whatever we did had to be done in love, peace and harmony. We were taught to love one another and to look out for one another. If one of us were ever in trouble we were to come to each other's rescue. We have always lived by those rules and George was more committed to them than anybody else. We knew we were doing what both he and mama would have wanted us to do, and what each of us knew we had to do for our daddy.

On January 6, 1998 we laid Brother George to rest in the spot he had picked himself at the foot of mama in the Blue Mountain Church Cemetery. Ironically, or maybe not so ironically, just the Saturday before he died, George had met Jesse Crosby in town and had asked him to go riding with him. They had spent the afternoon together riding around the county and talking. Sometime that afternoon they had come by the cemetery to see mama's grave and George had pointed out to Jesse where he wanted to be buried when he died. That is the spot where he was laid to rest. His memorial service and funeral was just as big as mama's or even bigger in terms of the numbers of people who showed up. George knew a lot of people and had built many houses around the three county area just as daddy had before him.

A few days after we buried Brother George we all departed and left daddy in the care of Brother Claude and Sister Berdia. A few weeks later I returned to Mississippi to assist with getting the property deeded and assigned to them. We just knew daddy was going to resist and raise holy hell when we mentioned to him about assigning the property to just one of the children; which he did. But when we discussed the idea with him just Claude and I were there with him. He went on for three hours and the two of us sat patiently and listened for we knew there was no need trying to convince him to do other than what he wanted to do. But I knew that the next morning when it came time to go to the courthouse in town and sign the papers he would have forgotten all about the discussion we had with him the day before. What was important was that he be taken care of for the remainder of his life and that those papers be signed along with power of attorney for Claude and Berdia to be able to make decisions on his behalf expeditiously.

When Claude and I walked into the courthouse the next morning with daddy for him to sign the deeds and papers giving control of everything to Claude and Berdia neither of us knew how we would walk out of the courthouse or what would happen while we were inside. It was an act of total faith and trust in God that the right thing would happen. Brother Claude had spent most of the night pacing and praying; he had gotten almost no sleep. I had gone and spent the night in Jackson with Angela and her husband and returned early that morning to Bay Springs. I had prayed about the matter and turned it over to God and said what will be will be. I knew what had to be done and I knew we had to do it that day.

As we approached the room in the courthouse where the papers had to be signed and witnessed I walked ahead of Claude and daddy and went into the room and told the clerks what we needed to do. I had the folder with the papers we had picked up from the lawyer's office in my hands. The lawyer who drew up the papers for us was the same Lawyer J.E. Ulmer's son, Attorney Rance Ulmer, who was a very good friend of George's who refused to let us pay him for doing the legal work. He said it was the least he could do for George. When Claude and daddy entered the room I was standing there at the counter with pen in hand. I told daddy and showed him where he needed to sign both the deed and the power of attorney papers. He asked me what were these papers for and I told him they were to give Claude and Berdia authority to take care of the land, the taxes and the deeds. All he said was "okay" and signed the papers.

I looked back at Brother Claude and I could see him take a deep breath and sigh of relief. The clerks took the papers and stamped them and signed where they needed to sign and made copies for us.

I went to go in my wallet to get money to pay the fees and Brother Claude grabbed my hand and said "I'll pay this bill."

We collected our papers and receipt, thanked the clerks, turned and walked out of the building the same way we had come in. Both of us knew that the Spirit of the Lord was with us and that God had answered all of our family's prayers that day. We thought for sure we were going to hell that morning.

In July 2000 Brother Otha and I went together to visit Brother Claude, Sister Berdia and daddy to spend a few days. We had each been to Bay Springs several times since George had died to spend a few days but this was the first time we had been together since then. We all talk on the phone with them several times a month since they have been in Mississippi to keep check on them and to keep informed about how daddy is doing. When we were there on that trip we noticed how far daddy's mental capacity had deteriorated and how confrontational and combative he had become. We could see that it was time for different arrangements to be made for their safety and for daddy's well-being as well as theirs. We encouraged them to look into getting daddy into the nursing home before he became violent and unruly. We knew how difficult daddy could be when he was healthy and mentally well; we feared what he would do if he continued along the path we saw when we were there on that visit.

Before we left we encouraged Brother Claude to move with haste. The last thing we wanted to happen was for anybody in the family to be harmed. We knew from the time mama and George had died that eventually if daddy continued to live long that one day he would have to be committed to a nursing home. We wanted it to be in Mississippi because it would be impossible to get him away from Mississippi and to keep him away from there. Why he loved Mississippi so we still don't know; probably just because it is home.

A few weeks after we left Mississippi Claude called to inform us that he had committed daddy to the nursing home on August 25, 2000, the same day as George's birthday. The first few days he seemed fine, but as he came to realize where he was and that he would not be free to go and come back and forth to Rock Hill

Community when he wanted to, daddy went into a rage and tried to tear down the nursing home. The staff had to restrain him and he was sent to a hospital for behavior modification. He stayed in the hospital that time for two weeks and was returned to the nursing home. A few weeks later he was back in the hospital for behavior modification again. At 85 years old daddy still believed he was the same man he was 65 years ago. On the second visit to the hospital for behavior modification we all became fearful that daddy was not going to adjust and that they would dismiss him from the nursing home. We were worried because we didn't know what we would do then. We knew he could not come back home; he would surely be dangerous then and unrestrainable.

Upon returning to the nursing home after that second visit to the hospital for two weeks, daddy finally started to adjust to being in the nursing home. On one day he was coming out of the dining hall and there was a white man in a wheel chair sitting by the door of the dining hall raising a storm cursing. I understand daddy and the man had a run-in before because of his cursing and daddy had told him if he didn't stop cursing he was going to knock the hell out of him. Well, on this particular day that is just what daddy did; he hauled off and slapped the piss out of the man, whose name also happens to be Otha.

I called daddy on his birthday, March 18, 2001 to talk with him and to wish him a happy birthday. I asked him how he was doing and he said he was as happy and content as he had ever been in his life. He asked me when I was coming to visit him. I told him I would be there just as soon as I could. He said there was no need to rush because he was making it just fine. I guess there is no need for us to be GONE TO HELL THIS MORNING!!!

Daddy died on September 23, 2004 and was buried in the Blue Mountain Missionary Baptist Church Cemetery next to our mother, Hattie Denham Lang, on Tuesday, September 28, 2004 at 11:00 a.m.

ABOUT THE AUTHOR:

Dr. Marvel Lang is a Professor of Urban Studies at Michigan State University in East Lansing, Michigan where he has been employed since 1986. He grew up in rural southeast Mississippi on a farm five miles outside the small town of Bay Springs in Jasper County. His formative years were in the late 1950's and early 1960's when the Civil Rights Movement was at its peak in the South. His father, Otha Lang, Sr., was his hero although he lived in constant fear that the Ku Klux Klan would be coming to kill him because he would not bow or conform to the Jim Crow system but stood up and demanded the respect due him as a man. This volume is a testament to the life of Otha Lang, Sr.

Dr. Lang received his undergraduate degree at Jackson State University in 1970 with high honor; the M. A. at the University of Pittsburgh in 1975; and the Ph.D. at Michigan State University in 1979. He was president of the senior class at Jackson State in 1970 when the two students were massacred by state troopers just a few days after the Kent State massacre. He was previously a faculty member at Jackson State and also worked at the U.S. Census Bureau in Washington, D.C. as a professional researcher. He has written and published extensively on several topics.

Printed in the United States
119368LV00004B/1-99/A